KV-399-834

Developing as a
Reflective Early
Years Professional

A Thematic Approach

EARLY
YEARS

WITHDRAWN
Leeds Trinity University

LEEDS TRINITY LIBRARY

329384 2

You might also like the following books from Critical Publishing.

The Critical Years: Early Years Development from Conception to Five
By Tim Gully
978-1-909330-73-3

Early Years Placements
By Jackie Musgrave and Nicola Stobbs
978-1-909682-65-8

Early Years Policy and Practice: A Critical Alliance
By Pat Tomlinson
978-1-909330-61-0

Global Childhoods
By Monica Edwards, edited by Chelle Davison
978-1-909682-69-6

Language, Literacy and Communication in the Early Years
By Carol Hayes
978-1-910391-54-9

Learning through Movement in the Early Years
By Sharon Tredgett
978-1-909682-81-8

Studying for your Early Years Degree
Edited by Jackie Musgrave, Maggi Savin-Baden and Nicola Stobbs
978-1-911106-42-5

Well-being in the Early Years
By Caroline Bligh, Sue Chambers, Chelle Davison, Ian Lloyd, Jackie Musgrave, June O'Sullivan and Susan Waltham
978-1-909330-65-8

Our titles are also available in a range of electronic formats. To order please go to our website www.criticalpublishing.com or contact our distributor, NBN International, 10 Thornbury Road, Plymouth PL6 7PP, telephone 01752 202301 or email orders@nbninternational.com.

CRITICAL
PUBLISHING

Developing as a
Reflective Early Years Professional

A Thematic Approach

SECOND EDITION

CAROL HAYES, JAYNE DALY, MANDY DUNCAN,
RUTH GILL & ANN WHITEHOUSE

EARLY
YEARS

First published in 2014 by Critical Publishing Ltd
Reprinted in 2014
Second Edition published in 2017

All rights reserved. No part of this publication may be reproduced, stored in a retrieval system, or transmitted in any form or by any means, electronic, mechanical, photocopying, recording or otherwise, without prior permission in writing from the publisher.

The authors have made every effort to ensure the accuracy of information contained in this publication, but assume no responsibility for any errors, inaccuracies, inconsistencies and omissions. Likewise every effort has been made to contact copyright holders. If any copyright material has been reproduced unwittingly and without permission the Publisher will gladly receive information enabling them to rectify any error or omission in subsequent editions.

Copyright © 2017 Carol Hayes, Jayne Daly, Mandy Duncan, Ruth Gill and Ann Whitehouse

British Library Cataloguing in Publication Data
A CIP record for this book is available from the British Library.

ISBN: 978-1-911106-22-7

This book is also available in the following e-book formats:

MOBI ISBN: 978-1-911106-23-4
EPUB ISBN: 978-1-911106-24-1
Adobe e-book ISBN: 978-1-911106-25-8

The rights of Carol Hayes, Jayne Daly, Mandy Duncan, Ruth Gill and Ann Whitehouse to be identified as the Authors of this work have been asserted by them in accordance with the Copyright, Design and Patents Act 1988.

Cover design by Out of House Limited
Text design by Greensplash Limited
Project Management by Out of House Publishing
Printed and bound in Great Britain by TJ International Ltd, Padstow, Cornwall

Critical Publishing
3 Connaught Road
St Albans
AL3 5RX

www.criticalpublishing.com

MIX
Paper from
responsible sources
FSC
www.fsc.org   FSC® C013056

Contents

Praise for the first edition

... a vital source to enable students to develop the ability to reflect on the practice and to support their personal and professional development for employment within the sector.

Karen Hudson, NPTC

This book is easy to read, informative and provides clear guidance for students on how to be a reflective practitioner.

Denise Nannetti, North Hertfordshire College

Very useful text with up-to-date policy reviews; makes a lot of links to theory and practice. Highly recommended for early years practitioners.

Mehjabeen Shaukat, Tameside College

One of the best reflective practice books for undergraduate students that I've read. It has a friendly and approachable tone, with a sharp critical edge that makes you think further.

Clarrie Smith, Stockport College

This is an excellent book for higher education students as it offers a clearly laid out format with a wide reference list for each chapter. The text is up to date and reflects current government policy and practice within the field.

Leigh Jarvis, Vision West Nottinghamshire

This book is excellent as the content puts reflection within the context of early years practice in a comprehensive way. The writing is accessible for undergraduate readers.

Elaine Hallet, Institute of Education

Meet the authors

Carol Hayes

I have worked in the early years sector for over 44 years as a teacher and tutor. I lectured at Staffordshire University, the Open University and Glyndwr University (then NEWI). I helped to establish a thriving early childhood studies department with programmes from foundation degrees to masters in early childhood. I am currently National Chair of the Sector Endorsed Foundation Degrees Professional Association (SEFDEY) and, since retiring from full-time lecturing, have been writing and publishing works related to the early years. My main research interests are dyslexia, the early years and developing language and literacy.

Jayne Daly

My career in early childhood care and education began over 30 years ago as a nursery officer and manager of a number of settings. Throughout my professional career I worked within the public care, health and education sectors. My passion and love for my subject meant that I expanded my career into higher education teaching in 2007, as I recognised that it was time to 'give something back' to those new to providing quality outcomes for very young children and their families. Since 2007 my higher education career has expanded from lecturer in early childhood studies to senior lecturer in child, education and family studies at the University of Wolverhampton, where I am also currently studying for my PhD in education. In my current role I teach a range of subjects across the child, education and family studies programmes as well as outreach work and continual professional development (CPD) within the local community. My research interests are quality early years leadership, international early years curriculum development, children's creative development and childhood resilience.

Mandy Duncan

I began my career as a nursery nurse almost 20 years ago, before training as a teacher. I initially worked with children in primary schools in both inner-city and rural areas and later with young people aged 14–19 in a further education (FE) college. I am currently a senior lecturer at Staffordshire University, teaching on a range of BA and masters programmes. I have recently been awarded a PhD, having undertaken extensive research with young people undergoing child protection procedures.

Ruth Gill

My experience with children started as a children's nanny to bereaved families and progressed to working in a further-education-based nursery as an assistant. I quickly progressed to management, which was a real challenge. I am currently a senior lecturer in early childhood studies at Staffordshire University and have been an academic group leader for the Education, Human Development and Society programme. I am currently engaged in doctoral research and I am a Senior Fellow of the Higher Education Academy.

Ann Whitehouse

I started my career as an NNEB and worked for a number of years in nursery education, supplemented with valuable experience as a nanny, childminder, pre-school leader and teaching assistant. More recently, I worked as a further education lecturer in early childhood, where I played an integral role in developing a foundation degree in early years for experienced practitioners. I recently retired from my last role as a senior lecturer at Staffordshire University, where I was award leader for the part-time BA and FdA in early childhood studies. My professional involvement with early childhood care and education continues through my role as external examiner at three universities and as a regional chair of SEFDEY. My specific interests are related to the development of early years pedagogy and my research involves listening to practitioners' experiences and views. I also have two young grandchildren who make sure that I use my practical skills regularly and who provide me with endless opportunities for critical reflection on their early childhood experiences.

Foreword

It is universally recognised that reflective practice and being reflective are essential elements of being a professional in any workplace. However, these can also be difficult terms to explain, and, more importantly, translate into everyday practice, especially if you are working in the frenetic world of early years! Add to this the need for a critical evaluation and the task becomes seemingly impossible.

It is for these reasons that I am delighted that there is a second edition of this great book, which investigates these concepts in-depth, while retaining the relevance to early years practice. This group of outstanding early years experts highlight the relevance of different facets of reflective practice for practitioners, but they also encourage the reader to critically challenge their own thinking.

The breadth of this book's content is breathtaking. Reflection is analysed in specific circumstances, in collaborative work and there is even a global perspective. The specific early years examples used give direct relevance for practitioners, whatever type of setting they may be working in. This not only makes the subject more transparent but is also encourages the reader to be more analytical about their own practice, and maybe the practice of others too.

In this second edition there are two new chapters: Chapter 4, which is entitled 'Reflecting on work-based learning', by Ruth Gill and Ann Whitehouse; and Chapter 10, 'Reflecting upon childhood, creativity and play', by Jayne Daly. These are both excellent additions and demonstrate the changing nature of the early years sector. The rest of the book retains the thought provoking and beneficial chapters of the original edition, which range from writing for reflection to creativity and playfulness to working in a multi-professional team.

Chapter 1 is by Carol Hayes and is all about reflective practice. The examples of a range of reflective models are very usefully linked to early years practice and are used to explain professional judgement. The challenges to reflective thinking are thought provoking and I feel sure will help practitioners work through some of their own challenges. Ruth Gill tackles 'Writing for reflection' in Chapter 2. The RAIN framework, which stands for Reflects, Analysis, Interpret, Next steps, is invaluable and would be a good framework for practitioners new to reflection. Ruth also gives some excellent guidance for writing a reflective journal, including examples. Chapter 3, written by Ann Whitehouse, tackles the complex nature of a 'critical friend' – a seemingly contradictory phrase. Ann has cleverly dealt with this by using conversations between critical friends as case studies.

Chapters 4 and 5 move reflection into the workplace. In Chapter 4, Ruth Gill and Ann Whitehouse establish how collaborative working and shared understanding of the setting's expectations can improve everyone's professionalism. For those practitioners considering higher education, Chapter 5 by Jayne Daly should be essential reading, as she considers the challenges and benefits of learning. The case studies are excellent examples that many practitioners will identify with.

Whilst still in the workplace, Carol Hayes analyses the rationale for observations and assessments when working with children in Chapter 6. The what, why, who, when and how of observations are explored, with a useful flowchart of why you need to observe. For practitioners in England, there is a section on the EYFS and how a reflective practitioner can utilise observations as part of the curriculum. Carol also discusses some of the very current issues around male practitioners.

Arguably one of the most conflicted areas of reflection for practitioners is that of emotional availability, from discussions about cuddling to attachment to professional love. In Chapter 7, Ruth Gill considers emotionally available practice and the key person role from a number of perspectives, and, most importantly, how this role may be interpreted differently. Practical examples of 'professional love' are usefully included. Following this is Mandy Duncan's thoughtful and sensitive reflection on the complex issues around racism, especially in predominantly white settings. This is a contemporary issue for many practitioners. I would urge you to read this powerful chapter, opened with an equally powerful poem. Mandy then goes on, in Chapter 9, to scrutinise poverty around the world and its affect on children, including children in developing nations, noting that poverty 'has long term, permanent, physical, intellectual and socio-emotional consequences.' Some of these concepts go well beyond ordinary early years concepts, encouraging the reader to sometimes reflect on ideas that may be outside of their normal comfort zone.

Chapter 10 is one of the new chapters to the second edition of the book, focusing on childhood, creativity and play. Concepts of creativity and their strong links with Malaguzzi are examined, as well as some interesting examples of play and playfulness. The potential conflict between freedom and keeping children safe is discussed. In Jayne Daly's Chapter 11, on being a reflective leader, you will find reference to texts beyond the usual early years texts, including Goleman's *Emotional Intelligence*. Some of the classic leadership theories have been examined in relation to early years, making this a critically reflective, but practical chapter. Fittingly, the chapter on the multi-professional team is a collaborative chapter, written by Carol Hayes, Mandy Duncan and Ann Whitehouse. This fascinating chapter opens with reflections on the tragic case of Victoria Climbé, a young girl who many consider was failed by the lack of joined-up thinking between professional teams. The progress that has been made since then is explained, including the plethora of terms used to describe multi-professional teams. However, there are still plenty of challenges for such teams and these are investigated under headings such as trust, relationships, ethics and moral dilemmas.

The final chapter, by Carol Hayes, includes detailed analysis of action research, and the very useful role that a reflective research buddy can play during the research process.

Trustworthiness is analysed, which is an aspect that is deserving of reflection, as is professionalism.

The importance of reflective practice and professionalism cannot be overstated in the early years sector, especially in the modern age where practitioners are more and more frequently having to source their own professional development. It is a delight to have a book that not only critically examines the theories of reflective practice, but also makes the links to early years practice. Thus making this book essential reading for both new practitioners and those more academically minded.

Kathy Brodie, 2017

1 The nature of reflective practice

CAROL HAYES

Harry stared at the stone basin. The contents had returned to their original, silvery-white state swirling and rippling beneath his gaze.

'What is it?' Harry asked shakily.

'This? It is called a Pensieve,' said Dumbledore. 'I sometimes find, and I am sure that you know the feeling, that I simply have too many thoughts and memories crammed into my mind.'

'Err,' said Harry who couldn't truthfully say that he had ever felt anything of the sort.

'At these times,' said Dumbledore, indicating the stone basin, 'I use the Pensieve. One simply siphons the excess thoughts from one's mind, pours them into the basin, and examines them at one's leisure. It becomes easier to spot patterns and links, you understand, when they are in this form.'

(J K Rowling, 2000)

What is reflection?

Can you swim? When you go to the swimming pool do you dive in with a flourish or do you lower yourself into the water carefully and with trepidation? Are you comfortable at the deep end where you cannot put your feet down or do you wade in slowly ensuring that you know how to get back?

Reflection is a little like this. You can lean over the pool looking at the blue water glistening in the sunlight and see your reflection looking back at you and while the pool is not disturbed your image is clear and easy to see. Once other people enter the pool the water starts to move and ripple and your reflection gets more difficult to assess. When children enter the water, the splashing and energy with which they engage makes it even harder to see your reflection clearly.

When you see your reflection in the water do you say

- *Oh look there's me, or*

- *Is this what I want to be like?*

When you look into the water do you see who you expect to see or can you see someone else at your shoulder? Those of you who are confident swimmers, like confident practitioners, are happy to take the plunge and accept the challenges of the deep water with no armbands or life jacket. As you dive in, the water opens up for you to see as you explore the depths of the pool, touching the bottom, perhaps gathering new things from the floor of the pool. These practitioners perfect their style and levels of confidence by listening to friends and instructors, talking to others who have observed them and perhaps reading about how water is displaced, aerodynamic shapes, speed and velocity.

However, most of us slip gingerly into the cold pool, putting a toe into the water of reflective practice; needing instructors to keep us afloat and to help us to take our feet off the bottom, change our style and review our practices.

It is common to hear early years practitioners say:

- *We can do the job so why do we need to do more?*

- *I have been in the job for the last 30 years and have vast experience; I do not need to do more.*

- *Forget about what you were taught in college. This is the real world!*

Sylva et al (2004) documented, in The Effective Provision of Pre-school Education (EPPE) Project, that early years settings run by critically reflective, well-qualified staff were more effectively run, more reflective and more open to change and challenge. The evidence for the importance of reflective practice is so compelling that it cannot be ignored any more.

Like the experienced swimmer and diver, the reflective practitioner is the one with vision, the ability to judge the depth of the water, the temperature of the water and the content of the water and has creative flair as they dive. With this ability they are able to be responsive and creative in their practice. The experienced swimming instructor is there to take you by the hand and guide you through further training, which will give you better understanding, develop your confidence and resilience and encourage your reflection upon events, critical incidents and experiences past, present and future. So too is a book like this designed to take you through the processes and hold your hand when the reflection appears scary, to raise your levels of confidence and your image as an advanced practitioner.

Reflection could be considered a synonym for 'thought process' which involves looking back at events and asking questions, looking forward and crystal ball gazing. Reflection involves a self-assessment or self-appraisal of practice and competence at a given time and in a given situation. It is about looking for learning points within the reflection, about striving for better understanding and eventually identifying future developmental needs.

Is there really a definition?

The original definition of reflection in education probably came from Dewey (1933), who discusses reflection in the light of professionalism, and this was developed further by Schön (1983), into a process he called 'reflective practice'. How often have you heard the phrase *That's all very well in theory but what about here in the nursery, what use is that here in the real world?* from practitioners looking for real solutions to real problems? However, Schön (1983) saw this as a serious misunderstanding of the relationship of theory to practice. He thought that attributing to professionals' knowledge and autonomy in their work granted them extraordinary rights and privileges in return for their very special contribution to society. His concern about this led to his idea that there are two types of reflection: reflection on action and reflection in action.

Reflection on action

Reflection on action is looking back, so it can only be done retrospectively, once the situation has happened and a possible solution has been found. This then involves asking questions such as:

*   *Are these the right solutions?*

*   *Are there other solutions?*

*   *What would be the consequences if different solutions had been found?*

If you are a driver you could liken this to replaying a 'near miss' in your mind; as a practitioner this is perhaps an incident with a parent that was not resolved satisfactorily – the scenario of *If only I had … .*

Reflection in action

As a concept this is more debatable, and you could question whether it is even possible to reflect while entrenched within the situation. Remaining with the analogy of the driver there are times when actions are unconscious, for example changing gears and braking. For the practitioner this might be routines such as reading a story or serving a meal. You do them automatically, but reflecting in action is when you switch to conscious mode and start to 'think on your feet'. This might involve changing the activity in response to a new situation which has occurred and drawing more consciously on a range of familiar strategies. Schön's representation of reflection could perhaps appear to be somewhat simplistic or account insufficiently for the context and background of the reflection. Moon (1999) questions whether it is even achievable to reflect at the time and suggests that you need to step away from the situation and look back in context and time. However, looking back into the past can be limited by perception and what you remember, and if you ask several people what they remember about the same incident they will often 'remember' it differently. Psychologists such as Schacter (2001) have shown that the further away in time you are from a situation the less you remember about it and, more disturbingly, you may even appear to remember things related to the event that never transpired. Interestingly, in the legal system this is readily recognised and statements relating to an incident are known to be more accurate if they are taken as soon as possible or within 24 hours of the incident taking place (HSE, 2003). Schacter (2001) believes that there is a common misunderstanding that the memory is like a video or photograph, reproducing an experience. He reported that memory is more about active construction. The problem, according to Schacter (2001) is not storing information but retrieving it. He showed that the things that we block out are often the things that are often those with which we are most familiar and the link between recall and creativity is a power-ful one. This could be attributed to the fact that the same areas of the brain responsible for memory are also responsible for the imagination. Schacter (2001) showed that incorrect responses to memories increase exponentially with the passage of time even when given by a competent professional under favourable conditions, so completely accurate recall is rare. Schacter (2001) talked about the 'Seven Sins of Memory':

1. Transience – the weakening of memory over time.

2. Absent minded – the breakdown of the interface between attention and memory.

3. Blocking – temporary failures of retrieval.

4. Misattribution – assigning memories to the wrong source (incorrectly remembering trivia that you read, to a 'fact' that a colleague told you).

5. Suggestibility – memories implanted by others, leading questions or suggestions (Schacter (2001) believes this to be the most dangerous).

6. Bias – how current knowledge and beliefs affect how we remember events.

7. Persistence – recalling things we would like to forget.

This response to memory, according to the HSE (2003), can also be influenced by the practi-tioner's own values, culture, education, age, prejudices and assumptions. This emphasises the importance of reflecting upon the 'here and now' and even reflecting into the future, that is, on what you would like to happen, with a commitment to your extended professionalism. The more you do something, the more routine an activity is, the less likely you are to think about it, so activities in the nursery such as toileting, meal times and greeting times are often taken for granted and less likely to be put under the spotlight of scrutiny and reflection. The process of choosing which activities to reflect upon can also be a difficult one, with practition-ers often feeling that small events or routines are not worthy of close examination, wanting to reflect upon large projects, major incidents and key moments in the day. Frequently you may want to reflect upon things that went wrong, debating how they could have been better or how they could be avoided, but it is as important to reflect upon the things that you do well, and consider why they are so good and what makes them this way. In the things that go well you can see good practice that could be replicated in other contexts and used as solutions to the difficult moments or to help other situations that you find more challenging. It is impor-tant to reflect upon good practice to ensure that it remains so, and that it is challenged from time to time as groups change, systems change and contexts are different. Could the good practice be 'even better practice' or even 'outstanding practice'? The process of reflection in action, therefore, really means thinking about your assumptions and the everyday things that you take for granted. This does not imply that you need change for the sake of change, but that you develop a deeper understanding of your own practice and of why you do the things in the way that you do, that is to seek a rationale for their existence.

The whole concept of reflection moved on from Dewey and Schön, and Boud, Keogh and Walker (1985) describe reflection as:

> *an important human activity in which people recapture their experience, think about it, mull it over and evaluate it.*
>
> (p 43)

This is clearly a much broader and more fluid description and like Moon (1999) it equates reflection with learning. Moon (1999) suggests that you can reflect upon things for which there is not necessarily an obvious solution, and associates reflection with a range of feelings which can be emotional and even spiritual, but certainly a part of the mental processing. Moon (1999) also develops the concept of reflection by emphasising the purposive nature of the process. You usually reflect upon something in order to have an outcome, a solution, so it becomes a processing of knowledge, understanding and emotion:

> *a form of mental processing with a purpose and/or anticipated outcome that is applied to relatively complex or unstructured ideas for which there is no obvious solution.*
>
> (Moon, 1999, p 23)

Osterman and Kottkamp (1993) brought into the process the concept of analysis, ie that reflection starts with an element of curiosity, of asking questions and questioning accepted assumptions:

> *through reflection and analysis we strive to understand the experience.*
>
> (p 23)

Ruch (2002), like Schön, saw the importance of theory and research to the reflective process. She saw that practitioners are often reluctant to see research in the light of real experiences and tend to dismiss them as theoretically remote, impracticable and unusable. This builds upon Schön (1983) who talked about the 'technical rationality' where knowledge is divorced from experience, and the values and understanding that underpin practice are never questioned. Some practitioners believe that this is the way that it has always been done and do not question whether it is still appropriate despite possible changes to the team, changes in customer expectation, changes to the physical fabric of the setting or changes of local and national politics and policy over the years.

The reflective process

The human brain probably processes some 50,000 to 60,000 thoughts every day. As we encounter difficulties and problems in our daily lives we consult what Raelin (2002) calls our 'solution database', which contains all the elements that we have learned in the past to find answers to everyday problems. Of course accepting this means that there is a finite number of possible solutions and no elements of the database will enable us to tackle new, and so far unencountered, problems. This method of problem solving does not allow you to think 'outside the box'. However, by thinking about thinking and other such metacognitive processes, by reflecting on your thoughts and those of others, you are able to add to your 'solution database', to expand ideas and give new meaning to old ideas and older situations. Clearly this type of personal reflection demonstrates great benefit to professional practice, enabling new solutions, creative ideas and imaginative, resourceful thinking to flow into settings. By sharing your reflections with others you open up your thoughts and assumptions to public scrutiny and public examination, but this also allows your thinking to incorporate the ideas of others and you can thereby learn from your actions.

Every situation you may find yourself in will be different – different contexts, different employment cultures, different relationships and so on. Although your existing 'solution database' can lead you in certain directions and give clues for solutions, if no two situations are the same then it is likely that no two solutions will be the same either. This implies that, as you look at a new situation, you need to look for similarities with what you have already experienced, but you also need to look at the differences.

So you should put into the reflective process what you already know or believe, but add new material from your observations, from research, from peers, colleagues and even the children and families in your care, and then draw out something that relates to the reason for that reflection in the first place.

Grushka, Hinde-McLeod and Reynolds (2005) bring in a further suggestion of 'reflection for action'. This they describe as prospective reflection, and some refer to this as crystal ball gazing, allowing the practitioner to consider where they want to be in the future, reflection upon future developments, meeting perceived needs or career planning. However, the crystal ball gazing should not be so introspective that it becomes navel gazing, which narrows the process to such an extent that it ceases to take account of the wider context and the epigenesis (that is the bi-directional relationship) between the environment and the person. Prospective reflection can be likened to looking through a holiday brochure before you go away. You get ideas of what it might be like, what you might do, or who you might meet. It is like superimposing yourself into the picture and imagining the feelings, actions and experiences that will ensue, enabling you to be more prepared when you finally meet with this experience in the future.

So what is reflective practice?

Reflective practice requires practitioners who already see themselves as active researchers and learners, who explore their values and benefits and regularly set learning goals for themselves and their settings. It is about looking beyond reflection to a wider context which incorporates care and education in a political sphere, the curriculum, pedagogy and innovation. Not all practitioners are reflective learning practitioners and for many the learning stopped when they left formal education with their licence to practice. This is often evident in the quality of their practice and the experiences that they offer to the children in their care as well as their resistance to change and a change culture, as highlighted by the Nutbrown Review (2012).

> *An individual does not stop learning and developing once they have completed their initial training and become qualified ... they need further training to enhance and develop their knowledge and skills, and to keep pace with new research and developments.*
>
> (Nutbrown, 2012, p 4.23)

CASE STUDY

The brush-off

Practitioner: *Following my discussion with the parents of James, I am really concerned that we are not connecting with parents enough and the concept of parent partnership in the nursery is not working as well as it should. I would like to propose that we have a meeting with parents and staff to discuss this and find out how we could develop this relationship further.*

Manager: *Thank you for that suggestion but you will not remember that we did have a meeting a couple of years ago, before you arrived at the nursery, and it really did not work with only two parents turning up. The staff felt that it was a waste of time.*

Reflective activity

» *How do you think that the practitioner should react to the manager?*

» *How could you further develop the relationship with James' parents?*

» *What advantages can you see for James and the other staff within the nursery?*

Extended thinking

It can be so frustrating when you think that you have a great idea for improvement and it is met with opposition. It is possible that such resistance is the main reason why change is not implemented.

» *Consider for a moment how the practitioner in the case study could have better prepared for this resistance.*

» *For example could s/he have come better prepared with research data, facts and figures about how this approach to parent partnership has been tackled in other settings and their success rates?*

» *Perhaps s/he should have been more prepared for the emotional response to such change. For example perhaps the manager feels threatened or sees this as a criticism of her leadership. Could it be that the manager fears that if she agrees to these changes that more demands for change will be made?*

LeDoux (1999) looked closely at the emotional state of mind that is contributory to such a resistance to change. He reminds you that your most important tool to help to move from resistance to support is you ability to listen and understand. He talks about the importance of not taking the resistance personally but to remain open minded, calm and relaxed. He reminds us to start small, build trust and to try to involve everyone in the change process. by considering three fundamental questions:

- What is in it for me?
- What is in it for you?
- What is in it for us?

It is apparent that the manager in the case study is entrenched in his/her ideas and closed to any concept of change. Perhaps s/he even feels threatened by a practitioner who appears critical of the system that s/he has been responsible for for some time. There is no suggestion by the manager that reflecting upon what has happened in the years since parent partnership policies were last reviewed would achieve anything, despite the change in team, in customer base and the inspectoral requirements. If the manager continues to block new ideas and resist change and suggestions, there is a danger that eventually staff will give up thinking about what they are doing and will no longer strive for improvement through their reflection. This could produce a stagnation of the processes and procedures within the setting, which could leave children with a bland and unvisionary experience, lacking in creativity, thereby reducing the learning environment to one of benign and limited means.

Raelin (2002) describes reflective practice as the:

> *practice of periodically stepping back to ponder the meaning of what has recently transpired to ourselves and to others in our immediate environment. It illuminates what the self and others have experienced, providing a basis for further action. In particular, it privileges the process of enquiry, leading to an understanding of experiences that may have been overlooked in practice.*

(p 1)

The whole concept of reflective practice therefore carries multiple meanings, from solitary introspection to a critical dialogue of thinking and learning. Some have described this solitary dialogue as nothing more than self-indulgent but Ghaye (2000) refers to this inter-subjective reflection or the relational context and mutual collaboration as a 'reflective conversation'. Practitioners can formalise it and record it, even manufacture it, as may be required for inspection purposes, or it may be a more ongoing and fluid experience which goes unrecorded and undocumented, but is nevertheless helpful as practitioners strive to make sense and meaning of the moral and social values that underpin their work.

CASE STUDY

Triggers Nursery

Triggers Nursery is a long-established setting of over 20 years. Many of the staff have been at the setting since the start. The nursery originally attracted large numbers of mono-cultural middle-class families, but over the years the demographics of the community have changed and these children and families have slowly been replaced by children from immigrant families, often with a poor grasp of English speaking skills and largely unemployed and on benefits.

As the population shifted many of the staff found themselves unable to understand the cultural lives of the children and their families and the quality of practice within the nursery started to decline, affecting the whole ethos of the setting.

Reflective activity

» *Imagine that you are the new manager of Triggers Nursery. How would you start to address the issues of equipping your staff with the reflective tools required to help them to better understand the dynamics and new remit of the setting?*

» *How would you create an open and unthreatening working environment where staff feel able to discuss their feelings and values with no fear of prejudice or reprisal?*

Extended thinking

» *With a colleague consider the following statement. 'The Early Years Foundation Stage (DfE, 2014) requires you to reflect on practice but in reality this is not practical as this requires the inspectorate to measure your ability to reflect. This is not easy, as without a clearly agreed definition and model for working, critical reflection may not be a definable phenomenon.'*

» *So what is the essential nature of reflection, that we can firstly recognise it and then be able to judge the practitioners performance?*

Reflective models

If you have looked at other texts on reflective practice you will have noted that there are almost as many models of reflective practice as there are writers in the field. Why is there such a proliferation of differing models of reflection? Is it just that researchers and writers cannot agree what it is, or do the models described simply lack consensus and clarity? Some of the key models are examined here to allow you a flavour of their similarities and differences. Most start by describing an incident and then encourage use of your own knowledge, that of your peers and colleagues, and evidence from theory and research in an attempt to understand what has been described.

The reflective pyramid

This relationship between the various forms of knowledge can be seen more easily as pyramidal (see Figure 1.1).

- At the top of the pyramid is you – *your personal reflection on your own life, aspirations, career plans, values and emotions.*

- Further down is what you share with your colleagues and peers. Consider how much you let them into your thoughts and reflections, and how much is within your control. Revealing your reflections can be likened to the 'dance of the seven veils' in which the dancer removes one veil at a time before exposing herself completely.

Figure 1.1 *The reflective pyramid*

- At the base of the pyramid is research and theoretical understanding and this really is the rock upon which all the rest is founded. You may not always appreciate how much this influences your everyday practice. It is not just your own understanding of the theories that you learned in college or through your reading, but it is how the wider context of government and society is influenced by new theoretical understanding and discovery that affects your conversations with colleagues and your own internal conversations. This in turn will allow you to see yourself within that context and how this will affect your practice. All models vary in how prescriptive they are but need to be seen not as a straitjacket – rigid, inflexible and mechanistic – but as a tool for learning. Different models may suit different contexts or the same context at different times. No one model will suit all of the people all of the time. Different models continue to be written to accommodate different professional groups and different groups within those professions. It is therefore likely that it is neither possible nor even desirable to use one definitive model.

The Kolb Cycle

Although Kolb (2015) is frequently referred to in the context of reflection, the Kolb Cycle (2015) originally referred to by Kolb in 1983, is just as often referred to as the Kolb Learning Cycle. Kolb was criticised by Boud et al (1985) for not specifically detailing the process of reflection within his diagram. However, the whole model is based very firmly in practice and in the personal experiential experience. Kolb lays great store by the importance of observation and in particular reflective observation (which is discussed in more detail in Chapter 6).

However, maybe experience is not enough. The practitioner who claims to have been in the job for 20 years and therefore has 20 years of experience to call upon when making decisions, could have had 20 years of the same experience and have been doing the same thing in the same way for all that time without really reflecting upon this in an intelligent and reflexive manner.

The Kolb model also talks of 'abstract conceptualisation', which moves from practical experience through an understanding of the 'why' as well as the 'what'. This is the point at which the reflective practitioner needs to say:

- *This is what I do but why do I do it like this?*

- *Are there other solutions, maybe better solutions, to the problems?*

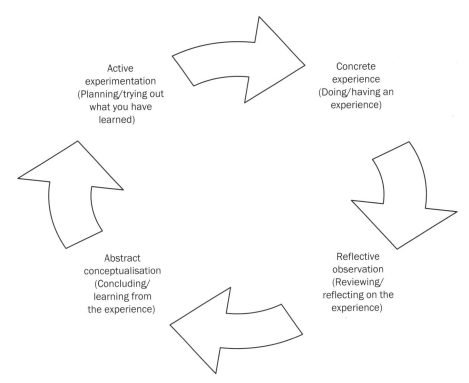

Figure 1.2 *Kolb's Reflective Cycle (2015)*

The practical experience is shaped and developed by an abstract conceptualisation of the issue. In Kolb's cycle this leads into planning and trying out some of the new ideas that have been developed from that interplay between theory and practice. Kolb (1984) can be accused of being too simplistic and sequential and lacking in an understanding of the effect that emotion can play on change and the reason for change at a particular time in a particular way. Kolb, like Schön, was concerned only with observable behaviour, what he called the 'objective observer', and the thoughts, feelings and values of a practitioner are not seen as important to the reflective process. This objectivity and evidence-based theorising is beneficial to the researcher as it appears open and transparent, and on the surface appears to add reliability to the model. However, it also has the potential to seriously limit the validity and reliability of the reflection by failing to recognise the part played beneath the surface by feelings, emotions, cultural values and moral dilemmas in the reflective process, which brings into sharp question its worth and merit.

Gibbs' Cycle

Gibbs (1998) attempted to build on Kolb's model and to incorporate an understanding of these emotive responses into a developed model (see Figure 1.3). Gibbs attempted to respond to the human nature element of reflection. However, as this is a frequently unseen element, a moving variable that cannot easily be replicated or understood, it is difficult to describe within a one-size-fits-all, two-dimensional model.

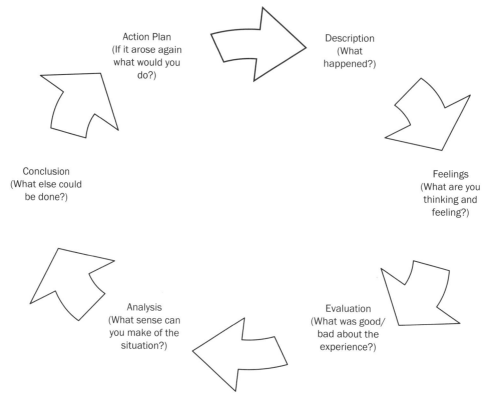

Figure 1.3 *Gibbs' Reflective Cycle (2015)*

However, maybe Gibbs' model is also too simplistic for such a complex process. It is steeped in concerns about practical experiences rather than recognising that the reflective process could be multi-layered and there may be differing levels of reflection. Within these levels it is important to examine the issues of value, change, commitment to quality, differentiation and diversity.

Jay and Johnson: three-tier classification

Jay and Johnson (2002), developed a three-tier classification of reflection based on a series of questions for the practitioner to ask themselves. This typology aimed to recognise this difference of levels and to build upon it by bringing in ethical and moral issues.

One problem with this model is that it does tend to retain Schön's idea of reflection on action, and of reflection only being a retrospective process with little scope for reflection in action or prospective reflection, reflection for action (Grushka, Hinde-McLeod and Reynolds, 2005).

Table 1.1 *Jay and Johnson (2002)*

Descriptive	What is happening? Is this working and for whom? How am I feeling? What do I not understand?
Comparative	How do other people explain what is happening? What do research and theory say? How can I improve?
Critical	Can I look at this from alternative perspectives? Given my own moral and ethical stance which solution is best for this particular issue? How does this reflective process inform and shape my perspective?

Race's ripples model

A model perhaps more suited to the experienced practitioner is Race's updated 'ripples' model (2014) (see Figure 1.4). This is based on the Vygotskian theory (1978) that the best way to learn is to become actively involved in the activity and that the best teachers are those who facilitate children's learning, rather than trying to pour in the learning from the top. Race (2014) places 'learning by doing' at the centre of a pool of water and shows how the ripples fan out from the centre to encompass other types of learning and reflection.

This model is similar to Kolb in that it is dynamic and based on experiential learning but it is not sequential requiring one aspect before and following another. Race describes this as *Intersecting systems of ripples on a pond* (Race, 2014).

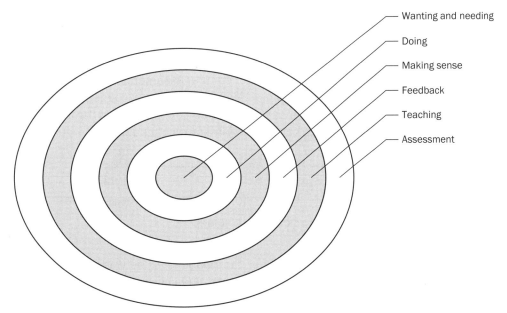

— Wanting and needing
— Doing
— Making sense
— Feedback
— Teaching
— Assessment

Figure 1.4 *The six stages of Race's ripples model of reflection and learning (2014)*

Raelin's five-stage model

Raelin (2002) suggests a five-stage model of reflection:

1. Speaking – with a collective voice – this is very group-orientated and involves being willing to express some of the uncertainties and assumptions.

2. Disclosing – sharing doubts, assumptions, impatience and expressing passions. Presenting a story to uncover the depths.

3. Testing – through open enquiry to uncover possible new ways of thinking. Considering norms and taken-for-granted assumptions.

4. Probing – non-judgemental consideration of other people's views, drawing out facts, assumptions, reasons and consequences and considering alternatives.

5. Being – Raelin sees this as the most influential of the five, which can also be referred to as 'mindfulness', an awareness of a situation without trying to input meaning, but considering what we can learn from it and how the practitioner becomes a part of the whole process.

He suggests that, generally, most practitioners do not move beyond a basic approach to problem solving as shown in Figure 1.5.

Figure 1.5 Raelin (2002)

Reflexivity

You have already considered how reflective practitioners engage in critical self-reflection, examining the impact that their own background, culture, assumptions, feelings and behaviour have upon their practice. The reflexive practitioner also takes account of the wider political culture, current ideology, national trends and legislation. To understand the term reflexivity, Finlay and Gough (2003) describe the concept as forming a continuum (see Figure 1.6).

Figure 1.6 Finlay and Gough's (2003) reflexive continuum

This demonstrates the bi-directional nature of the relationship between cause and effect and giving meaning to experience. Therefore reflexivity goes beyond reflection allowing us to use our experience to make sense of complex professional judgements. Finlay (2008) talks of reflexivity as having five overlapping variants with critical self-reflection at the core.

- Introspection – this is the one-to-one dialogue with yourself, thinking about feelings and emotions.

- Inter-subjective reflection – thinking about the relationship between your practice and the context in which it is set.

- Mutual collaboration – what Ghaye (2000) calls *reflective conversations*, the dialogical relationship between professionals.

- Social critiques – this focuses upon the wider cultural and political context within which the professional has to work.

- Ironic deconstruction – this is the analysis of the discursive practices focusing upon the ambiguity and multiplicity of meaning.

Challenges to reflective practice

Although the process of reflection, as described here, may appear long and complex, there is no need for it to be so and it may involve no more than five minutes at the end of the day to reflect upon the critical moments. It is likely that when people say that they have no time for reflection they are talking about retrospective and prospective reflection. This makes the 'heat of the moment' reflection, what Schön (1983) calls reflection in action, all the more important. So the barrier is perhaps not one of time but of willingness to engage each other in reflecting thoughts, feelings and actions.

That reflective practice is desirable and was demanded by the original Early Years Foundation Stage documents (DfES, 2008) is often taken for granted, but does the process really yield satisfactory returns for the time invested in its development? The amended EYFS (DfE, 2014) has much less emphasis upon reflective practice, but it does assume that all early years practitioners should be skilful, thoughtful and critical in their practice. Busy and sometimes over-stretched practitioners may well feel that reflective practice is difficult and time-consuming and this could result in unthinking and unsatisfactory results. Mechanical checklists of simplistic questions are unlikely to yield a thinking and thoughtful workforce. Answering questions simply to satisfy inspection processes, with answers that the practitioner thinks the inspectorate want to hear, is also of little use to the process. One can understand why some practitioners, whose only experience of reflective practice has been of this sort, would not think that the time invested produces credible and innovative results and solutions.

Clearly the process of reflection should not overwhelm your practice and it needs to be used selectively. One of the aims of the New Labour government in 2006 was to professionalise the early years workforce and raise the quality of provision for young children (DfES, 2006). A set of standards was developed to enable graduates to achieve Early Years Professional Status (EYPS). This has since been superseded by the introduction, by the coalition government (2013), of the Early Years Teacher status. The two essential elements of this were to be able to lead and change practice and to be a reflective practitioner. '*8.6 Reflect on and evaluate the effectiveness of provision, and shape and support good practice.*' (NCTL, 2013: p5) These initiatives were largely influenced by research conducted by Sylva et al (2004) and the Effective Provision of Pre-school Education (EPPE) Project. This demonstrated that settings run by well-qualified critical thinkers were highly influential in producing the enabling environment required for young children to learn and thrive educationally. It is interesting that the category concerned with the standards of physical care was shown to be less influenced by the qualifications of the staff than any other. According to CWDC (2010a) such critical thinkers

> *have a clear grasp of reasons why they are acting in particular ways. They recognise their role in improving children's experiences and life chances and in maximising their opportunities. They make decisions based on the depth of their knowledge of the EYFS and relevant theories and research. They are alive to changing circumstances and respond flexibly with children's interests at heart. They review, analyse and evaluate their own and others' practice and then judge whether they are making a difference to the well-being, learning and development of children in their own and colleagues' care.*
>
> (Children's Workforce Development Council, 2010, p 7)

This public scrutiny of early years practice can clearly be a scary business, opening us up to the risk of ridicule and attack. If you see reflective practice in terms of success and failure then it can seem to be intimidating, which could result in defensiveness and closing down the open-minded thinking it is trying to create. Reflective practice needs to be a continuing process, not something with an end point, viewing every situation, no matter how difficult, as something that can be learned from if you have the mindset to improve and go forward with grit and determination. You need to move from an approach which asks:

- *What is right?*

- *What is good practice?*

to a more inquisitorial approach of:

- *How can I create effective learning environments?* and

- *How can I develop my setting to offer accessible and equitable practices?*

Reflective practice is not going to be effective if the profession as a whole or the setting/workplace does not value its role in providing for the environment with coercive institutional practices. Boud and Walker (1998) suggest that managers of settings need to work hard to provide a working environment that supports both individual and collegiate reflections and one that encourages staff to challenge the dominant culture and practice. This can be difficult and has the potential to promote discord and an entrenchment of negative views as they challenge the issues of power and control.

> *a culture that permits questioning of assumptions is difficult to tolerate because it requires that people in control lose their grip on the status quo.*
>
> (Raelin, 2002, p 68)

As a practitioner you therefore need confidence in your practice if you are to engage with an honest self-appraisal and belong to a strong and cohesive working team which is able to confront its working processes and outcomes. A team willing to embrace change and trans-formation can engage with the whole reflective process in a non-threatening and supportive capacity. This also allows the capacity to co-construct understanding, ideas and meaning alongside the children (see Figure 1.7).

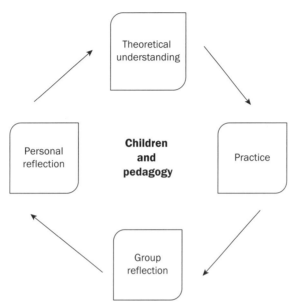

Figure 1.7 Co-construction of meaning

Reflecting, with the children taking a more active role in the process of co-constructing their learning, can have benefits for all parties. Through discussion and sustained shared think-ing, the children can be encouraged to ask questions and most importantly to look for solu-tions to their own problems creating learning from within rather than from above.

Another challenge could be that even using the term 'practitioner' could deter reflection. A practitioner is perceived as being involved with 'practice', a culture of 'doing', a busy person constantly on the move, rather than a thinker, reflector and researcher. Whilst there is much debate about the difference between a practitioner and a professional, a professional is more associated with words such as conscientious, engaging in constant evaluation, reflec-tion and striving for excellence. Perhaps a more accurate description should be a 'profes-sional practitioner'. Certainly those working with children need to be reflective, articulate, evaluative and highly knowledgeable, if they are to lay claim to being committed and autono-mous professionals.

Ethical issues

Professional practitioners engaged with reflective practice need to consider the risks involved with moral judgement and ethical concerns. Issues of sensitivity to confidentiality, privacy, informal disclosure, rights, consent and professional relationships must be explored. There must also be consideration of how reflections should be shared, when they should be shared and with whom. Such in-depth introspective thinking can potentially be what Brookfield (1990) called 'psychologically explosive'; he believed that there must also be attention paid to the personal, emotive and visceral nature of reflection. This constant striving for improved practice could result in the opposite of what is required, a lack of confidence in the practitioners and loss of self-esteem, causing negative attitudes to practices.

Seeing ourselves as life-long learners within the setting is probably the first step to engaging with reflective practice as well as understanding how practitioners making sense of their own beliefs, values and perceptions has important implications for their practice, teaching and learning with the children.

Reflective activity

Identify someone in your past who was a favourite teacher/carer/playgroup leader, etc. What characteristics do you think they had that make you remember them so many years later?

» *Make a list of their characteristics as you remember them.*

» *How do you think that you compare to these?*

The first one has been done as an example.

Characteristics of my favourite practitioner	Characteristics of me as a practitioner
He was understanding and tried hard to comprehend why I found something hard to do.	I try hard to see an incident from a range of perspectives.

» *Now examine the list of your characteristics and consider a recent incident in your practice; how do you think these affected the way in which you dealt with the episode?*

» *Can you find an example of each of your characteristics in your own experience?*

Chapter reflections

What we have seen in this chapter is that reflective practice is often hard to do effectively. The nature of the activity changes with context, different environments, organisations and relationships and all of these will demand different ways to reflect. The multiplicity and proliferation of models of reflection show that either there is simply a lack of consensus about a definition of reflective practice or there are genuinely different ways to reflect depending upon the context and area of professional practice. The problem with imposing a specific model is that it leaves little scope for practitioners to draw upon their own professional judgements, feelings and values. The practitioner who unthinkingly follows a particular model could render their practice more mechanical and mechanistic, which is the total opposite of Schön's original idea of 'professional artistry'. This suggests that, although different models are needed for the particular requirements of differing professions and contexts within those professions, there is no one model that can be held up as the perfect model and the definitive answer. Reflective practice should be a means to an end and not an end in itself.

> *Models need to be applied selectively, purposefully, flexibly and judiciously.*
>
> (Finlay, 2008, p 10)

What is ultimately important is that you learn from your reflections and from the investment of time and effort that you put into the process.

» *Pick up on apparently insignificant happenings and connect them to indicate patterns and consequences.*

» *Review issues by looking at them through another person's eyes or seeing things in a new light.*

» *Recognise how your own prior experience, feelings, values and emotions can affect your practice.*

» *Understand the importance of looking for innovative ideas and new creative solutions.*

» *Have the confidence in your own knowledge and practice to try new and innovative ways of approaching tasks.*

You are privileged to be working with young children and their families and you owe it to them to be as knowledgeable, skilful, ethical, moral and reflective as you can be. The following acronym may help you remember the key aspects of reflection:

Regular and relevant

Ethical

Feelings

Learning

Evaluation

Change

Time

Extended reflections

»   *Using the questions posed in the reflective model by by Jay and Johnson (2002) in table 1.1, critically reflect on a recent incident in your setting. Create a diagram or pictorial representation of your thoughts. Remember to include alternative ideas or solutions to your problem.*

»   *Share this with colleagues and invite their comments.*

»   *In the light of their comments would you now want to change the diagram?*

CASE STUDY

Aleesha's story

Three weeks after I started at Triggers Nursery I had to deal with a parent complaining about the way a junior member of staff had dealt with their child who had bitten another. I was required to help the staff member to write up the incident in an incident report book. After talking to the parent I was immediately worried. I was scared that I had not said the right things and was unable to answer her questions properly. It felt a bit like when I was training and had to give a presentation about a child being bullied, and the tutor was asking me questions. I didn't know what to say so thought that I could perhaps make up some good answers and bluster my way through it even though this was bluffing! On both occasions that was helpful in maintaining my confidence at the time but it could so easily have gone wrong and I have seen others come unstuck by making it up as they go along.

As I was a new manager it was important to me that all contacts with parents went well and that I could create a good impression, maybe I wanted too much to do well. I now toss and turn in bed at night thinking about it, and feel as though it was a disaster.

I need to think why the conversation with the parent had such an effect on me, my voice was 'wobbly' and my efforts to remain calm were frustrated. Colleagues in the nursery said afterwards that I looked in control despite what I was feeling, but did they really mean that or were they just trying to be kind?

As I think back maybe it was not as bad as it seemed. My colleagues seem to think that I dealt with the altercation well. Perhaps I need to think about how I will react to such a sensitive situation in the future and maybe I will do some research on the internet for some advice about assertiveness, or perhaps go on that leadership course that they do at the University.

One week later

I am feeling more positive about things now although I am still feeling a bit cross. I have started to read some material about appraising a situation and not letting one thing dominate my life. I think that I understand better now what was happening and this has given me more confidence in my ability to engage with parents in the future. As I write this I realise how useful it is to reflect on things and to write them down so that I can see the same situation from a range of different perspectives. I can see that there were things that I had not thought about in this situation, such as the parent's limited understanding of English, perhaps she had been bullied as a child, or maybe the child was unwell, tired or stressed on the day. I can also see the areas in which I could improve, knowing where I went wrong and admitting to the mistakes has perhaps given me the chance to improve.

Reflective activity

» *What challenges did the manager encounter both personally and professionally?*

» *How do you think that retrospective reflection (reflection on action) helped her to understand what happened?*

» *How could reflection in action have helped her to respond better at the time?*

» *How could prospective reflection help her to plan what she will do in the future?*

» *What could she now share with her colleagues in case they are ever in the same position, so that they could learn from her experience, and how could this be achieved?*

» *Can you think of a situation where you have struggled professionally and could the three types of reflection discussed in this chapter have helped you? Explain your answer.*

Extended thinking

» *Reflecting on the case study above you may want to consider the following questions posed by the flow charts.*

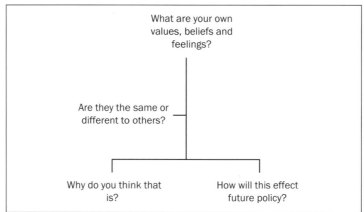

Further reading

Hallet, E (2013) *The Reflective Early Years Practitioner*. London: Sage.

This is a very vocationally orientated and grounded view of reflective practice which sets reflection into a range of different early years contexts. This book has something useful for all levels from level 2 to postgraduate staff, and contains several excellent practical and pedagogical examples to enable you to consider your problem-solving options. There is a particularly useful chapter to enhance your reading on 'Work-Based Reflective Pedagogy'. Hallet describes the learning journey of a critically reflective practitioner and the place of continuing professional development in the evolution of a unique, specialised and critically reflective early years workforce.

References

Boud, D and Walker, D (1998) Promoting Reflection in Professional Courses: The Challenge of Context. *Studies in Higher Education*, 23(2): 191–206.

Boud, D, Keogh, R and Walker, D (1985) *Reflection: Turning Experience into Learning*. London: Kogan Page.

Brookfield, S (1990) Using Critical Incidents to Explore Learners' Assumptions, in Mezirow, J (ed), *Fostering Critical Reflection in Adulthood*. San Francisco: Jossey-Bass.

Children's Workforce Development Council (CWDC) (2010) *On the Right Track*. Leeds: CWDC.

Department for Education (DfE) (2014) *Statutory Framework for the Early Years Foundation Stage: Setting the Standards for Learning, Development and Care for Children from Birth to Five*. London: Department for Education.

Department for Education and Skills (DfES) (2006) *Children's Workforce Strategy: Building a World-Class Workforce for Children, Young People and Families*. Nottingham: DfES Publications.

DfES (2008) *The Practice Guidance for the Early Years Foundation Stage*. London: Department for Education and Skills.

Dewey, J (1933) *How Do We Think?* Boston, MA: DC Heath and Co.

Finlay, L (2008) Reflecting on 'Reflective Practice', PBL paper 52, www.open.ac.uk/opencetl/ sites/www.open.ac.uk.opencetl/files/files/ecms/web-content/Finlay-(2008)-Reflecting-on-reflective-practice-PBPL-paper-52.pdf (accessed 23 February 2017).

Finlay, L and Gough, B (2003) *Reflexivity: A Practical Guide for Researchers in Health and Social Sciences*. Oxford: Blackwell Publishing.

Ghaye, T (2000) Into the Reflective Mode: Bridging the Stagnant Moat. *Reflective Practice*, 1(1): 5–9.

Gibbs, G (1998) *Learning by Doing: A Guide to Teaching and Learning Methods*. Oxford: Further Education Unit, Oxford Polytechnic.

Grushka, K, Hinde McLeod, J and Reynolds, R (2005) Reflecting Upon Reflection: Theory and Practice in one Australian University Teacher Education Programme. *Reflective Practice*, 6(2): 239–46.

Hallet, E (2013) *The Reflective Early Years Practitioner*. London: Sage.

Health and Safety Executive (2003) HSE Enforcement Guide. [online] Available from: www.hse.gov.uk/ enforce/enforcementguide (accessed 23 February 2017).

Jay, J K and Johnson, K L (2002) Capturing Complexity: A Typology of Reflective Practice for Teacher Education. *Teaching and Teacher Education*, 18: 73–85.

Kolb, D A (2015) *Experiential Learning: Experiences as the Source of Learning and Development.* 2nd ed. Upper Saddle River, New Jersey: Pearson Educational.

LeDoux, J (1999) *The Emotional Brain*. London: Phoenix.

Moon, J (1999) *Reflection in Learning and Professional Development*. London: Kogan Page.

National College for Teaching and Leadership (NCTL) (2013) *Teachers Standards (Early Years)*. London: Crown.

Nutbrown, C (2012) *Foundations for Quality: The Independent Review of Early Education and Childcare Qualifications*. London: Crown.

Osterman, K and Kottkamp, R (1993) *Reflective Practice for Educators: Improving Schooling through Professional Development*. Thousand Oaks, CA: Sage.

Race, P (2014) *Making Learning Happen*. 3rd ed. London: Sage.

Raelin, J A (2002) 'I Don't Have Time to Think!' versus the Art of Reflective Practice. *Reflections*, 4(1): 66–79.

Rowling, J K (2000) *Harry Potter and the Goblet of Fire*. New York: Scholastic Inc.

Ruch, G (2002) From Triangle to Spiral: Reflective Practice in Social Work, Practice and Research. *Social Work Education*, 21(2): 199–216.

Schacter, D L (2001) *The Seven Sins of Memory: How the Mind Forgets and Remembers*. Boston: Houghton Mifflin and Co.

Schön, D (1983) *The Reflective Practitioner: How Professionals Think in Action*. New York: Basic Books.

Sylva, K, Melhuish, E, Sammons, P, Siraj-Blatchford, I and Taggart, B. (2004) *The Effective Provision of Pre-school Education (EPPE) Project; Technical Paper 12 – The Final Report: Effective Pre-school Education*. London: DfES/Institute of Education.

Vygotsky, L S (1978) *Mind and Society: The Development of Higher Mental Processes*. Cambridge, MA: Harvard University Press.

2 Writing for reflection

RUTH GILL

I wonder if I've been changed in the night. Let me think. Was I the same when I got up this morning? I almost think I can remember feeling a little different. But if I'm not the same, the next question is 'Who in the world am I?' Ah, that's the great puzzle!

(Carroll, 1954, pp 20–1)

Introduction

You may have frequently asked yourself the same question *Who am I?* and tried to work out if you were the Mad Hatter or the White Rabbit. It may be that for early years practitioners (EYPs) we can all identify with the Mad Hatter, White Rabbit or Cheshire Cat. Whatever happens today will change the person you are tomorrow to a lesser or greater extent. The key to understanding the change is how you reflect upon each moment and understand the impact this has on you and others you work with.

The previous chapter considered critical reflection on the past and present to enable reflection for the future allowing you to feel confident that your actions and future practice are based on learning from those day-to-day changes. This greater understanding of yourself opens up the possibilities to be the best you can possibly be in the early years sector for the people you work with and for. The thought process is important but, as mentioned in Chapter 1, recalling events over time can be less effective as memories change and the thoughts and feelings surrounding an event change. Time alters perceptions of the event and inaccurate recall of the situation can change the way in which your future actions are formed and implemented.

You may feel, regardless of age and qualification, that the concept of reflecting is initially difficult to quantify: *What is it? How do I do 'it'? Am I reflecting properly?* Dyer and Taylor (2012) explore the anxieties expressed by undergraduate students who are required to reflect on their theoretical lectures and apply such reflection to practice. Reflection is personal, developmental and increases your ability to 'unpick' daily events that can be improved upon. Often the reflection process can be a negative experience and, while trying to understand 'what went wrong', your self-esteem may be affected too. Balanced reflection is vital for the reflective process to be meaningful and life-enhancing; remember to reflect on the positive events as well as those that do not 'go to plan'. Rolfe, Jasper and Freshwater (2011) confirm that often reflection is on a negative situation and, for the emergence of a greater sense of self as a professional, you will need to reflect on all situations that test your professional and personal self. You reflect on your everyday experiences sometimes without realising that you are reflecting.

Reflective activity

Reflect with members of your family about an event you all experienced.

» *What features of the event are the same in your own personal recollection as they are in the recollections of your family? What features are different or at odds?*

» *Why do you recall different aspects to those around you?*

» *Is your recall associated with strong feelings experienced during the event?*

Extended thinking

» *Sometimes you will replay these events over and over in your mind to make sense of them and to make new meaning. Think about how you could have acted differently and what the result may have been. This will help you to think before you act with future events.*

Your perceptions of events may differ because of the lapse in time and how you 'felt' about the event. Understanding that your recollection of events is based on your own perceptions will help you to appreciate that other people also have a different view of the event. Your reflection is not 'wrong'; it is your view. This is key in trying to understand your professional self and how workplace events will be interpreted and reflected upon differently by work colleagues.

Why write for reflection?

Reflection can be verbal or written, formal or informal. Writing reflections can be just one of the many ways in which to try to make sense of any event. Often writing for reflection is dismissed as a 'waste of time', 'a diary of nonsense' or something that 'only authors do'. You have made marks in a variety of ways from being a baby playing with yogurt on your highchair tray to the toddler years of writing on newly wallpapered walls! At school, children are encouraged to write about their holidays, birthdays and special events in their life, so writing about what has happened to you is not entirely new. As children you were asked to recall these events and describe what the event was and how you felt. Writing these experiences down assists with the 'thought process' of reflection and begins to help you understand the events. As they unfold, they play through your mind and you 're-live' that moment. Some of you may have even kept a diary when younger and this may have helped you through the turbulent teenage years when it seemed that nobody understood you. This 'diary writing' gave you a forum to release your thoughts and gain some relief from the anxiety you felt. You write all the time for personal and professional reasons, from shopping lists to end-of-year reports, for yourself or others. Yet pose writing for reflection to early years professionals and there is some trepidation at what is being asked for. Are you being asked for a life history, a résumé of your career or a 'daily diary' like that of Adrian Mole? The perception of writing is one of a private experience, as in a personal diary, and not to be shared with others. 'Revealing' innermost thoughts and feelings is not something you want to willingly partake in let alone share with others. So the beginning needs to be your story, an understanding of who you are and future possibilities, both personal and professional.

> *Reflective writing ... differs from other forms of writing only in that it has one primary purpose: it is undertaken for the specific purpose of learning; to enable us to come to a different, or deeper, understanding of whatever we are reflecting on.*
>
> (Rolfe, Jasper and Freshwater, 2011, p55)

Reflecting on the personal and professional 'you' is an important place to begin; effective reflection is only possible with this starting point and builds the foundations for a greater understanding of 'self'.

Reflective activity

» *Write two lists on an A4 sheet of paper, one for personal and the other for professional. Start by writing out facts such as your job title and how many siblings you have before exploring your values and beliefs in each list.*

» *How much of the personal 'you' is similar to the professional 'you'?*

The example shown below will help you to start your reflection.

Personal	Professional
I am a mother of two, wife, carer and have two siblings, one older one younger.	Nursery Practitioner. Worked in the same setting for ten years.
I believe that you should treat people with respect. Bad manners and rudeness are something I will not tolerate at home.	I aim for high professional standards and believe that parents are to be respected as the child's first educator.
I try to relax at home through reading novels and going for country walks. I need some time alone to contemplate what has happened each day.	I respect other practitioner contributions but find it difficult to understand others who do not seem to share my high-standard approach.

Extended thinking

» *You need to consider what the future may hold for you as a professional. Add an additional column to your chart to reflect on what you want to develop as a professional. This forward thinking will help you to make choices based on your hopes and dreams for the future.*

This starting point will underpin all your reflections and the personal and professional 'you' will evolve as your ability to reflect is enhanced. Taking time to reflect is critical, be that a few minutes at the end of the day or 30 minutes of quiet contemplation. Clutterbuck and Hirst (2003) examine the time taken by professionals to reflect as vital to be able to work more effectively and efficiently. Reflection should therefore evolve from a reactive behaviour to a proactive and instinctive way to look forward and anticipate how your actions and communication style influence your daily life. This can lead to greater influence and control of what lies ahead.

Although models of reflection can guide you in reflective practice, Thompson and Pascal (2012) consider that reflective practice is not simply a matter of process.

> *Professional practice is not a technical process of applying (scientifically derived) solutions to practice problems. More realistically, it is a matter of wrestling with the complexities of both theory and practice, using professional artistry to move forward as effectively as possible.*
>
> (Thompson and Pascal, 2012, p 314)

The more skilled you become at critical reflective practice the more likely you are to be able to think creatively about 'moving forward' rather than applying solutions to problems. Creative thinking can therefore be developed into creative reflective writing. Bolton (2005) phrases this creativity as 'exploratory' and 'expressive' and an essential part of writing reflectively to understand the hidden meanings within your practice reflections. This element of reflective writing or 'meaning making' is viewed by Thompson and Pascal as an omission in Schön's work. Essential to critical reflective writing is your ability to make meaning from your narratives of practice. You have lived through the experience and can recall it from memory. To then commit it to written words is the start of what Bolton (2005) calls 'storying'. 'Storying' your experiences is a way of working through each moment you have experienced. As with all stories there is a beginning, a middle and an end and this is your unique story of an event. Writing reflectively through a story technique will help you to examine all aspects of a situation to understand the difficulties or successes experienced. This 'storying' can lead to group collaborative reflections. The more confident you become, the more empowered you will be in writing reflectively and sharing this with others.

Where to start writing?

Introducing reflective writing to early years practitioners is often met with caution as it is not used formally as a 'tool' for reflecting or valued sufficiently enough. You may already use reflection in a number of ways to examine the provision offered to children and how to facilitate a child's progression. Writing in these situations tends to become evaluative rather than reflective. Indeed you have to reflect on your education provision but the writing aspect of this reflection results in an evaluation which looks at what the next steps are for children rather than being a holistic reflection on the event encompassing the 'you' in the scenario.

Reflective writing needs to be viewed as purposeful and to add value to a person; it is an investment of a greater development of self. Rolfe, Jasper and Freshwater (2011) explore key features of writing; one being as a purposeful activity. As soon as you assign a purpose and value to an activity you will find the time to commit to writing reflectively. This time the purpose, initially, is not about the children you educate or care for; it is about writing purposefully and, thus, making connections between events to make greater sense of them for self-development. Spending time on you, allowing yourself to take time to reflect will eventually influence the personal and professional 'you' but will also improve interactions and outcomes for those you work with. Explaining to your employer the value of writing reflectively and having the time to do so often causes tension, as a 'visible' outcome of your reflection is not easy to quantify or transfer to others. This results in reflective activity being overlooked in the workplace (Walsh 2009). Your reflective writing will yield positive results for you and those you work with only by having a long-term 'investment' of time.

Reflective writing allows for a deeper reflection and reflexivity creating rich meanings from what has been seen or heard. Bolton (2005) asserts that writing and talking are different; writing allows for connections between events to be realised, examined and developed; it is creative and enjoyable but requires courage to undertake. Writing uncovers parts of an event that can be uncomfortable and you need courage to face something that can reveal an unpleasant aspect of yourself previously ignored. Writing cannot be hurried which is problematic when you are a busy practitioner or setting manager. A common theme with all EYPs is that there is very little time to attend to such reflection when you have a full complement of children to nurture. The start of your reflective writing may begin with reflecting at home at the end of your working day on the events that have transpired. Bolton (2005) advises that to start the writing process you need to write about non-critical incidents. These could be the routine aspects of your day and how you felt each moment unfolded. This starting point will ease you into critical reflection and your courage can build the further you extend your writing.

Where to start sometimes involves reflecting on past experiences of writing and how your writing was viewed. For example at school or university writing was created as a result of directive lessons to produce something that was assessed by someone you viewed as an expert. This experience was often fraught with anxiety about whether you felt you had completed the work to the standard required. Rolfe, Jasper and Freshwater (2011) liken this to the difference between learning to write and writing to learn; a process we have all experienced through education. With reflective writing your starting point can be liberating as you break free from writing in a constrained way that will be judged by another person. You can begin to write reflectively, free from academic scrutiny to formally record your innermost thoughts. You are again learning to write, yet for a different purpose; not to meet learning outcomes of an assessment but learning to write for self-development. The writing to learn phase develops as your reflective writing increases and becomes more analytical and interpretive; an engagement with your inner voice creates a private but purposeful dialogue, your new proactive self.

Your reflective writing continuum will begin with small anecdotal comments either on a mobile, tablet device or a notebook. The beauty of using a mobile device is that you can keep your thoughts safe and secure, only accessible by you. A notebook is more difficult to keep private. The development of reflective writing can be seen in Figure 2.1.

Figure 2.1 *Development of reflective writing*

- **Notes and descriptive narrative** events reflect an early 'embryonic' reflective phase of writing.

- **Dialogic, analytical narrative** develops your ability to extend your earlier embryonic phase to consider the finer detail of an event. This leads to the concentrated moments of deep reflective writing; immersing you in the moment to realise and develop 'self' for professional insight. This will lead to a greater confidence and belief in your professional life.

Reflective writing is personal and not everyone will reach the optimum level of a proactive and deeply analytical reflective professional. This final proactive stage of reflective writing encompasses not only self-reflection but reflection on others. Reflecting on others may have emerged in the reactive 'embryonic' stage of reflection where you try to understand the event and the behaviours of those involved. Often this phase is associated with looking to others as the reason why an event was negative. Looking inwards to discover you are the reason the event was negative is an unpleasant experience revealing a hidden part of you, previously unknown.

Engaging in this level of reflection gives you greater confidence to encourage others to embrace reflective practice.

Extended thinking

» *Once you feel more confident reflecting on personal and professional situations introduce the reflective activity (page 27) to your work colleagues as a team development session. This will help individual staff to begin reflective writing and to start a dialogue about professional values and beliefs. Guidelines for sharing personal and professional reflections can be found on page 35 and will help you manage these team experiences. Not everyone will want to share at first but once individuals feel 'safe', they will do so following your lead and that of other more confident practitioners. The outcome of such an activity can lead to a greater understanding of each other in the team, what motivates each other and more importantly how to support each other when they need it most. Becoming self-aware is vital for professional growth.*

Increased self-awareness

Increased self-awareness through reflective writing engages you in the wider sociological context of your personal and professional life. Brechin, Brown and Eby (2000) conceptualise the criticality in deep reflection that reveals the wider context of any given event. You begin to look beyond your engagement in the event to critically reflect on the interaction of others, organisational influences and the wider political agenda that influences your professional being. Increased awareness of the internal and external forces at play will help you to define and implement the most appropriate course of action to take for the benefit of others in your care. This selfless notion is not uncommon in caring professions but you need to acknowledge and influence choices that help your professional and personal development as well as choices for the benefit of others.

Increased self-awareness is possible through uncovering hidden aspects of yourself which can be problematic. How can you know what you don't know? It is like reading for your studies; the more you read the more you begin to appreciate how little you knew before you engaged in that reading. Increased self-awareness through reflection will help you to uncover those hidden parts of you, making the unknown known.

Discovering the unknown is expertly defined by Joseph Luft and Harry Ingram, with the Johari window concept of making the unknown known which is explained as individually having *the capability to understand our abilities and limitations* (Thomas, 1992, p 225). Sole (1997) reconceptualises the Johari window and proposes that it can be used to frame questions, from the simple to the more complex, in order to gain a greater understanding of any given scenario (Figure 2.2, below). Reflective writing can enhance your capability to critically consider the simple and more complex events, increasing self-awareness.

On occasions, writing with increased criticality and reaching new heights of self-awareness can be detrimental professionally. Research students confess that the reflective writing process can become another form of procrastination:

Simple easy questions	Simple complex questions
Public	Blind
	self aware
Simple difficult questions	Simple complex questions
Private	Unknown

Figure 2.2 Johari's Window: discovering the unknown
Source: Adapted from Sole 1997 and Thomas 1992

> As far as my dissertation was concerned, journaling became my biggest procrastinator, because I just had to record all these things in my life, and each day I would end, 'and now I have to start writing my literature review!' If only I could have

just written it like I could my journal. However, recording this so many times just showed me how much I was procrastinating, so I stopped writing [my journal] for a bit and took on meditating, which is a little like journaling as I was able to reflect, and eventually I did get my literature review done.

(Final year dissertation student)

This student's reflection has revealed the difficulties with reflective writing and is a cautionary tale of when the writing needs to pause and other means of reflection need to take place. As with most 'tools' there is a time and place for all of them and you need to choose what to use and when. Likewise to immerse yourself in a high level of reflective writing over a long period of time can be exhausting. As your writing of events develops you can determine if the event needs close examination or notes and short sentences to help to see a pattern of events over time. Indeed, meditation may be something to consider in times of increased responsibility.

Timescale is not a feature of Figure 2.1 as learning to reflect and write reflectively is like learning to ride a bike; once you have mastered the skill you never forget how to do it. All that you have to appreciate is the more time you invest in writing, the greater the depth of reflection and mastery of the skill you will achieve. Thompson and Pascal (2012) go further and suggest that an increase in work pressure further validates the importance of taking time to reflect. With increased work comes increased responsibility and accountability and, therefore, you need a clear vision and direction associated with your role. You can only do this well through reflection. Having this clear vision is referred to by Cowan and Stroud (2016) as having focus. Having focus on an event involves constructive thinking that enables you to improve the quality of actions made in what Cowan and Stroud refer to as making the action more 'fertile'(2016, p 28). They propose a 'composting' feature of reflection:

...composting reflection digs around purposefully in what they have already accumulated, disturbing it, sifting through it, turning it over, letting in some fresh air, and then bedding it down again for a while.

This captures the process of reflection and the unhurried nature of deep reflective engagement.

RAIN framework

Deep engagement is sometimes difficult to start in the initial stages of reflective practice and you may feel a formal structure or framework will aid your focus of an event. Using the RAIN framework will help you to write reflectively until you find your own style or, if you prefer, this format may continue to support your reflections.

To begin the process use RAIN to structure your writing. This eliminates the evaluative aspect of reflection and encourages deeper consideration of the moment.

Reflect – Setting the scene

- What is the moment for reflection? Who was involved? Length of time? Conversations detailed verbatim. Reactions, tone of voice and gestures of others noted.

Analyse – Thinking through the events

- What was your involvement? Did your interactions shape those of others? Did those involved use effective listening skills? Was communication effective – if not, what barriers, visible or otherwise, were evident? Was a resolution identified?

Interpret – Thinking through the possibilities

- What, if anything, could you have done differently to improve the outcome? Was the outcome determined by those involved and the environment you work in? Was your communication effective to fully extend the meaning of those interactions experienced?

Next steps – Feeding forward the reflection

- What will happen now after this reflection? Further reflection or purposeful action?

Reflective activity

Reflect on your day at work. Begin to write about interactions with staff, children and parents. Consider the following when writing your reflections.

» *How were you feeling about the day ahead before you arrived at work?*

» *Were your interactions shaped by the previous day's situations?*

» *What was the biggest challenge experienced?*

» *Now look at these using RAIN. Re-read your reflections and take time to consider each aspect below. Remember to start with a non-critical incident.*

- **Reflect** – *What was the incident? Is your account thorough? Is this incident in context? Does your written account include your feelings associated with the incident?*

- **Analyse** – *What are the features of this incident? Who was involved? What were your interactions and reactions to the incident? How did others contribute to the incident? How did you feel after the incident?*

- **Interpret** – *Which part of the process raised questions of practice or personal concern? To what extent have your reactions and interactions changed the outcome of the incident? What, if anything, could be changed?*

- **Next steps** – *What does this incident raise for you as a person and as a professional? Will this change how you 'deal' with future incidents of this nature? Write in your reflection the uncertainty or affirmation of your experience.*

Critically reflecting on any incident will illuminate the finer details that are sometimes overlooked; these missed moments are essential for a complete and thorough reflection on the incident. Regular written reflections starting with this framework will enable you to piece together a wider context of you as a person and professional. This gives you a greater professional insight and one which is described as being reflexive in nature (Thompson and Pascal,

2012). You are utilising your professional expertise to its fullest as a result of your heightened sense of self-awareness which, in turn, comes from your reflections.

Extended thinking

» *After writing a series of these events you will need to revisit them to recognise reoccurring themes. Which are the dominant themes: the environment you work in, the people you work with, the demands of the role you have? Or are they triggered by a personal event that altered your professional performance? This will help you decide how you might begin to share your reflections with colleagues.*

Brookfield (2002) uses four critical lenses to examine teaching practice through reflection. The third lens looks to the colleagues you work with and how they may be able to help you see another dimension of the specific event. Reflective practice can isolate you through fear of sharing your perceived shortcomings with others. Seek out a trusted member of the team who you work closely with; they will be your 'critical mirrors and sounding boards' (Brookfield, 2002, p 34). They can offer a different perspective that you had not previously considered which begins to change your initial reflection on the event. Enhanced reflection with others such as this can help you to feel supported when you need it most, and can support other staff too as your reflective skills develop.

Narrative reflections

Writing your reflections can be structured following the RAIN framework or completely free from structure, a narrative or story. Boudreau, Liben and Fuks (2012) examine narrative or storying as a way to write reflectively for individual purposes or for group reflection. This 'contemplative writing' involves putting pen to paper to recount an event. The authors further assert that reflective writing allows for review and analysis, time and time again, with the opportunity to review and extend the initial narrative. Further to this Charon and Hermann (2012) purport that the act of writing itself teaches reflective skills; the more you practise writing the more competent you will become at reflective writing. Reflective writing is personal to you and can be in any format or structure you choose; the RAIN framework will help to start the process but thereafter you may feel more confident to write a narrative-based text that is unstructured.

Bolton (2005) examines the concept of storying and telling your own story as a narrative of text to create meaning. As the writer, you will have your own view of an event and, as a reader of such material, you will have a different view. This is why writing reflections is so important; becoming a reader of your own work can sometimes give you clarity which you would otherwise not be able to capture. Reading your own reflections over a period of time, and revisiting particular sections of your narrative, will help you to deconstruct events developing critical reflection. Bolton (2005) continues to explore the nature of narratives and how these can be enhanced by others' perceptions of the very same incident. You have already started to do this at the beginning of this chapter with the recalling of a family event. Consider the following activity for professional development.

Reflective activity

Consider a recent experience at work that you and other staff were involved in. Try to choose an event that was not a crisis event, for example, an interaction with a parent as they were leaving their child in your care.

»   *Write down your narrative surrounding the event and ask other staff involved to write down their own reflections.*

»   *Once complete, sit together and pass round each person's writing for others to read. When the writings have been around all involved, re-read your own and add to this what you now know from others' perceptions of the situation.*

Ask yourself the following:

»   *What was noted by others that you had not considered or omitted from your narrative?*

»   *Did others write in a factual or interpretive context? Were feelings associated with their perceptions?*

»   *How has your reflection changed with this additional information?*

Noting the perceptions of others might encourage you to seek the perspectives of work colleagues so that you can reflect on the complete event rather than just your perception of it. This form of inclusive team reflection is achieved as seen in the shaded area in Figure 2.1 and can enhance the proactive element of reflection and the ability to reflect for future moments (Wilson, 2008).

Extended thinking

»   *Collective reflection can often turn into an opportunity to 'gossip' about an event. Regardless of your role and responsibility in the setting you are ethically bound by the nature of the sector you work in to keep such reflections professional. At each collective reflection meeting ask yourself the following at various time intervals:*

1. Is the conversation inclusive?

2. Is the conversation respectful?

3. Is the conversation focused?

If your answer is 'no' to any of these during the conversation you need to intervene and bring the conversation and reflection back to the original focus. It may even be that you have exhausted all avenues and the reflection needs to end.

Writing reflectively for group collaboration

Bolton (2005) explores how writing reflectively can be shared and mitigate the apprehension sometimes faced by sharing your thoughts with others. She suggests the formation of peer mentors who, in pairs, can meet and discuss their reflective narrative and are a supportive feature of those initial stages of sharing something that once was a solitary reflective moment. This supportive aspect can 'filter' any contentious reflections before sharing with a wider group of professionals.

Sharing reflective journal entries with a team of professionals is described by Bolton (2005, p 88) as *deeply educative, and can be powerfully team-building*. That said, some professionals do not want to be involved and this could reduce the overall effectiveness and team collaboration possible. As with any personal and professional sharing activities, there need to be some guidelines to create a 'safe' environment in which to share. You may choose to form the following guidelines for professional reflection sessions with your own team or study group:

- mutual respect and trust is given to all who join each and every session;

- all shared information remains confidential unless a safeguarding concern is raised;

- listen to others, be supportive and value contributions;

- consider the professional and personal elements in all reflections to aid others' development of self;

- respect that all members can join and leave the group at any time.

You could stipulate some strict rules and boundaries. This might, however, be counterproductive, resulting in unsuccessful sessions and low participation. The group will gradually build a sense of identity and purpose leading to increased reflection, collaboration and greater team cohesion. This type of group collaboration can be used effectively between professionals who do not work together but share the same role in the sector, as seen in the following case study.

CASE STUDY 1

Group collaboration

A group of nursery managers met frequently over a period of ten years to share a variety of concerns and dilemmas they faced. Although they did not formally write down their reflections this opportunity, once per term, allowed them time to listen to each other's 'stories', to share similar scenarios and outcomes so that individuals were professionally supported. Often those staff who had more responsibilities felt more isolated as they were unable to share professional dilemmas with their own team, especially if the information related to employment difficulties. This group was unique in that they were not in direct competition with each other, their workplaces were similar and their roles and responsibilities were varied enough to generate experiences for each to draw upon.

This example shows how group collaboration doesn't have to be based on workplace teams but can have group membership of national appeal for professional development and enhancement.

Reflective writing for emotional incidents

Some reflections can be emotionally charged and to avoid writing these incidents could prolong the personal and professional dilemma you face. Engaging in deep reflection and becoming reflexive is essential for personal and professional development (Bolton, 2005). Goleman (2004) ponders that all judgements made, rational or personal, are affected by the emotions and emotions override the rational part of our thinking. When your emotions are involved with incidents, in practice your judgement can be compromised either in a positive or negative way.

Hickson (2011, p 836), explores *structured uncertainty* through reflective writing and proposes an *emotional scaffolding* that aids stability in times of change and uncertainty that arise from new knowledge gained from reflection. Emerging from this uncertainty was the understanding that change can be positive and reflecting on your own abilities and assumptions can be empowering. Indeed, reflective writing of emotional incidents will enable you to articulate a situation you may not have been able to verbally express. Emotional events are cited as one of the most common triggers in reflective writing (Brown, McNeill and Shaw, 2013); those moments that are the most difficult to comprehend can be retold and revisited for a deeper understanding. An Early Childhood student suggested that, for moments of great emotional turmoil, reflective writing enabled her to write the event to be revisited once she had calmed down. This is key to learning how to manage emotional events with clarity and often occurs afterwards when any strong emotions have subsided.

Reflecting on past events for future practice

CASE STUDY 2

Nursery manager

I started to write about my work 'events' during my foundation degree in early years as this was something I had not previously considered. Some days I would have nothing to write; I didn't feel I needed to with something as routine to me as staff being off sick, arranging cover for staff training, and making sure the child to adult ratios were correct. Initially I wrote about 'crisis' events that held really strong emotions for me. Re-reading one event that was minor was a revelation to me and highlighted an area of my management skills I needed to improve. I was so consumed as a new manager to a large team that I felt I had to 'fix' everything and solve all the day-to-day issues to relieve my busy staff. What I discovered was that I had made my staff dependent on me for basic day-to-day issues they should have the confidence and independence to do for themselves to enhance their professional practice. Reading my reflections on the event brought back strong memories and emotions that I'm sure I would have forgotten had they not been written down. I understand now looking back at this written reflection that I may have changed my practice as a manager but as a person I would always feel the need to take care of the practitioners who worked for me. That's who I am as a person and that will not change. I can now lead staff in being the best they can be supporting them rather than stifling their creativity and drive. My journal helps me to 'unpick' the personal and professional me so that I don't make the same negative professional judgements again.

Reflective activity

»   *How has your professional role conflicted with your values and beliefs and what is the 'right' way to lead or manage others?*

»   *Have your personal views influenced your professional practice and been detrimental to those professional people around you?*

»   *How might you begin to separate the personal and professional 'you' to understand how you react and interact with others? How do your values and beliefs underpin your professional practice?*

The case study above demonstrates how the personal and professional 'you' are evident in your daily practice with staff and children. Who you are as a person is not something to change per se but to reflect upon to ensure that your professional role reflects your professional judgement. Being an early years practitioner involves 'caring' about others and this can be difficult when faced with those crisis moments. Writing can help to relive the experience with clarity over time and to examine other situations. Rolfe, Jasper and Freshwater (2011) explain this as emancipatory reflection that opens up the possibilities to explore the situation, the thoughts and feelings associated with the event, leading to contextualising the event for actions to take. In Case Study 1 there is a strong sense of justifying the personal in the professional practice and it is sometimes difficult to professionalise interactions with people you work closely with. Writing these moments can help to examine whether your personal feelings have negatively contributed to a professional situation.

Extended thinking

»   *It is inevitable that the personal and professional will merge. However, being mindful of personal 'triggers' can help to minimise the negative impact of those in your professional life. Using your reflective writings think about what personal demands led you to a response you felt was negative or could have been handled differently. Was your behaviour triggered by an incident at home, a long term worry you have or are you feeling unwell? Reoccurring triggers need further exploration.*

Some personal things we just cannot and should not change, such as the mad rush of family life every morning; it's hectic but not usually detrimental. It's the feelings of hurt and upset that you carry around that are the most harmful to you and the children and families you support. Take care of yourself first, then your skills and expertise will take care of everything else.

Writing a reflective journal

The challenge faced when writing a reflective journal is to sustain this over time. You may begin by writing entries every day only to then write when crisis incidents occur. The purpose of a reflective journal is to use it as a daily tool to think deeply about practice, analyse those reflections and increase self-awareness, leading to informed reflective practice. Otienoh (2009) studied teachers' reflective journaling and found that very few maintained their journals after one year. The issues here then are of motivation to maintain written reflection and understanding the value of reflective writing. Otienoh (2009) found that enforced journal writing among trainee teachers was counterproductive and Gadsby and Cronin (2012) claim that reduced reflection limited professional development and change.

Reflective journaling can therefore only be described as an experience to try and find your own system of recording this reflective information; your journal is for you to form and use as and when you decide. So, while authors and tutors alike may assert that journaling is vital to professional development, the extent of your journal is for you to determine.

A key part of reflecting is interpreting the details to inform future practice as suggested with the RAIN framework. Reflection on the future (Wilson, 2008) is possible through revisiting past experiences in order to explore future potential and anticipate consequences of future practice. It is concerned with making the future a reality; making informed decisions.

> *In order to create a future we need firstly to be able to identify where we wish to go. Through reflection on current and former experiences we may project a variety of scenarios and examine what might happen. It is a form of future reflection and it allows us to examine pathways without the necessity of expending energy and other resources on inefficient or futile courses of action.*

> (Wilson, 2008, p 180)

Part of your journal may therefore address the matter of where you want to be in the future. This is particularly relevant if you are nearing the end of your studies or considering a change in career. You may have some life-changing choices to make and writing these down as a future plan will enable reflection on the barriers and the possibilities as well as clarifying your ultimate goal.

Student reflection on journal writing and personal and professional development

The following case study marks an important time during the dissertation studies of a final-year, part-time student who started to use a reflective journal.

CASE STUDY 3

During this time, I was also going through big changes in my personal development, mainly being assertive, and listening to ME and what protected me and how this could give me self-worth. I recorded this in quite some detail, and can honestly say that when reading back, I am so proud of how I have handled some situations and that I was able to reflect and be disappointed on how I handled others. Most importantly it embedded in me the importance of assertiveness for the protection of self-worth and enabled me to research this further, and this went from being assertive to mindfulness and meditation – all elements that have made me stronger. While I may always have known that I needed to be stronger and not let people walk all over me, I did not have the skills to do it.

My writing and reading back on it enabled this for me. I am able to write more freely about my feelings and how I want to be, how I want to react and how I want to be perceived by others but now I can do this and feel great about myself. I also started recording my levels of frustration, annoyance all the way to anger. I was able to detect my triggers, and how to manage these. While I did not always get it right, knowing the symptoms and being mindful of my actions in these situations, I was able to put strategies in place to deal with these effectively. I have always displayed high levels of empathy (my strength and weakness) though it has taken time and been very difficult. I think my writing and research helped me be balanced in my outlook so as not to allow other people's sorrow, hurt, anxiety, etc affect me so that I too became helpless.

Reading back on the journal is good as it allowed me to see how far I had come in different areas of my life and showed me where I could improve on things. It also showed me how so many times when I was feeling sorry for myself that I could have put in strategies to have coped better. I think the best thing I find about journaling, especially since I took on this 'positive thinking' stance to life, is that at times when you want to have a good moan, cry and breakdown, no one is looking at you saying 'feeling sorry for yourself again' and then I was able to go back and see how to deal with things differently.

My husband says I am more positive and have a better outlook in life – and I suppose that is just because he does not get it in the ear all the time now; my journal does. However, I also put in all the good things, when I find new research, how I share this with others and how I want to make changes for the better, so hopefully it is a balanced outlook. Now as I have almost finished my dissertation, my journal is not for its intended purpose, but I do a lot of meditating, which is very soothing; in doing this I always reflect on the past 24 hours and recall five things I am grateful for and then I record this in my journal; my gratitude lies in my children, my husband, my friends and family, my home and lastly that I have the skills to be a skilled reflective learner to make improvements to my life and those around me.

This student has demonstrated the flexible nature of journal reflection with honest and direct expression. Your journal is personal and you will decide how best to use it and in what situations.

Your journal can take any form from using words to express your reflections to pictures and drawings that capture a moment. Hallet (2013) considers a reflective journal as a purposeful space to include articles of interest from the internet, magazines, books or lectures. Documenting your professional work formally allows for the review of items of interest. Think of it as academic scrapbooking! A collection of new and exciting ways of personal and professional development captured for all time. Whether a computer-based journal or a hardcopy book, your journal will expand and you will be able to look back at your journey so far and the extent of your learning through reflection.

Insert for your journal

Hallet (2013) has charted the personal and professional learning journeys of early years student practitioners through visual representations. Some students drew pathways or curved lines to express the changing nature of their development along with notes of important events or times of great change. Consider what visual representation of your reflective learning journey might be. Is it a pathway with smaller paths leading in other directions? Is it a tree where you can add more branches and twigs with every development you chart in your personal and professional life? Perhaps this is a useful tool to use with colleagues to visually represent where you are as a team and where you want to be.

Chapter reflections

At the beginning of this chapter you were posed a thought: 'Who in the world am I?' Hopefully, through reflective and reflexive practice, you will recognise changes in your personal and professional choices and interactions. You are now at the point where you can have a strong sense of who you are and reflective writing will further this ability to define the 'self' personally and professionally. This journey of identity is only measured through looking back at your writing and reflecting further on those transition points in order to really appreciate how far you have developed and changed for the benefit of yourself and others. How you choose to document your reflections is personal and can remain private or shared with others. Self-development to move forward involves looking at what has gone before and making sense of this so that the reflection on the future phase can be fully appreciated. You just need to know where you want to be in that future realm.

Extended reflections

The extended thinking points throughout this chapter will help you to find a way forward and keep focused on what you believe in, value as a person and a professional and how to engage with your early years team. Reflection for the future needs some thought for you to feel in control of your destiny.

Further reading

Bolton, G (2005) *Reflective Practice: Writing and Professional Development*. London: Sage.

This book will help you to fully understand the concept of reflective writing and in particular will give you clarity on creative writing and 'storying'.

References

Bolton, G (2005) *Reflective Practice: Writing and Professional Development*. London: Sage.

Boudreau, J D, Liben, S and Fuks, A (2012) A Faculty Development Workshop in Narrative-Based Reflective Writing. *Perspect Med Edu*, 1: 143–54.

Brechin, A, Brown, H and Eby, M A (2000) Introduction, in Brechin, A, Brown, H and Eby, M A (eds), *Critical Practice in Health and Social Care*. London: Sage.

Brookfield, S D (2002) Using the Lenses of Critically Reflective Teaching in the Community College Classroom. *New Directions for Community Colleges*, No. 118: 31–9.

Brown, J M, McNeill, H and Shaw, N J (2013) Triggers for Reflection: Exploring the Act of Written Reflection and the Hidden Art of Reflective Practice in Postgraduate Medicine. *Reflective Practice: International and Multidisciplinary Perspectives*, 14(6): 755–65.

Carroll, L (1954) *Alice in Wonderland*. London and Glasgow: William Collins Sons and Co.

Charon R and Hermann, N (2012) Commentary: A Sense of Story, or Why Teach Reflective Writing? *Academic Medicine*, 87: 5–7.

Clutterbuck, D and Hirst, S (2003) *Talking Business: Making Communication Work*. London: Butterworth-Heinemann.

Cowan, J and Stroud, R (2016) Composting Reflections for Development, *Reflective Practice*, 17(1): 27–33.

Dyer, M and Taylor, S (2012) Supporting Professional Identity in Undergraduate Early Years Students Through Reflective Practice. *Reflective Practice*, 13(4): 551–63.

Gadsby, H and Cronin, S (2012) To What Extent Can Reflective Journaling Help Beginning Teachers Develop Masters Level Writing Skills? *Reflective Practice, International and Multidisciplinary Perspectives*, 13(1): 1–12.

Goleman, D (2004) *Emotional Intelligence and Working with Emotional Intelligence*. London: Bloomsbury.

Hallet, E (2013) *The Reflective Early Years Practitioner*. London: Sage.

Hickson, H (2011) Critical Reflection: Reflecting on Learning to Be Reflective. *Reflective Practice, International and Multidisciplinary Perspectives*, 12(6): 829–39.

Otienoh, R O (2009) Reflective Practice: The Challenge of Journal Writing. *Reflective Practice: International and Multidisciplinary Perspectives*, 10(4): 477–89.

Rolfe, G, Jasper, M and Freshwater, D (2011) *Critical Reflection in Practice: Generating Knowledge for Care*. Basingstoke: Palgrave Macmillan.

Sole, D (1997) Johari's Window for Generating Questions. *Journal of Adolescent and Adult Literacy*, 40(6): 481–3.

Thomas, F B (1992) How to interpret yourself/Johari window, SIGUCCS '92, Proceedings of the 20th annual ACM SIGUCCS conference on user services, December, ACM.

Thompson, N and Pascal, J (2012) Developing Critically Reflective Practice. *Reflective Practice*, 2(13): 311–25.

Walsh, A (2009) Modes of Reflection: Is It Possible to Use Both Individual and Collective Reflection to Reconcile the 'Three-Party Knowledge Interests' in Workplace Learning? *European Journal of Education*, 4(3): 385–98.

Wilson, J P (2008) Reflecting-on-the-Future: A Chronological Consideration of Reflective Practice. *Reflective Practice: International and Multidisciplinary Perspectives*, 9(2): 177–84.

3 Critical friends: the reflective facilitators

ANN WHITEHOUSE

It is the obvious which is so difficult to see most of the time. People say 'It's as plain as the nose on your face.' But how much of the nose on your face can you see, unless someone holds a mirror up to you?

(Isaac Asimov, 1967, p 96)

Introduction

Those new to critical reflection are frequently encouraged to start by focusing on themselves as individuals and by engaging in a process of self-reflection on the personal attributes, skills and experiences that they bring to their professional roles, alongside those required as part of their professional development or for career enhancement. Recognising and understanding something that has previously been hidden from your view, such as the 'nose on your face', indicates transformative learning. This enables you to become more aware of what you do and to evaluate your practices in order for change to take place (Gornall and Burn, 2013), which is central to developing your ability to be critically reflective (Canning and Callan, 2010).

Self-reflection has its limitations, however, as challenging your own assumptions and established practices can be a difficult and somewhat uncomfortable process that we tend to avoid as much as possible. Asimov (1967) argues that you really need help to focus clearly on what may be as obvious as the 'nose on your face' and it will soon become apparent that, if you wish to self-reflect in any depth, you will need to seek the perspectives of other people. We all need someone to engage with in critically reflective dialogue if we are to really begin to review our professional selves and practices. Every time we interact with someone, we are facing a mirror and, during critical conversations, other people can *reflect back to us different versions of the events we experience* (Brookfield, 1995, p xiii).

Brookfield (1995) recommends that to become critically reflective, you should look at your practice through four different lenses: your own autobiographical lens which focuses on your emotional responses to your own experiences, the lens through which the children and families using your provision see you, the lens used by your peers, colleagues and other professionals in the field and the lens of theoretical and philosophical research literature. This chapter aims to persuade you of the benefits of seeking the perspectives of peers and colleagues. This will enhance your critical reflection through developing relationships with critical friends as reflective facilitators who can help you see through any combination of these lenses in the mirror they present to you.

During the chapter you will have the opportunity to read real conversations between Debbie and Michelle, two early years professionals who have reflected on their experiences of having and being critical friends from the point when they started on their journey through higher education as mature, part-time student practitioners until now, when, as graduates, they are each running their own successful childminding businesses and still highly value their relationships with critical friends.

What is a critical friend?

The concept of a critical friend seems to have developed as a professional support mechanism within the field of education during a period in the 1970s, when it became popular to engage in a process of critical pedagogy which aimed to transform established, dominant educational concepts into more democratic and equitable ways of thinking (Brookfield, 1995). The term has frequently been associated with establishing internal and cross-organisational professional relationships for the purpose of critical reflection on practice, such as within school leadership support networks. Although this is where the majority of the literature is positioned, there is no reason why the concept cannot be equally applied within the context of early childhood care and education (ECCE) where the need to develop critically reflective practice has now been identified as integral to the growth of a highly skilled and professional workforce in the UK. To this end, critical friendships are already a feature of some university awards for early childhood practitioners engaged in professional development activities to facilitate their reflection as they apply theoretical and philosophical perspectives to their practice. Critical reflection can frequently occur as a result of participating in practitioner (or action) research in early childhood settings. Whitebread et al (2005), from the University of Cambridge, have shown that, in their collaborative research project on young children's independent learning, the researcher could encourage reflection and empower groups of practitioners through building critical friend relationships with them. In New Zealand, where professional early childhood workforces are already well established, Hedges (2010) also found that, when conducting research in two kindergartens, she was able to facilitate practitioners' reflection through all four of Brookfield's (1995) lenses by adopting a critical friend's role alongside that of researcher.

The literature suggests critical friends can be involved in one-to-one relationships or be supporting a group of people. In my experience, the critical friend relationship can develop a reciprocal nature that can benefit both parties by offering mutual support, and you will read how Debbie and Michelle support each other in excerpts from their conversation presented later in the chapter. The ambiguous nature of this concept and the diversity of its applications make the term 'critical friend' difficult to define. Furthermore, it can be considered an oxymoron: a term deliberately constructed using two words with contradictory meanings. Indeed, all the definitions found in literature suggest the critical friend's role lies somewhere

The critical friend provides an appropriate balance of
support and challenge along a continuum

Total friend	Total critic
Provides **support**: offering comfort, empathy, reassurance, affirmation or approval	Provides **challenge**: offering critique, provocation, prompts, debate or motivation

Figure 3.1 *The role of a critical friend*

along a continuum between giving unconditional support as a friend and being totally challenging as a critic (see Figure 3.1).

Reflective activity

Consider your own experiences as a professional.

» *When would you have found (or have already found) the support of a total friend beneficial?*

» *When would a total critic have been more appropriate or effective?*

» *What conditions affected your decisions about the most effective role in each of these situations?*

Being on a continuum infers that the balance of the relationship may not be fixed at any one point along it and your critical friend relationship may well take on a variety of different shapes as it progresses. Furthermore, its contradictory and complex nature means that your critical friend may almost simultaneously seem nurturing yet challenging. Confusing perhaps, but it is possibly the reason why these relationships appear so effective.

John MacBeath, Professor Emeritus at the University of Cambridge and Director of Leadership for Learning: The Cambridge Network, cited by Association of Colleges (2014), confirms that this may be the main strength of the role:

> The Critical Friend is a powerful idea, perhaps because it contains an inherent tension. Friends bring a high degree of unconditional positive regard. Critics are, at first sight at least, conditional, negative and intolerant of failure.

This highlights the common assumption that critics are associated with making negative judgements; however, Costa and Kallick (1993) helpfully remind us that to critique is integral to evaluation: the highest in the order of thinking skills, according to Bloom's taxonomy of skills within the cognitive domain (Bloom, 1956), and has been proven to be an effective way to enhance performance.

MacBeath (cited by Association of Colleges, 2014) comes to the conclusion that:

> *Perhaps the critical friend comes closest to what might be regarded as 'true friendship' – a successful marrying of unconditional support and unconditional critique.*

The following description of a critical friend given by Costa and Kallick (1993, p 51) is probably the definition most cited within the literature:

> *A critical friend, as the name suggests, is a trusted person who asks provocative questions, provides data to be examined through another lens, and offers critique of a person's work as a friend. A critical friend takes the time to fully understand the context of the work presented and the outcomes that the person or group is working toward. The friend is an advocate for the success of that work.*

How does a critical friend compare with other models of support?

Comparing and contrasting the roles of coach, mentor and counsellor, it is apparent that they share many characteristics and because interpretations differ so greatly, it is difficult to provide clear distinctions between them. For example, if you read our interpretation of the mentoring role in Chapter 4, *Reflecting on work-based learning*, you will see that we use Robins and Callan's (2009) definition to suggest that mentors in early childhood care and education (ECCE) nurture and encourage their mentees to take ownership of their own learning and professional development; this could be regarded as similar to the approach used by a critical friend. Gornall and Burn (2013), however, consider that mentors are frequently expected to disseminate their greater knowledge and expertise to their mentee, a view shared by Swaffield (2003), who likens the mentoring relationship to *that of a master and apprentice* (p 1). Furthermore, Gornall and Burn (2013) relate mentoring to the formal support structures put in place by organisations for trainees who need to meet specific criteria, where they argue that a rigid agenda leaves little flexibility for individual learning. While there may be some evidence to support their view, plenty of examples from ECCE demonstrate that even when prescriptive targets need to be achieved, such as the Teachers' Standards to meet Early Years Teacher Status, individual trainees have sufficient freedom to direct their learning according to their own interests with the support of mentors (see Chapter 3).

Coaching and critical friend relationships are not normally constrained by a prescribed agenda and the emphasis is on empowering others to find their own solutions to problems. Swaffield (2003) adds that coaches, like mentors, are expected to be experienced in the role of those they are supporting.

Although counsellors have many characteristics in common with critical friends, they are more concerned with people's feelings and personal matters (Swaffield, 2003). Also, there is more emphasis on learning from the past to inform the present than the other type of relationships, where the focus is on using present experiences to shape future practice (Gornall and Burn, 2013).

This confusion over terms and approaches leads to the conclusion that it is important to negotiate and clarify the boundaries and mutual expectations of any relationship set up to offer you professional or personal support before you start, no matter what title it is given.

As the boundaries between other roles appear blurred and the dynamic and evolving nature of critical friend relationships has already been established, we can also conclude that the characteristics associated with each model of support are not exclusive and may equally be adopted by critical friends as they respond to practitioners at different stages of their critical reflection and professional development. Debbie and Michelle illustrate this in the following conversation excerpt, where they conclude that critical friend relationships can vary and you may need more than one critical friend to fulfil your needs over time. Swaffield and MacBeath (2005) warn that without a precise definition, the term could be used indiscriminately, yet I would argue that the flexibility that a critical friend relationship can offer gives it the potential to be richer than either mentoring, coaching or counselling alone.

CASE STUDY

Conversation excerpt 1

Debbie: *For me, it was more of a mentoring role that I needed at the beginning of the relationship, because I was very unsure ... but I needed more of a critical friend at the end of my course ... because your confidence has grown ... and you have more of your own ideas ... there's less of that 'nurturing' that needs to go on ... the relationship changes as you go along – well for me it did anyway ... and sometimes there comes a point when you need to move on. You used to have Eve as your critical friend, didn't you? So when did you start talking to other people ... and me?*

Michelle: *Yeah, I reached a point when I felt I knew more about what I was talking about than Eve did ... it sounds really unkind and makes me look so ungrateful, but before that she had always given me the confidence I needed ... so if I hadn't developed the confidence, I would never have got to the stage when I could say 'right, I need someone new!' It's like laying the foundations, isn't it?*

Debbie: *Yes that's right, it is more like having a mentor and then they step back. I had Elaine and I think she did feed and nurture me ... it was supportive and confidence giving, but at some point she stepped back and then I moved on to someone else who was a different kind of critical friend.*

What makes a good critical friend?

Further understanding of the role may emerge from considering what you should look for when choosing critical friends. Some of the qualities required to successfully perform the role can be deduced from the definitions. Most importantly, it is clear that critical friendships should be founded on mutual respect and trust so that you can be confident that any support sought and issues discussed will be treated confidentially and in a non-judgemental manner.

Several aspects of the relationships will be considered here with regard to choosing and being a critical friend who can effectively switch between the roles of facilitator, supporter, advocate, challenger and critic. In summary, these aspects include:

- availability;
- interpersonal skills and emotional intelligence;
- knowledge and experience;
- positions and balance of power;
- shared responsibility.

Availability

Critical friends need to be available to offer support; this can be in terms of physical time, immediacy and proximity which need to be negotiated with those involved at the start of the relationship, but availability should also be considered with regard to the friend appearing approachable and open to considering any aspects of practice that arise within any boundaries that may have been established.

Interpersonal skills and emotional intelligence

Good interpersonal skills and emotional literacy are clearly essential. A critical friend needs the ability to listen, question and interpret what is being said initially, so that they can hold up a mirror that accurately reflects the situation, as Swaffield (2003, p 5) confirms:

> The critical friend's viewpoint has credibility if it is informed by an understanding of the situation, developed through listening as well as observation.

They must then demonstrate skills in communicating ideas and giving constructive feedback in a sensitive and respectful manner, as well as being able to summarise what they are reflecting back through the mirror by selecting an approach that will be meaningful for the recipient. The following four categories of personal competences, originally identified by Goleman, Boyatzis and McKee (2002) as contributing to emotionally intelligent leadership, have been applied equally well here to being an emotionally intelligent critical friend.

- ***Self-awareness:*** being able to recognise their own emotions and understanding their emotional triggers and responses underpins each of the other three categories. They are confident about their abilities and understand the strengths they bring to the relationship, as well as when they will need support.
- ***Self-management:*** being attuned to their inner feelings, critical friends will be able to self-regulate and control their emotional responses during conversations. They will be flexible and be able to adapt their approaches to suit the people they are supporting. Critical friends will be able to model open and honest reflection on their own values, beliefs and practices in order to encourage others to do the same.
- ***Social awareness:*** social awareness includes the ability to empathise with others, and critical friends will be able to assess the appropriate thing to say or do and to

sense the values and priorities that are important to their partners at particular moments in their conversations. They will be able to find commonalities with people from diverse cultural backgrounds and understand forces of power at play in groups or organisations.

• **_Relationship management_:** critical friends will be able to motivate by articulating a shared purpose for the relationship that will inspire their partner's involvement. They will demonstrate a genuine desire to help others in the relationship to achieve a critical perspective. Critical friends need the ability to act as an advocate for change by demonstrating the confidence to challenge the status quo and the ability to offer practical solutions to the barriers their partners may face in the change process. They need to be able to manage conflict and have the resilience to avoid collusion and to resist going outside the boundaries of their role by knowing how and when to refer people, to a counsellor for example.

Knowledge and experience

There are differences of opinion as to whether or not a critical friend is required to bring relevant expertise to the relationship from the specific area of practice being considered. Swaffield (2004) considers this is not a necessity, suggesting that:

> _not being an expert enables the critical friend genuinely to ask the powerful yet possibly naïve questions._

(p 273)

Having to formulate an explanation of a situation you are facing within a political, social, theoretical or practical context, for someone without the specific knowledge or experience to understand, can certainly help you see more clearly by bringing the _familiar into focus_ (Swaffield, 2003) and facilitating independent problem solving. Hedges (2010) argues, however, that although possessing the skill to pose naïve questions would certainly be useful in the role, a critical friend needs to be at least familiar with specific theoretical knowledge and research from within the area of practice before undertaking the role. This is particularly pertinent to the early childhood care and education sector, where policy influences on practice may be distinctly different to those affecting other sectors or disciplines. This does not mean that you should restrict your selection of critical friends to those within your own setting or organisation as the cross-fertilisation of ideas can be significantly beneficial to the process of critical reflection.

Positions and balance of power

Line managers or other senior colleagues are often chosen to perform the role of critical friend for practitioners engaged in professional development and they can be in a position to provide you with specific materials, suggest relevant aspects of practice to focus on or facilitate your professional development within the workplace in a variety of ways. According to Baskerville and Goldblatt (2009), however, being able to engage in _unguarded conversations_ is the ultimate goal of a critical friendship and you may find it difficult to reveal your innermost thoughts, professional dilemmas, mistakes or insecurities to your line manager for fear of risking your position within the hierarchical structure of your organisation. There can also be an imbalance of power within hierarchical relationships, as line managers may have invested significantly in your professional development in order to meet self-imposed or external outcomes which may lead to their agenda or ideas dominating your reflective conversations. Debbie and Michelle reflect on this issue in Conversation exerpt 2. Brookfield (1995, p 43) states that:

> for critical conversations to stand any chance of happening, participants must feel safe in declaring imperfection. They must know that no person or ideology will be allowed to dominate.

CASE STUDY

Conversation excerpt 2

Michelle: *To be a truly critical friend, I think they probably do need to be at the same sort of academic level as you ... because they have to challenge you a bit, don't they ... or make you think?*

Debbie: *Yes, but not your boss. Some people use their heads or managers, but actually they have not always made good critical friends, even though they might be academically superior. They are not always able to see things from your perspective ... they have a different agenda – a vested interest in your professional development.*

Michelle: *Mmm, if I had a boss who had been through the same kind of experience, then they probably could be supportive, but on the other hand, if they are your boss ... personally, I think a peer would be better because you can be nervous mentioning things to your boss ... you don't want them to think you don't know what you are talking about ... you can actually say to a peer 'am I being daft here?' I guess some people might have that kind of relationship ... not that I never have.*

Debbie: *So, are we saying that we need someone with the same sort of background, or are their skills more important?*

Michelle: *They need to know how to make you ask the right questions ... which suggests a similar academic level so that they understand what you are aiming to get out of it ... but they have to have an interest as well ... if they're not interested, they are not in tune with you. Do you remember when Cath, that tutor on the foundation degree was getting us to focus on our research projects? She asked us completely naïve questions because she knew nothing about early years ... she went right back to basics.*

Debbie: *Yes that's right, but she really made us think, didn't she? So, is it also about the way we project our ideas ... our confidence? You've got to be able to project them in a way that they can kind of understand them ... explaining them clearly ... you've got to be able to tell them about it.*

Michelle: *You also need a person who can confidently say 'should you really be doing that?' … someone that you can trust enough to listen to … if you want to strive to do better, then you would be willing to think about what they say and not take it too much as a criticism.*

Debbie: *Yeah, that's the critical bit, isn't it? It's about having trust and respect in them.*

Michelle: *I think the most important thing is to have a like-minded critical friend … either academically or as a childminder … someone who you can openly talk to about things without fear of retribution … and without everyone in the town finding out, either.*

Debbie: *Yes, I know just what you mean!*

Colleagues and peers can make excellent critical friends, especially in situations where they have shared similar experiences to you, such as working in a comparable environment, being on the same academic course or mutual involvement in a professional development activity or research project. At times it is very reassuring to know that you are not alone; other practitioners have experienced similar issues to you and colleagues or peers may be able to offer solutions that you may not have previously considered or even known about. If you are paired with your critical friend by a third party, it might take you a while to develop a trusting and respectful relationship, but it is likely that care will have been taken to select critical friends who are able to demonstrate the skills required and to marry up like-minded peers or colleagues during the process. If you are in the position of being able to select your own critical friend, you will most probably ask someone with whom you have already established elements of trust and respect and whom you know to be empathetic to your views. When attempting to see yourself and your practice from a different perspective, critical reflection may be prevented by the fact that most of us would naturally choose someone to support us whose mirror will reflect familiar images back to us, instead of one that might startle us into stopping to think. It is therefore worth considering seeking a critical friend from outside your own pedagogical context who can challenge your attitudes and introduce fresh ideas as opposed to merely reaffirming the ones you currently hold.

Shared responsibility

Critical friendships may develop into relationships where partners take equal responsibility for supporting and challenging each other as the situations they face demand. Although this type of friendship can prove very effective, particularly if you want someone who can act as a 'sounding board' for your ideas, there are two potential difficulties to consider alongside the advantages they can bring. Firstly, you may find you are facing difficult situations at the same time and are consequently unable to give each other the time and attention required to play the role of a critical friend. Secondly, individuals may make unequal demands on the friendship, which is to be expected in the short term, but has the potential to cause the relationship to break down if the situation is allowed to continue over an extended period of time. Having stated the disadvantages, my own experiences lead me to believe that critical friendships that develop over time, between colleagues or peers who are in tune with each other, can lead to either party instigating the type of reflexive conversations that demonstrate deep mutual trust and an unconditional regard for the other person's perspective. Ironically, there appears to be a positive correlation between the strength of the friendship and the depth of critical challenge that can be offered in such relationships.

Reflective activity

» *Who would you choose as a critical friend and why?*

» *Do you think it might be an advantage to have several critical friends to approach when you are in need of different types of support, or might it be better to concentrate your efforts on developing one critical friendship with the aim that deep and meaningful critical reflection will flourish?*

How do conversations with critical friends work?

A social-constructivist approach to learning has become widely accepted within early childhood care and education in many parts of the world in recent years and critically reflecting on practice through engaging in meaningful conversations within critical friend relationships sits well with Vygotsky's (1978) sociocultural theory; that we construct our own knowledge and understanding through social interactions with other people who will also influence our attitudes and beliefs within the cultural context of the environment. Through your conversations, an effective critical friend will use their skills to ascertain your current level of thinking and understanding and offer an appropriate balance of support and challenge that will facilitate critical reflection, enabling you to see new possibilities and ways of thinking that are within your own zone of proximal development: a clear example of a familiar strategic approach to facilitating learning that Bruner (1960) described as 'scaffolding'.

One way to gain an understanding of how the dynamic interactions between partners within a critical friend relationship work is through using the principles and terminology of transactional analysis, which was originally developed by Eric Berne (1968) as a counselling tool based on Freudian ideology, but has since been applied to many other contexts where developing effective communication is important, including education and personal development. In transactional analysis, each partner is viewed in terms of being in one of three ego states which describe their ways of thinking or acting: the Parent (P) who models behaviour on parent figures; the Adult (A) who behaves by tackling issues in the here and now; and the Child (C) who behaves in child-like ways. Whatever type of relationship you have, the ultimate aim is for the interaction between you and your critical friend to be based on responses reflecting the Adult ego state (as shown in Example 1 in Figure 3.2), as this is considered to be the most effective way to communicate with each other. At times in the friendship, it can be more appropriate for the critical friend to adopt behaviour that is more akin to a parent figure in response to the partner who may feel like a child seeking approval and needing nurture (Example 2 in Figure 3.2), for example, as Debbie and Michelle describe at the very beginning of their professional development. Communication can still be effective in this type of interaction, as the Parent (P) and Child (C) ego states adopted by both partners complement each other. This is not the case, however, when you are both trying to communicate using ego states that are not compatible (Example 3 in Figure 3.2), causing a mismatch of responses which do not fulfil the relationship or achieve your goals.

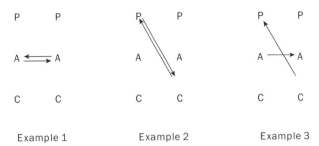

Figure 3.2 *Examples of communication between partners in critical friendships using the transactional analysis model*
Source: Berne, 1968

Being more aware of the way you are both communicating can really benefit your critical friendship interaction and make your relationship more effective, particularly if you can work towards the stage where you are mostly communicating in the Adult ego state, which infers that you will be open to the synergy it can provide to facilitate your critical reflection. As the process of critical reflection progresses and you become more knowledgeable and confident, you may find yourself in a position where you adopt the Parent role offering guidance and support to other people, including your own critical friend who may start seeking your advice, and so the cycle continues and friendships may grow to be reciprocal. The continuous movement in and out of each state can create a relationship of critical equality based on deep mutual respect.

Reflective activity

»   *Draw upon some of your own experiences of communicating with critical friends, colleagues or peers and consider whether the transactional analysis model can be applied to explain their degree of effectiveness.*

It appears, therefore, that the very nature of effective critical friendships is reciprocal and that they cannot be anything other than mutually stimulating and rewarding. They are continuously evolving and being reshaped by the contributions of each of the persons involved as they co-construct new understandings of pedagogy and practice through their reflective conversations, confirming Swaffield's (2005, p 56) claim that *there are no sleeping partners in a successful critical friend relationship.*

How can critical friendships support practitioners within early childhood care and education?

Critical reflection is fast becoming an integral part of professionalism in all sectors, but having the support of critical friends may be particularly beneficial to those of you emerging as new professionals in early childhood in the UK. You are possibly struggling to overcome some of the characteristics commonly associated with members of the sector workforce that may hinder your critical reflection on practice.

Reflective activity

» *Read the following characteristics commonly associated with mature early childhood students engaging in critical reflection for the first time as they embark on higher level professional development courses. Reflect on those that relate to your own situation at the same stage of your personal and professional development.*

   – Have had little or no previous encouragement to aspire to career development or academic achievement: *I always wanted to work with children, but was told I would never have the qualifications when I left school.*

   – Feel isolated and unsupported by colleagues in their workplace: *I wanted to share what I was learning on the course, but I could see them rolling their eyes as if to say 'here she goes again!'*

   – Have a low self-image which is reinforced by lack of recognition for their role: *I usually stay in the classroom over lunchtime – we are not really encouraged to go into the staffroom.*

   – Lack status and pay in the workforce: *my employers pay their cleaner more per hour than they are willing to pay me.*

   – Have little confidence in their study skills and their ability to achieve academically or professionally: *I'd only got a few CSEs and never thought I could go into higher education.*

(Adapted from Canning and Callan (2010 p 76), illustrated, in italics, by typical statements from HE students.)

Extended thinking

Canning and Callan (2010) explain that this lack of self-belief needs to be overcome before the transformation process of reflective practice and professional development can begin. Imagine you have become the critical friend of an early childhood practitioner demonstrating a combination of these characteristics.

» *What types of support would you need to provide to help them move from a position of emotional dependency to a point where they have the confidence to voice and act upon their own ideas?*

Once you have started the process of critical reflection, possibly initiated as part of professional development activities, maintaining your formal or informal critical friendships provides at least one way for you to continue reflecting on your practice.

In excerpt 3 of their conversation, you will read how Debbie and Michelle found their ability to critically reflect developed as they progressed through higher education and reflecting through conversations with their critical friends continued to be an important feature of their professional practice as they developed their graduate careers.

CASE STUDY

Conversation excerpt 3

Michelle: *Discussing things with your critical friend is in addition to getting advice from your lecturer.*

Debbie: *It's like the further you get, the more you look for a wider range of opinions ...*

Michelle: *Yes, you do!*

Debbie: *... because other people will see something different ... so you might see one thing, someone else will see something different ... and you take them all into account.*

Michelle: *Yes, yes that's perfectly true ... when you're at uni, you listen to your tutor's ideas and then you discuss it with the people on your table and take their views on board ... and then I might think 'I wonder what Debbie would make of that?' so I come back and ask you to discuss it with me ... it's another way just to check really ... with someone in a different context ... before deciding to do it your own way.*

Debbie: *So you take all the views on board first, because everyone will have a different approach.*

Michelle: *It's a bit like on your first assignment on the foundation degree, you might have ten sources that you look at, but when it comes to your final dissertation you have looked at a hundred or more and you have learned how to sift out what is relevant to you ... it's just the same really!*

Debbie: *Yeah ... we've supported each other a lot, haven't we? Do you remember when you were trying to decide on your research topic? We had a great conversation one day about 'men in childcare' as we followed the children round the park!*

Michelle: *Yes, I do! They were up and down all the slides ... with us following and deep in discussion ... and you helped me see how I could give a different view on it.*

Debbie: *I really miss the stimulation of discussions with my university peers. I'm in the EYP network and they have some great meetings, but I'm not able to get there because of the timing ... I was never allowed to go when I worked in the children's centre either, because only one person could be released.*

Debbie: *But it was good as a new person setting up in business ... us bouncing ideas off each other, being okay to disagree ... but having enough in common to understand each other's perspective.*

Michelle: *Yes, we know each other's strengths ... so I come to you, as you have much more expertise with the children ... but I can help you with the business side.*

Debbie: *Yes, sometimes it is reassuring just to know that you are doing the right thing, that you have got it right ... you know you have really, but it is nice when you confirm it.*

Michelle: You still have the self-doubts though sometimes ... I know you do too, don't you?

Debbie: Yeah, I'm terrible sometimes! You just need someone to reassure you.

Michelle: But now it's often about sharing ideas and knowledge and information ... after talking with you, I often go back and look up some of the concepts we have discussed to understand more. That's particularly important for childminders, as the onus is on finding out information for yourself ... there are a lot of myths out there that go round like 'Chinese whispers', so you have to find the original source so that you know the truth.

Debbie: Yeah, but I know it can be just the same for those working as part of teams in settings, professional development can be devalued in some settings and you can feel on your own, particularly where the managers are not graduates and you can seem like a threat.

Facilitating critical reflection of practice in the workplace is not easy, however, and it cannot happen without certain conditions being in place. Firstly, engaging in reflective conversations with colleagues and peers takes time; a commodity in very short supply when you are all busy practitioners coping with the demands of young children, their parents and your other professional responsibilities. Despite good intentions to foster reflection by setting aside regular times to discuss practice in ECCE settings, these meetings are all too often filled with discussions about practical, day-to-day concerns and they rarely leave time for the type of critically reflective conversations that I advocated earlier in the chapter. Secondly, a culture has to be established by leaders that is open to different perspectives and where everyone feels their contributions will be valued and respected, irrespective of their status (Brookfield, 1995). As part of this culture, Hanson (2012) suggests you and your colleagues need to acquire a reflective disposition which includes developing the following characteristics:

- listening to other people's ideas and being willing to try them out;
- sharing your ideas;
- self-awareness and an ability to be honest with yourself and your colleagues;
- open-mindedness and willingness to be challenged;
- ability to challenge your assumptions;
- critical-thinking skills and the ability to argue;
- having evidence-based values about early childhood;
- knowledge of theoretical concepts underpinning practice.

The culture should also foster trust and a sense of security and mutual support, according to Potter and Hodgson (2007), who concluded that practitioners need to feel safe before they could start to reflect. They found, in their research on a professional development activity designed to enhance early childhood pedagogical practice, that the extent of practitioners' reflection appeared to be dependent upon the level of mutual trust within the staff team.

Critical reflection is a social process and feelings of isolation are sometimes experienced by lone workers such as childminders like Debbie and Michelle, but also by individuals working within groups where the culture is not open to critical reflection. Critical friends can provide the support and challenge that is missing from day-to-day interactions with colleagues, as well as enabling the practitioner to seek ways to transform the culture in the workplace to overcome isolation, if appropriate. Brookfield (1995) reveals how susceptible we can all be to 'impostor syndrome' when feeling vulnerable and doubting our self-worth. This may be particularly true for members of the early childhood profession in the UK who continue to struggle with status and recognition on a regular basis. Critical friendships can enable you to grow in confidence as you come to realise that your critical reflection is having a positive impact on your practice. Having a relationship where you feel secure makes it easier to check, ask or admit mistakes without fear and your critical friends can provide a scaffold to support you until you develop your self-confidence once more.

The ripple effect

The impact of becoming confident and critically reflective practitioners spreads far, like a ripple, reaching children, parents, colleagues, peers, organisations, communities and the wider society. You will pass on the skills and knowledge you have gained, from being part of a critical friendship, to other practitioners who may be at the beginning of their professional development and you may continue to find support, stimulation and critique from well-established critical friends that will spur you on to join other like-minded people in organisations where your voice may be heard on a new level and influence social policy. Your careers will continue to develop as you take on roles as Early Years Teachers, leaders and researchers where you may be in a position to recommend that others find critical friends. You may establish critical friendships as part of collaborative and reflective learning cultures, such as communities of practice where there is an expectation for practitioners to converse and share knowledge on a regular basis (Wenger, 1998). Debbie and Michelle appear to have joined that pathway.

CASE STUDY

Conversation excerpt 4

Debbie: *As your confidence grows, you give others the courage to have a go too ... I hope I have played a part in a lot of other practitioners' CPD ... I persuaded you to do the top-up, didn't I?*

Michelle: *Yes, you did! It's all about building confidence really ... like in our childminding network ... I had the confidence to **ask** for support from the others ... then this encouraged others to do the same. So now we have like-minded childminders coming from far and wide to our group, because they want to extend their knowledge and improve what they do.*

Debbie: *Yes, it's becoming quite a reflective community, isn't it?*

Michelle: *It's like we've had good critical friends, so now we want to give something back ... and the more you know, the more you realise you know very little at all!*

Chapter reflections

More knowledge about the role a critical friend can play will enable you to select the right person to hold the mirror and reflect back to you different perspectives of your experiences. A greater understanding of how critical friendships function can help you get the best out of your formal or informal professional relationships, whomever you may class your critical friends to be. Critical friendships are as flexible and as diverse in composition as the practitioners involved in them; that is their strength. It is worth remembering that not all conversations with peers and colleagues are reflective: participating in a critical friendship is a reciprocal and active process that empowers you to control its direction, shape and approach to reflecting on practice.

In writing this chapter, I have reflected on some of the professional relationships that have developed throughout my own varied career in ECCE and have acknowledged, in some cases for the first time, how much I have benefited from the stimulation and synergy generated by engaging in reflective conversations with those whom I now recognise as being my critical friends. I hope to have persuaded you to think of critical friends as being more than just a name on a form and that you too will go on to enjoy rich critical conversations and relationships that will develop to stimulate, challenge, nourish and sustain you throughout your career as a reflective professional. I will leave you with two concluding statements from Debbie and Michelle, who seem to be able to summarise articulately exactly how critical friends are our reflective facilitators.

Debbie: *Our critical conversations are highly motivating ... I come away on a high .... buzzing ... I don't want them to end.*

Michelle: *It's not until you discuss it with someone else that you realise you have a passion for something ... it feels like they act like a mirror ... reflecting it back at me, so I can really see it!*

Extended reflections

Debbie and Michelle are fortunate in having developed an informal critical friendship that continues to nourish and sustain them as professionals and to support their businesses. Reflect on the difficulties currently facing practitioners within ECCE settings and the decrease in government funding available to support them through changes to policy and provision.

»   *Would all practitioners benefit from having the support of a critical friend, or is it only of value to those working in isolation?*

»   *How can practitioners find a critical friend and develop mutually beneficial friendships to provide the support they need to implement changes and overcome difficulties?*

»   *Do ECCE practitioners need their own professional body with a critical friend system in place to support their professional development?*

Further reading

Hedges, Helen (2010) Blurring the Boundaries: Connecting Research, Practice and Professional Learning. *Cambridge Journal of Education*, 40(3): 299–314.

As part of her 'co-constructed, participative reflective inquiry' approach to research with kindergarten teachers in New Zealand, Hedges adopts a critical friend model based on Costa and Kallick's definition (1993) to facilitate the teachers' critical reflection on their practice.

Extended reading activity

» *Reflect upon the effectiveness of some of the strategies Hedges uses in her dual role as critical friend/researcher.*

» *Consider how you could engage in a collaborative research project with your colleagues. Could critical friendships be utilised to facilitate critical reflection at any stage of the process?*

» *You could compare Hedge's use of critical friendships in research with the approach used for The Cambridgeshire Independent Learning in the Foundation Stage (CINDLE) project described in Whitebread et al (2005).*

References

Asimov, I (1967) *I Robot*. London: Dobson Books.

Association of Colleges (2014) Guidance Note: What Does It Mean to Be a Critical Friend? [online] Available from: www.aoc.co.uk/sites/default/files/Being%20a%20critical%20friend_0.pdf (accessed 9 January 2017).

Baskerville, D and Goldblatt, H (2009) Learning to Be a Critical Friend: From Professional Indifference through Challenge to Unguarded Conversations. *Cambridge Journal of Education*, 39(2): 205–21.

Berne, E (1968) *The Games People Play: The Psychology of Human Relationships*. London: Penguin Books.

Bloom, B S (1956) (ed) *Taxonomy of Educational Objectives, the Classification of Educational Goals – Handbook 1: Cognitive Domain*. New York: McKay.

Brookfield, S (1995) *Becoming a Critically Reflective Teacher*. San Francisco: Jossey-Bass.

Bruner, J S (1960) *The Process of Education*. Cambridge, MA: Harvard University Press.

Canning, N and Callan, S (2010) Heutagogy: Spirals of Reflection to Empower Learners in Higher Education. *Reflective Practice: International and Multidisciplinary Perspectives*, 11(1): 71–82.

Costa, A and Kallick, B (1993) Through the Lens of a Critical Friend. *Educational Leadership*, 51(2): 49–51.

Goleman, D, Boyatzis, R and McKee, A (2002) *The New Leaders: Transforming the Art of Leadership into the Science of Results*. London: Little, Brown.

Gornall, S and Burn, M (2013) *Coaching and Learning in Schools: A Practical Guide*. London: Sage.

Hanson, K (2011) 'Reflect' – Is This Too Much to Ask? *Reflective Practice: International and Multidisciplinary Perspectives*, 12(3): 293–304.

Hanson, K (2012) How Can I Support Early Childhood Undergraduate Students to Develop Reflective Dispositions? A thesis submitted for the degree of Doctor of Education, Exeter: University of Exeter.

Hedges, H (2010) Blurring the Boundaries: Connecting Research, Practice and Professional Learning. *Cambridge Journal of Education*, 40(3): 299–314.

Potter, C A and Hodgson, S (2007) Nursery Nurses Reflect: Sure Start Training to Enhance Adult–Child Interaction. *Reflective Practice: International and Multidisciplinary Perspectives*, 8(4): 497–509.

Robins, A and Callan, S (2009) Mentoring and Supporting Teams, in Robins, A and Callan, S (eds), *Managing Early Years Settings*. London, Sage.

Swaffield, S (2003) Critical Friendship. *Inform No. 3* Leadership for Learning. Cambridge: University of Cambridge Faculty of Education. Available from: www.educ.cam.ac.uk/centres/lfl/about/inform/PDFs/InForm_3.pdf (accessed 9 January 2017).

Swaffield, S (2004) Critical Friends: Supporting Leadership, Improving Learning. *Improving Schools*, 7(3): 267–78.

Swaffield, S (2005) No Sleeping Partners: Relationships between Head Teachers and Critical Friends. *School Leadership and Management: Formerly School Organisation*, 25(1): 43–57.

Swaffield, S and MacBeath, J (2005) School Self-Evaluation and the Role of a Critical Friend. *Cambridge Journal of Education*, 35(2): 239–52.

Vygotsky, L (1978) *Mind in Society*. Cambridge, MA: Harvard University Press.

Wenger, E (1998) *Communities of Practice: Learning, Meaning and Identity*. Cambridge: Cambridge University Press.

Whitebread, D, Anderson, H, Coltman, P, Page, C, Pasternak, D P and Mehta, S (2005) Developing Independent Learning in the Early Years. *Education 3–13*, 33(1): 40–50.

4 Reflecting on work-based learning

RUTH GILL AND ANN WHITEHOUSE

Pooh had accidentally dropped a fir-cone into the river near to the bridge.

'That's funny,' said Pooh, 'I dropped it on the other side,' said Pooh, 'and it came out on this side [of the bridge]! I wonder if it would do it again?' And he went back for some more fir-cones.

It did. It kept on doing it. Then he dropped two in at once, and leant over the bridge to see which would come out first; and one of them did; but as they were both the same size, he didn't know if it was the one he wanted to win, or the other one. So the next time he dropped one big cone and one little one, and the big one came out first, which is what he said it would do, and the little one came out last, which is what he said it would do, so he had won twice...

And that was the beginning of the game called Poohsticks, which Pooh invented, and which he and his friends used to play on the edge of the Forest. But they played with sticks instead of fir-cones, because they were easier to mark.

(A A Milne, 1928, pp 91–2)

Introduction

Nowhere more than in early childhood care and education (ECCE) has it been established that we learn experientially: learning 'by doing' is fundamental to all the principles underlying our practice. In the excerpt above, Pooh, the bear reputably with very little brain, clearly demonstrates his ability to observe what is happening in his environment (cause and effect), identify problems and solutions, experiment and collect data, reflect on his findings and implement new ideas to improve processes (action research) in order to create a very successful activity to be enjoyed by his friends and, indeed, the countless other adults and children who have read or heard about his game of *Poohsticks* over almost 90 years.

Learning through practical experience in the workplace has always been accepted as a vital element of becoming a practitioner and you will most probably have spent many hours gaining work experience in settings, either as a student or an apprentice, to attain your initial qualifications near the beginning of your career. Participating in vocational training or work-based learning programmes is often considered more valuable than academic-based studies within the early years sector. A considerable number of practitioners enter the early years sector with few academic qualifications and little confidence in their academic abilities, making work-based learning opportunities appear more attractive to them and their targets more attainable. It seems valid to argue that you cannot possibly perform the role of caring for and educating young children without having had the experience to acquire and perfect the practical skills and competences that it requires. Becoming a *competent technician* (Osgood, 2010) is undeniably essential, but we need a workforce that can do more than merely follow policy or curriculum guidelines, if we are to offer the high-quality provision that we know our babies and young children need to get the best possible start in life. By engaging in professional development activities in the workplace, you can grow into the *critically reflective emotional professionals* (Osgood, 2010) required to achieve this aim.

Many of you will currently be studying at a higher level, having recognised the need to gain deeper knowledge and understanding of young children and how they are affected by their early childhood experiences. You will most probably have realised very early on in your programme that your learning and development relies predominantly on gaining greater understanding of what is happening in your ECCE environment through engaging in critical reflection.

This chapter will discuss aspects of learning in the workplace at different levels and stages in your career as a practitioner.

Communities of practice and social learning communities

It is widely believed that, while we may learn from actively engaging with our physical environment in isolation, social relationships and interaction with other people can offer the best learning opportunities. Social constructivist theorists recognise that learning is enhanced through working together within a social context, facilitating discussion of events, sharing and challenging thoughts and clarifying what is important. Indeed, there is evidence in the opening literature excerpt to suggest that the final version of Pooh's game evolved as a result of interacting with his friends and incorporating some of their ideas for improvement. Furthermore, the most meaningful learning usually occurs as we respond to the challenges presented within the familiar context of our own environments.

Their composition and purposes

A community of practice, also known as a learning community, is formed by a group of practitioners who share common prior experiences, beliefs, principles and concerns and are working towards similar aims. It is not necessary for the practitioners to be working together as a team, although this may sometimes be the case, but sharing a desire to impart knowledge and learn from each other is a key element. The development of such communities, resulting from dynamic social interactions between groups of individuals across many types of business environments, has been the focus of several studies, for example, Lave and Wenger (1991). According to Aubrey (2007, p 80), where these learning communities are successfully developed within ECCE:

> the culture will become one where learning, self-development and development of others through reflective conversations is the norm.

We would argue that even the most isolated of you are members of at least one community of practice, with the majority probably belonging to several. Some of your communities may meet regularly and/or frequently, such as a team working together in the same organisation. In others, you may only meet occasionally, at a conference or training event, for example, or you may rely on non-verbal forms of communication in the main, such as through online forums or journal articles. Members will have differing perspectives based on their individual experiences and you may not agree on every aspect of practice, but improving provision for young children through increasing knowledge and understanding will remain each community's primary aim.

England's current economic climate has resulted in ECCE providers increasingly being left to fund and develop their own opportunities for training and professional development, as limited government resources are seemingly prioritised, in the main, to support those judged in need of improvement to reach the statutory required minimum standards (Grenier, 2016). Communities of practice have the potential to fill the gap left by the diminution of local authority support by providing the social learning opportunities crucially needed to continue your development as professionals and for improving the quality of ECCE provision.

Learning through practitioner research

After perfecting the game of Poohsticks, on pages 94–9 of *In the House at Pooh Corner,* A A Milne (1928) describes a further incident where Pooh and his friends find a problem, identify and discuss possible solutions and try one of them out. Eeyore has fallen into the middle of the river and appears unable to climb out unaided, so the friends evaluate Pooh's idea to throw stones in an attempt to make waves that would wash him to one of the banks. They decide the plan might work and implement it. As you can imagine, the plan does not go as expected, but a positive result is achieved and Eeyore is rescued. They evaluate the plan and conclude it was a *good idea*, approximately demonstrating completion of a cycle of research as a learning community.

One way for your communities of practice to develop professional learning and effective collaboration is to engage in some practitioner (or action) research. This could expand your community by involving several settings seeking solutions to similar issues in your local area or organisation, adding to the amount of data collected and the range of perspectives included in the project. In Chapter 13, *Reflection and change*, Carol Hayes writes about the nature of action (practitioner) research and we thoroughly concur with her view that participation in research offers real opportunities for learning that are relevant to your own context. As a result, learning from your research is often more meaningful and improves practice to a greater extent than other types of learning experiences. Your ability to observe behaviours and social interactions will be fundamental to your roles as practitioners and those of you who have engaged in higher education will most probably have undertaken small-scale research. Your research knowledge and skills have been developed in preparation for conducting research in the workplace to enhance your understanding of social situations and people's attitudes and to evaluate aspects of practice. We are not suggesting that you will find it easy to conduct research processes in isolation; however, it is possible to gain expert support by inviting the collaboration of external colleagues, such as partners in a local university, for example.

Reflective activity

There are many excellent examples of professional development being offered by national and local ECCE organisations, networks and individual settings. Finding out about these will extend your own understanding of how effective communities of practice can be at developing collaborative initiatives and specific training to tackle issues identified within their localities.

» *Use the link below to read one such example from the article* Partner up! *(Sargent, 2016), which describes how Sheringham Nursery School and Children's Centre, a National Teaching School in East London, is successfully working in collaboration with other local schools, ECCE providers and universities to improve outcomes for children, within the East London Early Years and Schools Partnership.*

   www.eleysp.co.uk/wp-content/uploads/2015/05/Partner-up-East-London-Partnership.pdf

» *Reflect on how this community of practice has developed and how it benefits its members.*

Extended thinking

» *Consider how National Teaching Schools move on from merely disseminating good practice to working in two-way partnerships with practitioners working in other forms of ECCE provision.*

Some possible barriers to learning as part of a community

Communities of practice may not always function as effectively as they could and not all practitioners will find it easy to be involved. We have identified just a few of the barriers that you may encounter here, but having an awareness of them may help you to critically evaluate your performance as a community and take actions to minimise their potential effect on your endeavours.

• **Individual confidence:** individuals may lack the confidence they need to contribute to discussions or projects, fearing that their ideas may be thought irrelevant or too simple for consideration. Individuals may also hold back due to feeling insecure about their 'technical' abilities, such as their use of correct terminology, or their grammatical and spelling skills.

• **Complacency:** members may simply comply with behaviours accepted and established within the community, instead of seeking alternative pedagogies and practices and being prepared to make 'risky' decisions.

- **Exclusivity:** communities may become exclusive due, for example, to differences in practitioners' working patterns or conditions, the location or timing of events. Invitations may not be extended to professional partners from other disciplines. As a result, valuable contributions may be lost, causing gaps in shared knowledge and understanding and impacting on the success of projects.

Reflecting on your professional identity as part of a developing learning community

According to Wenger (2000), we are primarily driven to continue learning and sharing our knowledge so that we can feel part of a community. He purports that our identities bring a sense of belonging and enable us to use our experience and competencies to make informed decisions about what is important to us when:

- positioning our pedagogy and developing our practice;
- understanding with whom we should share our knowledge;
- understanding the boundaries of our roles and to whom we are accountable.

These are all considered by Wenger (2000) as vital elements of an effective social learning system.

Reflective activity

Strong and healthy social identities are dependent on the three interrelated and inter-dependent qualities identified along the top of Table 4.1.

» *Think about the progress you are making in developing your own professional identity, as an individual and as part of a learning community, by focusing on how each of Wenger's modes of belonging contributes to the process.*

Table 4.1 *Interrelated and interdependent qualities of social identity. Adapted from Identity Dimensions (Wenger, 2000, p 240)*

	Depth of connection / belonging	**Breadth and scope**	**Effectiveness**
Engagement	Do you interact as a team? How do you interact? Do you have formal forums or informal chats, for example? How long has the team been established? Is there a feeling of mutual trust?	Do you go on visits, attend conferences, invite other agencies or experts to contribute to your forums? Do individuals provide feedback on CPD events? Do you research topics to inform discussions?	Do you have opportunities to develop new ideas or try out innovative practices? Is your team accepting of your experiences and ready to embrace them in practice?

Table 4.1 (cont.)

	Depth of connection / belonging	Breadth and scope	Effectiveness
Imagination	Do you have meaningful discussions? Are you a good listener? Are you able to share aspirations and deeply held values?	Do you participate in wider networks within the local community or as active members of national organisations? Do you contribute to national consultations to inform social policy? Do you share your pedagogy widely, through the use of media, for example?	Do you have sufficient understanding of local, national and global policy to appreciate the part you play within society and how your pedagogy relates to the global picture?
Alignment	Are you fully committed to your team and to upholding the principles and values underpinning ECCE? Do you give and receive feedback?	Do you follow guidelines that will help improve the life experiences of families and the wider community as a whole, as well as outcomes for young children?	Do you understand the lines of accountability within your organisation and the most up-to-date national requirements by which your practice will be judged?

Practitioners' sense of belonging has been clearly established as an important factor to consider when evaluating the effectiveness of any learning community. In particular, Vinales (2015) concludes that feeling included plays a significant role in the levels of confidence and ultimate success of students and trainees in the workplace. Most of you will be unsurprised by this finding, but it is well worth remembering how it can feel to join a new setting or community of practice and evaluating how your behaviours may be perceived by colleagues.

Reflective activity

» *Consider what aspects of your ECCE environment and practice could be adapted to help novice, short-term practitioners feel more involved and gain a better sense of belonging in your setting.*

In reality, students, trainees and less experienced members of teams are learning from all the practitioners with whom they come into contact; this may be intended or non-intended learning. Indeed, we are all continually learning from our colleagues in communities of practice, a concept reinforced by the social learning theory established by Albert Bandura, who stated:

Most human behaviour is learned observationally through modelling; from observing others, one forms an idea of how new behaviours are performed, and on later occasions this coded information serves as a guide for action.

(Bandura, 1977, p 22)

This implies that as practitioners in a setting, you have individual and joint responsibilities as role models for the professional development and learning of other members of your team, whether they are short- or long-term colleagues, currently engaged, or not engaged, in formal learning programmes.

Reflective activity

We frequently consider the role models we are portraying as practitioners and how they may affect the children and their parents, but do we fully appreciate the impact we may be having on our colleagues? Role models can have both positive and negative influences on others' practice.

» *Reflect on times when you have adopted approaches as a result of observing the practice of colleagues. If you are honest in your reflection, you may also realise that you have emulated what you know to be less than best practice at some stage... we must admit to occasions when we certainly have!*

Mentoring and ways it can support professional learning and development

Mentoring has become widely accepted across all sectors of education, with mentorship schemes frequently put in place to support staff in developing aspects of work-based practice as part of professional development qualifications. Mentoring within ECCE has frequently been associated with the development of leadership practice in recent years, as leadership has been seen as key to improving the quality of provision. Later in the chapter, you will also read about the important role mentors play in the current process of achieving Early Years Teacher Status (EYTS) in the workplace. Aubrey (2007) considers it beneficial to extend this type of support to developing other aspects of professional practice, stating that:

If mentoring becomes an integral part of the early childhood setting there is a genuine chance that the organisation will become a learning community.

(Aubrey, 2007, p 80)

Robins and Callan (2009) suggest that we have already established a mentoring approach in ECCE practice through the way that we nurture the young children in our care; they provide the following definition:

mentoring in practice is largely about identifying, and then nurturing, the potential within an individual in a way that enables them to set and own their own goals.

(Robins and Callan, 2009, p 103)

This fits in well with the original concept of mentorship found in Greek mythology, where Homer describes how Odysseus entrusted the care and education of his son to his wise friend named Mentor, before going away to war. There are, however, several approaches to mentoring being adopted within ECCE; although their characteristics may differ, each shares the aim of supporting individual practitioners as they direct their own development as professionals.

External versus work-based mentors

Many professional development programmes require you to have a mentor to facilitate reflection on aspects of your own practice and progress through making links between your academic learning and practical experience, recognising strengths and areas for improvement and planning actions to achieve goals.

External mentors are sometimes provided by the academic institution, which generally means they have mentoring skills and experience in the role, as well as specific knowledge of the criteria you are expected to meet. Strengths of this approach include the following.

* Your mentor will have a good understanding of the programme aims, content and how it is run, so they can help you interpret what you are required to do in the workplace to achieve your targets.

* Your mentor will be in a position to observe your practice in the workplace objectively and to provide an external perspective. They could suggest alternative approaches that may be beneficial to your own professional development, the development of other colleagues in the team and your provision for young children and families. Robins and Callan (2009) articulate this point succinctly, stating that *Outside mentors can perhaps challenge in ways that close colleagues cannot* (p 119).

* It may be easier for you to raise concerns with an external mentor about practices or opportunities being provided for your professional development in the workplace as they are emotionally detached from the setting. They will have the credibility and authority to come in to mediate and plan actions with you and your colleagues to help you achieve your targets.

Although you may have regular meetings with your mentor in your academic institution, it may not be possible for them to continually visit you in the workplace and at times you will require immediate support or feedback from work-based colleagues. Furthermore, as an infrequent visitor, your external mentor cannot profess to know the children and staff thoroughly, or to be fully aware of everyday pedagogical practices in the setting. This suggests a necessity to complement external support with a work-based mentor, and in best practice these are practitioners who are given the time and training to perform the mentoring role effectively.

Although work-based mentors may not always be so familiar with your programme, they can:

* normally arrange regular formal and informal interactions with you and are available to give on-the-spot feedback, reassurance and support when you need it;

- fully understand the context of your ECCE setting, the children and families, the staff, the whole organisation and the local community;

- provide up-to-date knowledge of statutory requirements and inform you how these relate to practical policies and procedures in your setting.

Internal mentoring schemes run at various levels of individual or team development within ECCE organisations: from the induction of newly appointed staff or the supervision of newly qualified staff, for example, to the enhancement of quality provision through continuous peer mentoring. If you are involved in mentoring, it is advisable to access some training to fully understand the process and the skills required to make the relationship effective. To be worthwhile for professional learning, it is equally important to extend your own knowledge and understanding and be open to considering alternative perspectives and methods with your mentees. This ensures that the process does not lead merely to the continuation of embedded practices or pedagogy previously established in the setting, which can potentially be a limitation of work-based mentoring. This will demonstrate your own learning disposition and commitment to continued professional development for mentees to emulate. Vinales (2015) reminds us that *Mentors as role models shape the future workforce* (p 534) and your influence on learning in practice cannot be underestimated.

Reflective activity

Reflect on becoming, or being, a mentor in your workplace.

» *Why might you consider becoming a mentor?*

» *How might the role impact on your current role and responsibilities?*

» *What do think you have to offer a mentee?*

» *Are there any new skills or knowledge that you would need to help you perform the role?*

» *How you would expect an effective mentor/mentee relationship to transpire in practical terms?*

» *What boundaries for the role would you feel the need to establish?*

Team mentoring

Taking a team mentoring approach in an early childhood setting usually means that several practitioners take responsibility for the mentoring of trainees, students and apprentices, rather than the role being allocated to just one person. This approach can offer the mentee distinct benefits in comparison with the more usual practice of having a named mentor, including the following:

- it may empower them to approach someone with whom they have developed an affiliation and feel comfortable;

- they can legitimately seek differing pedagogical views and emulate different approaches to practice;

- they may benefit more from an individual practitioner's specific areas of expertise;

- they may gain improved access to regular support and immediate supervision, as and when it is required.

Reflective activity

» *Reflect on how a team approach to supporting less experienced colleagues could work, or does work, within your setting. Consider the possible disadvantages that may be experienced by both parties and how they may be overcome.*

During your reflection, you may have considered that receiving feedback and information from several practitioners may be confusing for a mentee, although colleagues on higher level programmes should be encouraged to critically evaluate a range of perspectives. You may also have thought about how the responsibilities of mentoring may impact on other aspects of the practitioner's role. If not managed effectively, practitioners may not receive recognition for the role or the time required to perform it. Some may be overwhelmed by requests for support, which could lead to added pressure, inequalities in roles and eventually resentment within the team.

Challenges to good mentoring in early childhood care and education workplaces

Recognising some of the challenges to maintaining effective mentoring approaches within settings may help you establish practices and boundaries to avoid them, or at the very least, enable you to be realistic about the amount of mentoring you and your colleagues can be expected to provide.

- As a work-based mentor, you will normally be performing the role in addition to the many other pressures of your role as a practitioner. Your responsibilities to children, families, other colleagues and the smooth running of the workplace may be considerable and may need to take priority during most of your working day. It can be challenging to find time to seek out your mentee and focus on their progress and needs. It is helpful if this aspect of your role is given due consideration by colleagues and you can set aside regular time slots for meeting and supporting your mentees. You may also need to establish realistic boundaries for your mentoring role with mentees and colleagues.

- Commitment to mentoring processes within settings can be challenged by long-term staff shortages or continual changes within the team. This situation may result in confusion for mentees and mounting pressure for the few constant practitioners. Priorities and expectations for mentoring may have to be reassessed until stability returns to the team.

- ECCE remains a sector affected by continuous change to its policy and procedure. It can be a challenge for you to continually update the knowledge, understanding and skills you need to meet statutory requirements and perform your roles with confidence. Opportunities for relevant and affordable continuous professional development are needed to keep abreast of the latest policies and practices, not only to perform your role as a confident professional practitioner, but also for your role in modelling good practice and providing support as a mentor. Furthermore, understanding the learning outcomes your mentee needs to demonstrate in the workplace can be challenging and you may need to be proactive in accessing opportunities to gain training and information about their programme and the assessment criteria.

Work-based learning for Early Years Teacher Status

Workforce reform has paved the way for what the then Labour government saw as a graduate-led workforce to raise standards in early years and for child outcomes leading to longer term educational success (HM Government, 2008). Ultimately this will lead to an early years workforce that can contribute to raising quality in early years settings and ...*make a lasting, positive impact on children's well-being and development...* (DfE, 2016). The Early Years Professional Status (EYPS) saw the beginning of government investment in creating a graduate-led workforce and by 2011 over 6,000 EYPS staff were working in the sector (Whalley, 2011). This has now been enhanced further with the creation of Early Years Teacher Status (EYTS) and Teachers' Standards, which reflect standards evident in other teacher training professions.

There are currently a range of routes available, all with the same entry requirements as other sector teacher training, and all routes require you to demonstrate competence across the Teachers' Standards in Early Years (DfE, 2013). The minimum training requirement that must be met is that 120 days of teaching practice are completed, with a minimum of two weeks in Key Stage 1, across a minimum of two settings (DfE, 2014). This can be easily achieved through the routes available; however, the challenge is demonstrating your competence and ability to 'teach' to meet all eight standards. This is primarily due to the concept of 'teaching' in early years.

Your perception of teaching may be at odds with the sector as you appreciate the need for care and education to work as one. That does not mean that you do not teach; the word *teach* conjures up images of a very formal activity, often characterised by school-based provision. Ofsted (2015) explored the notion of teaching and play with a range of providers in the most disadvantaged areas and summarised that teaching and play were not separate endeavours and that every interaction and *playful encounter* (p 5) they observed was a form of teaching.

Reflective activity

Take ten minutes to reflect on your own practice, or have a discussion with your staff team, and consider what teaching practice is in early years.

» *What does teaching 'look' like?*

» *How do you know that teaching is evident in practice?*

» *How would you define teaching in early years?*

Extended thinking

»   *Read the Ofsted (2015) document and consider how as a trainee Early Years Teacher, or leader of an ECCE setting, you might convey to staff and parents how teaching and play coexist.*

On pages 9 and 10 of the document there are some interesting views of what teaching and play are and how practitioners define themselves. Perhaps it is time for all in the sector to start believing that we are teachers of young children, and once we believe this, and can convey it with confidence, our status will be one step closer to greater recognition.

Expectations of Early Years Teacher Status work-based learning

Managing expectations of work-based learning opportunities must be considered *before* entering the setting. Building strong foundations is fundamental to the success of a teacher training early years placement. It is built upon a shared understanding of what the setting expects from you and what you can hope for in support from them. The following *Seven steps for success* will assist anyone new to a work-based learning setting, or currently employed, who is training towards the EYTS.

Seven steps for success

1   **Background** – For each work-based environment, you need to fully understand the context of the setting you are joining or are employed in. Settings evolve and change and appreciation of the finer details of the setting can help you to achieve your professional goals. What is their philosophy? What area do they serve? What needs might children have? Is there a variety of religious beliefs represented? What do parents and Ofsted say about the setting? Often the setting website will have this information along with freely available local authority information. If already employed, you may need to consider how your training can help to further the aims of the setting and facilitate professional growth for all staff.

2   **Your own beliefs** – You will have preconceived ideas and prejudices as a result of your own experiences in life and therefore it is essential that you identify what those are and how you can work in a team in a professional manner without jeopardising your professionalism.

3   **Reflective audit** – Reflecting on your own practice can be enlightening, especially when set against the Teachers' Standards in Early Years (DfE, 2013). Measuring your own progress with a reflective audit will bring your performance into sharp focus. Against each standard identify how you can demonstrate your practice and how you might improve on it. Summarise these improvements into short- and medium-term aims to keep you on target.

4   **Initial arrangements** – Your first formal interaction with the setting as an EYTS trainee is about agreeing parameters. This will take time so ensure that you have requested an hour with your mentor to chat through what is expected of you and to ask questions. Check setting policies, times of operation, lines of reporting and ask to be introduced to the team you will be working with. This is an enhanced qualification and should be considered as such by following up all mentor conversations with an email to your mentor, detailing what you have discussed and the actions in place and dates when they will be met. This way your mentor can see if you have fully understood the guidance offered or if you need any further support.

5   **Communication** – Every setting is different and you need to assess quickly how the setting prefers you to communicate with staff and parents. It is easy to feel welcomed and part of a team, but be mindful that you are training and of the need for professionalism at all times. Replying to a polite request about your weekend can be managed professionally.

6   **Implementing actions** – Meet your mentor every week; if not a face-to-face meeting, an email to a busy mentor can assist with your progress towards meeting the Teachers' Standards. When planning provision with staff, ask for certain duties that will help you meet your short-term targets. Review your reflective audit every four weeks to ensure you are progressing and if not take action to address them.

7   **Seeking feedback** – Without feedback on your daily interactions you will not be aware of how to enhance your practice. It is not about asking staff for an appraisal of your performance; every conversation you have with staff can be a reflective conversation sharing practice to understand what can be changed to make children's learning more meaningful.

These steps instigated by you *and* maintained by you throughout your training are vital to gain the most from your work-based placements. Being an active and reflective student (Hallet, 2013) and making the most of opportunities available to you will ensure that your EYTS training will be beneficial for you, the setting and most importantly the children with whom you engage. Lindon and Trodd (2016) further express that this initial training should enable you to be more confident and competent at reflecting on your practice.

A significant part of this success is the relationship with your work-based mentor. Student experience has revealed mixed responses from students about mentor involvement and participation. Where problems do occur, it is in relation to differing expectations between the mentor and trainee. Engaging with the *Seven steps to success* will alleviate some of the issues before they even arise. Each setting mentor will have different expectations of you based on the setting context and you need to respond to any work-based situation with the points below.

- Be organised and prepared – at the end of each week communicate with the team how you hope to extend learning opportunities for children. Share your intended planning, seek feedback on how appropriate this is and be adaptable to making changes where necessary.

- Enrich the setting with your academic knowledge in practice – this means sharing what you are learning academically and demonstrating this through your practice. Practitioners need to be able to share and observe good practice to learn not just from each other but *with* each other.

- Offer additional support – if you can support the team further they will be appreciative of your commitment and dedication. Assisting with wider setting arrangements can help you to forge new networks with other professionals and can be a source of essential evidence for your teaching portfolio.

Engaging with the wider setting can help gain more recognition for you and the status. Trainees express frustration that EYTS is still not widely understood by all staff in work-based settings, but staff are 'open to the concept' in practice. Likewise, mentors in early years are embracing the role of mentorship, but seek further guidance from training providers about what is required of them. There is clearly still much to convey to all involved with EYTS training programmes, and the development of school-based teacher training non-statutory mentor standards has begun to assist with understanding what the mentor ideally should be able to offer a trainee (HM Government, 2016). That said, these non-statutory standards are school based not early years, and therefore could be used as a guide when training new mentors to ensure parity across mentoring support for trainees.

Reflecting on Early Years Teacher Status work-based learning experiences

Reflecting on work-based experiences will enable you to improve on your practice but also help you to identify where future employment opportunities may lie. Your perception of a particular age range may fill you with dread or joy, but remaining open to the experience will allow you to explore each age group fully. A recent survey of undergraduate trainees asked them to reflect on their experiences and comment on their preferred age range.

> *I enjoy working with the age group 0–2 years because you can make sure you have a positive impact on the foundation to their development.*
>
> (Trainee A)

> *2–3, as they are capable of speaking to you in response to anything you ask them.*
>
> (Trainee B)

> *I enjoy working with the toddler age group, 2–3s, as they can respond back and interact with you, and are very playful, and a joy to work with.*
>
> (Trainee C)

These trainees have found their ideal age range that could shape their future career choices. One trainee reflected further:

> *I have enjoyed all although with regards to the teaching side I would say preschool. At the moment I am in the baby room and trying to follow the weekly activity sheet is difficult as there is not really anything in the EYFS relating to numeracy for this age.*

> (Trainee D)

This trainee recognises that teaching numeracy is different across age groups and may prefer to work with children from age three, which they enjoy the most. With all experiences you need to be able to provide evidence for your teacher portfolio that you can demonstrate your competence to teach across the age range.

Abrahamson (2015) examines each Teachers' Standard and provides a wealth of examples to assist you in deciding what evidence to include. More importantly, she goes on to explain how 'good' evidence that meets the Teachers' Standard well is more important than providing multiple documents that are vague and do not accurately demonstrate your competence. For example, including a certificate of training is not a strong piece of evidence. A written reflection of what you have learned, how you have shared this with staff and parents and what has changed in your practice as a result of this training is a much stronger piece of evidence to provide against a particular standard. Avoid cross-referencing multiple standards to one piece of evidence as this too reduces the strength of what you provide overall in your portfolio. Below are some aspects to consider when collating different types of evidence.

Leading learning across the setting is an important feature of EYTS and one you need to embrace early on in your training. This can be problematic as you may view yourself as a trainee and feel unable to lead an established team with a management structure in place. This perception is daunting and you should consider smaller leadership aspects, for example, leading a change in the setting. This can be achieved in consultation with others in the team. Abrahamson (2015) suggests that with some sensitive communication you can explain to the team how making a small change in the room will help you to achieve your EYTS. You could arrange an after-work brief meeting to share your idea and gain others' perspectives. Leading change can be successful if all of those who are affected by the change are involved – that includes children and parents too.

Trainees were asked to reflect on how they could or have influenced change as part of their training programme.

> *... if I have an idea about something that I can contribute to, then I speak to the room leader and put my idea across to them and see what they think. It depends where you are based, a lot of setting staff are very helpful and will help you to get to where you want to be.*

> (Trainee D)

It allows me to have a multidimensional approach to each situation and allows me to analyse information thoroughly.

(Trainee E)

Some trainees could already analyse situations and negotiate how to gain support from others in the setting. This proactive approach to leading change will result in you being a catalyst for change in the sector.

Influencing change and leading others requires reflection on what is currently in place and the intended outcome following a change. One example may be that you want to formally recognise the transitions children go through from home to the setting and from room to room. The following steps can help you begin to manage the process.

- You need to know and understand attachment theory, and in consultation with the setting team plan how you can foster positive attachment relationships through transition periods.

- Before you commence with any change, communicate your 'new initiative' to parents and seek feedback from them.

- Be clear on the timeline for implementation and review and evaluate the initiative at set time periods to measure if it is effective in meeting the needs of children, parents and staff.

Implementing a successful change takes time and there will be some negativity along the way, but if you have planned this well and based it on theoretical concepts in practice you should feel confident that the change will be of benefit.

Reflective activity

Leading change requires you to reflect on the team you work with and how change affects others. Tuckman's small group theory (Tuckman, 1965) demonstrates the different phases teams go through to reach performativity. This can take time and you need to appreciate this is a process that cannot be rushed; your team will reach performativity by working together, with you supporting their professional development through the change. As a leader of change consider how you:

» *communicate with and consult others;*

» *collaborate on realistic targets the team can work towards;*

» *review progress as a team and review goals if required.*

Leading others can inspire teams to share best practice, reflect on their own abilities and make positive changes. Allen and Whalley (2010) confirm the importance of inspiring others once your training is complete. Reflecting on your own journey and the successes and barriers experienced can help you to support other trainee Early Years Teachers (EYTs). ECCE is constantly evolving and your training will be vital going forward, enabling you to keep pace with the changes ahead and raising outcomes for children.

Chapter reflections

This chapter has considered aspects of work-based learning from the perspectives of practitioners at different phases of their career in ECCE; from those entering the profession as trainees, to others who have reached a stage where they have the confidence and competence to formally support less experienced colleagues, including all those situated between these two points who want to continue their professional development in collaboration with colleagues in, and beyond, the workplace. None of your paths are easy and we commend you all for devoting time and energy to improving your provision for the youngest children in our society and their families.

In your busy professional lives, your main focus is rightly on the children's development and learning, and your own learning may take low priority as you juggle seemingly more important aspects of your role. On reflection, however, it is clear to see that by focusing more on your own learning in the workplace and investing time in professional dialogue with colleagues, you are providing positive role models that will significantly influence everyone you meet in your professional life; including the children, their parents and families, your immediate colleagues, your professional partners and the wider community. This chapter highlights the importance of establishing collaborative practices and democratic social relationships where you can demonstrate that all participants are learning from each other. This approach will facilitate a sense of belonging, which can impact greatly on the success of learning in the workplace. We should all be encouraged by Pooh, who despite having very little brain, has a strong sense of belonging that empowers him to contribute ideas in dialogue with his friends, even though he is not confident that they are 'good' ones.

We end the chapter by urging you to take ownership of your professional learning in the workplace: don't wait for colleagues to instigate learning processes if they are not already established. You might need to begin by taking small steps in modelling learning behaviours to colleagues and children; start a reflective dialogue in the staffroom, ask a trainee about their learning programme, volunteer to attend a network meeting or voice your ideas for changing the environment. You may be ready to extend this by forming or engaging in learning communities in your workplace or communities of practice in the form of local networks, by joining relevant professional organisations and attending training events and conferences or by enrolling on programmes to enhance your learning or gain new skills; to become a mentor or an EYT for example. You will soon come to realise that there is no end to the learning process and you may well find yourself presenting research findings from your workplace at a conference. Wherever your work-based learning takes you, we know that it will enhance your professional practice, inspire and motivate others and improve standards in ECCE and the status of the workforce as a consequence.

Extended reflections

Hammond, S, Powell, S and Smith, K (2015) Towards Mentoring as Feminist Praxis in Early Childhood Education and Care in England. Early Years, 35(2): 139–53. *www. dx.doi.org/10.1080/09575146.2015.1025370*

This article focuses on approaches to mentorship relationships in ECCE settings in England and their dynamics with graduate trainees from a feminist perspective. An interesting vignette from a case study is included to illustrate how mentees' success is influenced by issues of power, status, assessment and leadership styles (among others).

» *Use the article to deepen your understanding of a work-based mentor's responsibilities and reflect on how your mentoring approach can either facilitate or inhibit the further development of professional practice.*

Further reading

Abrahamson, L (2015) *The Early Years Teacher's Book*. London: Sage.

This is a 'must-have' book for anyone studying towards the EYTS. The first part of the book introduces the Teachers' Standards and considers assessment, placement preparation and action planning along with mentor guidance. The second part of the book dedicates a chapter to each standard, breaking each down into smaller components, suggesting evidence to gather, offering case study examples, reflection on practice and further reading to underpin each standard.

References

Abrahamson, L (2015) *The Early Years Teacher's Book*. London: Sage.

Allen, S and Whalley, M E (2010) *Supporting Pedagogy and Practice in Early Years*. Exeter: Learning Matters.

Aubrey, C (2007) *Leading and Managing in the Early Years*. London: Sage.

Bandura, A (1977) *Social Learning Theory*. Englewood Cliffs, NJ: Prentice Hall.

DfE (2013) *Teachers' Standards (Early Years)*. Available from: www.gov.uk/government/uploads/ system/uploads/attachment_data/file/211646/Early_Years_Teachers__Standards.pdf (accessed 28 November 2016).

DfE (2014) *Early Years Initial Teacher Training (ITT): A Guide for Providers*. Available from: www.gov. uk/guidance/early-years-initial-teacher-training-a-guide-for-providers (accessed 28 November 2016).

DfE (2016) *Get Into Teaching*. Available from: https://getintoteaching.education.gov.uk/explore-my- options/become-an-early-years-teacher (accessed 28 November 2016).

Grenier, J (2016) All About…Raising Quality, EYFS Best Practice. *Nursery World*, 13–16 October 2016: 21–25.

Hallet, E (2013) *The Reflective Early Years Practitioner*. London: Sage.

Hammond, S, Powell, S and Smith, K (2015) Towards Mentoring as Feminist Praxis in Early Childhood Education and Care in England. *Early Years*, 35(2): 139–53.

HM Government (2008) 2020 Children and Young People's Workforce Strategy. Available from: www.webarchive.nationalarchives.gov.uk/20130401151715/http://www.education.gov.uk/publications/eOrderingDownload/CYP_Workforce-Strategy.pdf (accessed 28 November 2016).

HM Government (2016) *National Standards for School-based Initial Teacher Training (ITT) Mentors*. Available from: www.gov.uk/government/uploads/system/uploads/attachment_data/file/536891/Mentor_standards_report_Final.pdf (accessed 28 November 2016).

Lave, J and Wenger, E (1991) *Situated Learning: Legitimate Peripheral Participation*. Cambridge: Cambridge University Press.

Lindon, J and Trodd, L (2016) *Reflective Practice and Early Years Professionalism*. London: Hodder Education.

Milne, A A (1928) *The House at Pooh Corner*. Suffolk: Richard Clay (The Chaucer Press) Ltd.

Ofsted (2015) *Teaching and Play in the Early Years – A Balancing Act?* Available from: www.gov.uk/government/publications/teaching-and-play-in-the-early-years-a-balancing-act (accessed 28 November 2016).

Osgood, J (2010) Reconstructing Professionalism in ECEC: The Case for the 'Critically Reflective Emotional professional' *Early Years*, 30(2): 119–33.

Robins, A and Callan, S (2009) Mentoring and Supporting Teams, in Robins, A and Callan, S (eds), *Managing Early Years Settings*. London: Sage.

Sargent, M (2016) Partner Up! National Teaching Schools. *Nursery World,* 11–24 January 2016. Available from: www.eleysp.co.uk/wp-content/uploads/2015/05/Partner-up-East-London-Partnership.pdf (accessed 8 January 2017).

Tuckman, B W (1965) Developmental Sequence in Small Groups. *Psychological Bulletin*, 63: 384–99.

Vinales, J J (2015) The Mentor as a Role Model and the Importance of Belongingness. *British Journal of Nursing*, 24(10): 532–35.

Wenger, E (2000), Communities of Practice and Social Learning Systems. *Organization*, 7(2): 225–46.

Whalley, M (2011) *Leading Practice in Early Years*. Exeter: Learning Matters Ltd.

5 Reflecting on the transition from vocational practice to university study

JAYNE DALY

Setting the scene

Imagine that you have had a hard day at work. The children in your work setting have been hot on your tail and you on theirs! You have had the tears and the tantrums, the runny noses, and even the odd lollypop in your hair!

You have answered question after question, nursed one or two children to sleep, and laughed at their jokes and stories. Now it is time for reflection ... So put the kettle on, dim the lights, put the TV on, get out that DVD your friend brought you for Christmas (that you haven't had a chance to watch) and that bag of popcorn and bar of chocolate you have been hiding at the back of the fridge for just the right moment!

Now you are ready to sit back and watch *Educating Rita*.

> Educating Rita *clips on YouTube (2014) Available from: www.youtube.com/ watch?v=12m9_yuC9Dg (accessed 20 November 2016).*

This film portrays the transitional experiences of a hairdresser, Susan (Rita), as she embarks on her higher educational journey.

This YouTube scene is particularly poignant as this is the one where 'Rita' is explaining to her tutor why she had not attended a social gathering at his home. She firstly makes the excuse that the type of wine she brought was wrong, and that's why she did not come. Obviously, Frank insists that he didn't want Rita to bring wine, he just wanted Rita's company, as she was amusing. Rita was not happy with the suggestion that she would be funny at all. This was not what she wanted to hear from her tutor. Rita wanted to be taken seriously; after all, she was now embarking on an academic journey.

Rita *had* turned up to Frank's house, but found that once there (looking through the window) she could not take those steps to make that final transition into his home. She walks home, bottle of cheap wine in hand, and meets her family in the pub. When she arrives her family are singing a song that is playing on the jukebox. Everyone that is, except her mother. Her mother had stopped singing and now she had begun to cry. Obviously Rita is concerned, and she asks her mother why she had stopped singing. Her mother tells her that there must be better songs to sing. Rita realises by listening to her mother's words that she does not want to sing the same old song and returns to her study the next day (as this scene shows) to explain to Frank her reasons for not attending his function.

Introduction

Whenever I see this screenplay and this scene in particular, I reflect upon my early days as an undergraduate early years practitioner. I remember I had mixed emotions. I was excited at the prospect of becoming a university student, but afraid that I would not *fit in* to the life-style university promoted. University was something that was only for the rich and the clever. I said this once to a friend of mine who asked me to define clever (she knew I would never be rich!). If you have ever tried to look for definitions of clever, as I did, you will know what she meant!

Making the transition into higher education was not easy for Rita either. The screenplay shows her transformation through many identity changes (even changing her name from Susan to Rita) only to reflect upon her pretence, and revert back to Susan later. It clearly focuses on the mature female learner that sets out to find a better 'song to sing', which was impacted by choices that Rita was not ready to commit to, including that of being a mother. Rita's experiences here are used as a basis for the introduction to this chapter, to set the scene, and to foster reflective thought processes in you as a reader. We will return to some of Rita's experiences later.

Whether you have been (or are about to go) through this experience yourself, or whether you are about to support someone who is taking this step for the first time, this chapter will hopefully give you a little insight into making that journey, as you reflect upon what has been, and what will be. It is important to note that the case studies used in this chapter are based on real-life experiences of early years practitioners who have taken, are undertaking, or are con-sidering undertaking this step. A further point I must highlight is that all of these experiences were recorded by women. Unfortunately I could not locate a male early years practitioner to take part in the writing of this chapter. According to Nutbrown (2012), less than 2 per cent of early years practitioners are male despite drives to encourage more males to enter the early years workforce. This is still a shocking revelation as we consider that in 1999 Cameron, Moss and Owen commented in their book how one of their male case study practitioners felt that it was the individual that made a difference to children's lives and it was not the gender of the practitioner (Cameron et al, 1999). This to me is a valuable point. Even at that time these authors were considering the inequality that male practitioners faced in early years practice. Their conclusions highlight their reflections in making the issues and dilemmas of the male nursery worker visible as they consider such issues as gender pay gap, whereby the male practitioner might be dissuaded from undertaking care work due to restrictive financial reward. Their arguments also reveal that male practitioners are treated differently due to the concerns around safeguarding which has been debated many times, as you can do, by reflect-ing on the Vanessa George case and noting that women are abusers too. Rushforth writing in

Nursery World in 2010 reflects upon the serious case review of this case commenting on the poor policies and recruitment procedures of Little Teds in Plymouth. She further notes failings of how staff were recruited in terms of lack of thorough checks highlighting the need to seek out the cultural background of new recruits not specific to their gender (Rushforth, 2010). In 2006 Cameron revisited the issues addressed in the collaborative text of 1999 (Cameron et al, 1999) and still highlighted the rarity of the male workforce in early years. Cameron does however make an interesting point that in order to develop change in the acceptance of male practitioners we much develop a reflective approach to our practices embracing discussion, debate and interest in new ways of working to support the cause. As practitioners we need to reflect and consider the difference of male co-workers and perhaps look at the world through their eyes. Cameron (2006) further explores the issues of the marginalisation of the male workforce even when a setting has been lucky enough to recruit. She further comments that these attitudes do little to support the case for the need for more male workers in the sector. Whatever the reasons for the limited male workforce within the sector I want you as a reader to understand that this chapter is not purely a female read as many of the issues discussed can just as easily be reflected upon by the male practitioner.

Extended thinking

Are you a male practitioner who works in early years? Or do you know of a setting that has successfully recruited a male practitioner? If so, what are the success stories? What are the failings of the setting?

»   *Consider the issues the male practitioner may face in a female dominated workforce. List them and reflect upon how the setting could develop their policies to make them more inclusive in terms of gender differences and similarities.*

»   *In doing this consider if there is a difference in the way male practitioners might be treated or does equality mean that all workers should be treated in the 'same' way?*

»   *Why might male workers feel marginalised?*

»   *How might this be overcome?*

Background: transitions in early years

When I watch *Educating Rita* as a screen play, it is easy for me to reflect upon and associate with some of the feelings Rita went through. Being able to converse at *university level* and bringing the *wrong wine* was always a fear of mine, as I am sure it is, or has been, for many of you reading this chapter now. So where did this all come from? Why was I, as both an early years practitioner and setting manager, and many others like me, thrust into the world of academia?

In 1997 the White Paper *Excellence in Schools* (HMSO, 1997) identified the need for our youngest children to have a better start to their education. This was then developed further by the Labour government in their decision to introduce Early Years Development Partnerships (EYDP), updated to Early Years Teacher (EYT) in September 2013. In 1998, the Green Paper *Meeting the Childcare Challenge* (DfEE, 1998) recognised the need to support the links between care and education in the early years, leading to an approved childcare plan. For every local authority this meant that free childcare places were offered by September of the same year, for any 4 year-old whose parents wanted to take this up, with plans to extend this to 3 year-olds by 2004. It was clear that if public funds were to be spent, then better regulatory controls and a curriculum needed to be in place in order for settings to qualify. In September 2000, the Foundation Stage Curriculum Framework (DfES, 2000) was introduced for children from three years to the end of the Reception year. All settings claiming free funded places were required to conform to the use of this framework. By September 2001 the regulatory controls were in place and Ofsted became responsible for ensuring the quality of provision. By 2003, this had been extended to children from birth to three with the *Birth to Three Framework* (DfES, 2003). In 2007 there was change once again, as both the *Foundation Stage* and *Birth to Three* frameworks were amalgamated into one Early Years Foundation Stage (DfES, 2007). The Early Years Statutory framework was revised in March 2012 and came into force in September of the same year (DfE, 2012).

In 2003, the Association of Teachers and Lecturers called for a recognition of the status of Early Years Teachers and the complex role they carry out (ATL, 2003). By 2007, the amalgamated curriculum had been introduced in response to the childcare strategy (UK Childcare, 2013) and Childcare Act 2006 (DfES, 2006). Central government capital, the Transformation Fund and Graduate Leader Fund (DfE, 2013b, 2013c) was provided in order for early years practitioners to gain their Early Years Professional Status (EYPS) and to become the agents for change within the sector. This public purse was to provide finance for individual higher education funding, to ensure there was a graduate leader (EYP) (now Early Years Teacher) (EYITT, since 2014) (DfE, 2016) in every private, independent and voluntary (PIV) setting by 2015 (DfE, 2013a, 2013b, 2013c). This is discussed further in Chapter 11.

There was now an expectation for the new non-traditional higher education student, in the form of the vocational early years practitioner, to become an undergraduate. Widening participation within higher education became policy following the Dearing Report (1997), which expanded the higher education explosion predicted by the Robbins Committee in 1963 (HMSO, 1963). There was now a strong emphasis on the new non-traditional student, from various under-represented groups in society, taking the opportunity to develop their education by undertaking degrees, and subdivision degrees such as foundation degrees, with the help of national and local government bursaries.

Social and cultural capital and access to higher education

Christie et al (2008) help us to reflect upon the fears of many of these non-traditional students taking their first steps into the unknown world of academia. The fear of failure and lack of confidence can be likened, as Morgan (2013) discusses, to the feelings of any young A level student entering higher education for the first time.

The factors involved in the transition of the non-traditional student are further highlighted by Brine and Waller (2004), who draw our attention to their past educational experiences. Baxter and Britton (2001) argue that the mature learner now uses the opportunity to make transitions to higher education to reshape their perception of themselves, and to make conscious decisions about shaping their future. Very often this can mean a significant change from past life experiences.

Returning to Rita's experiences, it was clear that she wanted to change her self-perception and identity by changing her name, as she craved for a new 'song to sing'. Bourdieu's (1977, cited in Sullivan, 2002) cultural capital concept determines that this is not always easy for individuals such as Rita. Bourdieu (1977) identifies his theory and suggests that

> *cultural capital consists of familiarity with the dominant culture in a society, and especially the ability to understand and use 'educated' language. The possession of cultural capital varies with social class, yet the education system assumes the possession of cultural capital. This makes it very difficult for lower-class pupils to succeed in the education system.*
>
> (p 494, cited in Sullivan, 2002, p 145)

In Rita's case within Russell's screenplay her early engagement with higher education meant that very often she misunderstood 'educated language', but was quick to engage with this with deep and dogged determination. According to Bourdieu's theory (1977, cited in Sullivan, 2002), social capital in education can have demoralising consequences for many, in terms of their academic expectations. The growth of new cultural capital (1977, cited in Sullivan, 2002) becomes the academic stimulus to the eradication of past lives, and to movement between the social classes creating social capital. Modood (2012) explores the *capital metaphor* (p 17), as being somewhat appealing, but argues that Bourdieu's study has limitations and would prefer to call for social and cultural capital through equality in society. Modood's concern surrounds lack of equality through individual life circumstances, which is something that became a focus of the coalition government in 2010 in Britain. In 2010 new government policy was introduced, resulting in higher university fees and the expectation that universities would improve incentives for encouraging mature learners (both male and female), learners of lower social class and learners from ethnic minorities with traditionally low participation rates in higher education (Clayton, 2012).

Sullivan (2002) concludes in her research that cultural capital as defined by Bourdieu can be contradictory at times, by suggesting that Bourdieu has failed to explore the prejudice in society that prohibited many lower socio-economic classes accessing the education environment. Khan (2007) also recognises the weaknesses in this concept. Sullivan (2002) does, however, admit that cultural capital has in some cases had an impact on academic identity achievement. This was evident in Rita's case: initially she was highly motivated, mentored and encouraged by her tutor Frank, but also by her own intrinsic motivational qualities and aspirations. Once her confidence grew, she realised that she needed more than just Frank, and went off to summer school to expand her horizons.

Basit and Tomlinson (2012) contemplate the motivational aspirations of the working class through cultural and social capital to seek out higher education opportunities. In turn, they consider the work of Christie et al (2008) with regard to the disadvantaged student from a non-traditional student perspective, and the effects upon them emotionally and psychologically because of their transition.

Risk factors in the transition to higher education

What are the risk factors in entering higher education?

Morgan (2013) notes:

> *Studies that have focused on the transition experiences of non-traditional students suggest that going to university may be seen as a time of risk, including financial risk, risk to identity and self-concept, risk to family life/children and the risk of failure as well as feelings of not being able to cope or make friends.*
>
> (Morgan, 2013, p 3)

Baxter and Britton (2001) consider the risk of breakdown in family life is far greater for the mature female learner than the mature male learner. Wright (2013a) found that within her study many female learners

> *wanted the best of both worlds: to work and to study but always in a context that protected their families' needs.*
>
> (Wright, 2013a, p 206)

Wright argues that, no matter how we try to avoid it (even in the twenty-first century), it seems that most of the family workload falls to the female.

Challis (2006) recognised that mature students often have serious doubts as to their ability to study in higher education, which he argues is significantly different to the younger learner. Challis suggests that mature students worry more about the *quality of their reading and listening* (p 212). However, one poignant point that Challis makes is that mature students come to higher education because they want to be there rather than the student straight out of school who may simply be fulfilling a societal expectation. It is true, however, that some mature students now feel that they are being forced into higher education because of government policy and fear for their future employment within the sector without higher education qualifications, something which is highlighted in Case Study 1.

So it seems that the transition into higher education, for the non-traditional vocational Early Years practitioner, is not an easy one. If we look at these risks it is a wonder that we ever succeed at all but many do, just like Rita.

CASE STUDY 1

Diane

Diane is a part-time early years practitioner, qualified to NVQ level 3. Diane's manager knows she is exceptional at her job. She is an excellent team player and recognises the individual needs of all of the children while working in the toddler room. Diane has a young family, a girl and boy both under the age of ten, a partner and her elderly mother living with them. Diane has been asked by her manager to undertake a foundation degree at university. A colleague has recently qualified and, although Diane sees the value in undertaking this qualification in order to benefit the family's future, she is concerned about the commitment of time and energy that she will have to make. When explaining this to her manager and to the owner of the setting where she works, they are both unsympathetic stating that the qualification will be a requirement of her continued employment. Diane cannot afford to lose her job, but the pressure she finds herself under is immense. She finds herself torn between the risk to family life and the risk to her role within the setting. There seems no choice. Diane reflects upon this situation.

Reflective activity

»   *What would be the best thing for Diane to do?*

»   *Explain whether you think Diane is ready to commit to higher education.*

»   *What may be the potential risks for Diane?*

»   *How could she approach this situation?*

Commentary on Diane

It is evident here that Diane is being 'bullied' into undertaking her foundation degree by her managers. This is not something that Diane has chosen to do herself. This will make it all the more difficult for Diane to commit to the rigours of studying at higher education level. Students attending higher education frequently report managers trying to take control of their staff in this way, especially in the early days of the early years foundation degree when government funding was freely available. The main risk that Diane will face here is the risk of being 'set up to fail', not through lack of academic skill but through the pressure that she is being put under before she begins this educational journey. In the case of *Educating Rita*, Rita was in a position to make choices; these choices were not always easy and she suffered the break-up of her marriage because of her choice not to have children during the time she was studying. If we go back to the words of Wright (2013a) having the *best of both worlds* cannot always be possible and it is here that we need to turn our attention to the choices and sacrifices we may have to make when we enter higher education for the first time.

So let's reflect upon the questions. Ideally it would be fantastic if Diane could have the best of both worlds but, unless Diane can freely commit to higher education with the support of her family, it is unlikely although not impossible that she will succeed. Goleman (1996), draws our attention to the importance of emotional intelligence (EQ), highlighting that unless we are emotionally ready we will not learn. Mytton and Rumbold (2011) also recognise the impact of emotional intelligence as the transition process into higher education begins. To be emotionally ready, Diane must take into consideration her own needs, her roles and responsibilities within her family. If we try to reverse this situation and give Diane the choice, Diane would have no doubt considered her family and their needs first and, if they are happy and supportive, she will be ready. Currently Diane faces many potential risks if she is not ready to commit: financial risks, relationship and family life risks, and of course the risk of failure (Morgan, 2013).

Diane needs to now decide who *she* is, her self-identity and what *she* wants.

Extended thinking

So, before you read on, given Diane's story, put yourself in her position as a practitioner.

» *What would you do?*

» *What have you done when faced with a similar situation?*

Developing a new identity and self-perception in higher education

According to Wright, human beings develop a sense of personal identity by reflecting and developing *courage to be different from others* (1982, p 5). It is interesting how Wright uses the words *courage to be different* suggesting there is an element of bravery in this process. Craib recollected the momentous shift from class identity in pre-war and early post-war years. He highlighted the focus upon individual and diverse identity as *an element or process within a self* and further remarks that personal identity *catalogues the individual* (1998, p 1).

Sometimes as individuals we may lose our sense of personal identity. Who are we? What do we want to achieve? What must we do to get there? How do we make a start? We must ensure, according to Craib (1998), that we gain experience in order to develop our inner self and to use our inner self to support others. Craib affirms the diverse elements that Wright (1982) posits but he does not allude to courage or bravery in this process. Perhaps this was because in 1998, with the eve of a new millennium fast approaching, the shift towards finding one's own identity was a much more poised process in this time of global change, and 'millennium goals' (United Nations, 2007) supported global communities in reaching equality in many, although not all, countries.

Both Craib (1998) and Illeris (2014) share the view that, although contentious in 1895, Freud was the first psychoanalyst to distinguish changes in the self-perception of his patients, often connected with emotional conditions which had transpired earlier in their lives. Illeris asserts that since that time, although the process of psychoanalysis has been developed by many (both Erikson and Rogers within their neo-Freudian positions posited their views surrounding personal identity and change), *all deal with some sort of learning as change* (Illeris, 2014, p 17).

Rogers (1969) noted links between changes in self, self-perception and identity through continued transformative learning, something which he suggested would bridge the gap between emotional therapy, education and learning. Erikson, although not centrally concerned with education within his philosophy, suggested that as humans we need to go through individual stages throughout our life. He highlighted that the stage from youth to adult was the most significant, as this would determine our personal identity (Illeris, 2014, p 4). From this we can propose that learning accomplishment, that Wright (1982) posited in terms of identity, may not be complete in childhood, and that through the changes we face throughout human development and lifelong learning we continue to strive to achieve the personal identity that Erikson and Rogers theorised.

Cavallaro-Johnson and Watson (2004) highlight in their study '*Oh Gawd, How Am I Going to Fit into This?': Producing (Mature) First Year Student Identity* that success in developing student identity in higher education is determined by successful engagement with the student in the learning environment. This enables them to grow in confidence and to change their view of what it is to *be successful* (p 477). Cavallaro-Johnson and Watson (2004, p 479) refer to the work of Archer et al (2001) and suggest that *mature age identity and issues of educational access ... can be conceptualised usefully as multiple, fluid, and shifting*. Therefore, his concept reveals that as adults our self-perception and confidence are continually evolving with the more experiences that we encounter; in this case in the learning environment.

Willians and Seary (2011) liken the transformative learning process for the mature learner to:

> a novice paintball player, who unless well positioned and attuned to the rules of the combative game, is bombarded and worn down by constant 'hits'.
>
> (p 199)

The *hits* that Willians and Seary reflect upon are used as a metaphor for the personal challenges that many learners go through, when seeking to test their perception of their own identity within the transformative learning process.

CASE STUDY 2

Sally

Sally is a specialist teacher of children with dyslexia and she now has her own freelance business. She has worked in early years for a number of years. Her transition into higher education was not an easy one as she had to consider her very young family. She has had various positions in the early years field, but always had a desire to teach. Sally had deep feelings about her transition into higher education: financial costs mounted, as well as variances in teaching styles and methods, as she progressed. But as Sally's children grew up so did her confidence and her family continued to support her in her lifelong journey. Sally discusses her feelings regarding the benefits of embarking on a higher education journey. She states:

The benefits of embarking on a higher education course are simply that you are able to become the person you know you are; you can reach out for your potential and you can fulfil it.

Sally also reflects upon the risks, and notes:

If you have friends or relatives who like you in the 'pigeonhole' they are used to seeing you in, then they might react differently when you begin to evolve. She continues confidently, this isn't necessarily a bad thing, because if people don't want to see you fulfilled, then it's probably no great detriment if they disappear from your life – they'll just hold you back! ... I feel that now I am a fully qualified specialist teacher, my capabilities and passion have not changed. It is great to have those pieces of paper to attach to your CV as evidence of your dedication and hard work. I think it also gives you a feeling of equality and pride in your work environment ... I am proud to be called a specialist teacher. I feel I have taken off the shackles of my 1970s secondary education and come through to the other side. Eventually, I proved them wrong and me right. That feels good. I like who I am and what I represent.

Extended thinking

Watch further clips of Educating Rita.

» *Reflect upon barriers to higher education for the non-traditional student. How might these be overcome?*

» *Would it have been possible for Rita to overcome the barriers she faced without making sacrifices?*

Commentary on Sally

Considering Sally's comments, it is clear that, although she had barriers to overcome in undertaking the higher education transition, she has recognised now who she is, and what she wanted to be. Sally has reached her dream and become that specialist teacher. Sally also recognises that others in her circles did not want this transformation to happen for their own selfish reasons and *'pigeonholed'* her. This was also highlighted in *Educating Rita* as Rita became something that her own family did not want her to be. This is why it is important, as with the case of Diane, to reflect upon your entry to higher education and discuss all options with your family as they too are going to have to make sacrifices. Sally highlights how she has changed her life with her family's support. She considers how she has undone the past as Baxter and Britton (2001) predict. But most of all what is clear in this case study is the way Sally feels after undertaking this transformative learning process ... it *feels good!*

Extended thinking

Sally has obviously found happiness and she has recognised that potentially there will be others that may stand in your way as you embark on your journey. Sally sounds strong in her beliefs that if others are not supporting you then they should 'disappear from your life'.

»   *Discuss this point.*

»   *What are your views?*

»   *Should those that are not supportive be set aside so that you can move forward on a new journey to avoid being pigeonholed as Sally suggests?*

Transformative learning in higher education

The Leitch Report (HM Treasury, 2006) outlined recommendations for change within the UK in its suggestions for workforce skills development to improve economic growth and social justice. The introduction of foundation degrees in the UK, and the call for widening participation within higher education, has meant that more and more mature learners (particularly with the expansion of part-time options for study) are able to access these degrees to improve professional skills. Students may also gain personal benefits, in terms of personal fulfilment, by receiving graduate status and potentially financial gain through improved employment prospects.

The concept of transformative learning, according to Illeris, very often means that something needs transforming. Illeris posits that external events or events that lead into *new life situations* (2014, p 91), may impact upon the learner's decision to change. In the case of students in early years, changes within the sector already discussed identified the need for this change, but there may be other reasons for entering higher education. Britton and Baxter (1999) identify from their study that the female mature learner sought to want to *develop a career and move away from the domestic sphere of the home* (p 90). These views are supported by the work of Merrill (1999, cited in Wright, 2013b, p 90), who noted *that the women in her study found education to be a mechanism for personal change and development* and *they no longer wanted to be dominated by domesticity.*

According to Illeris, the concept of transformative learning was further developed, following in the footsteps of theorists such as Dewey and Rogers, by Mazirow in 1978. Mazirow, as discussed in Illeris (2014), concerned himself with investigations into the transformative changes of women undertaking further and higher education opportunities. Mazirow posited that this gave these students *new meaning* in their lives. This suggested that adults could create new *meaning schemes* and *meaning prospective* in their lives (Illeris, 2014, p 6). In order to gain these new meaning perspectives, and to understand one's inner self, the learner will require an element of personal critical reflection which, as Mazirow determines, is the *core of transformative learning* (Illeris, 2014, p 67).

By being open to viewpoints of others, allowing yourself to take constructive criticism, being prepared to take the 'hits' that Willians and Seary (2011) propose, as well as showing empathy and concern for others (including your family) and being able to reflect upon personal assumptions, and of course the assumptions of others, you are more likely to succeed in the transformative learning process within the higher education environment. If you return to Chapter 1, you can reflect upon Schön's (1987) theory of 'Reflection in Action', in order to move forward to change past lives and past negative experiences of education.

CASE STUDY 3

Louise

Louise is the manager of an early years pre-school setting. She is currently in the final year of her full-time BA (Hons) degree which will enable her to go on to complete her Early Years Teacher (EYT) status. Louise is passionate about the care and education of the youngest children and decided to undertake her current qualification because she felt that it would improve her knowledge and confidence in her current role. Louise also wants to achieve her degree for personal fulfilment, following a difficult start in further education. Louise needed to change her perception of education through her transformative learning process.

Difficulties that Louise faced when embarking upon her higher education journey were balancing childcare and work commitments, but these were soon resolved following initial adjustments. She tells us: *I have had very positive experiences as a mature student thanks to supportive input and guidance from my tutors.*

Louise states: *as a working mum with … a husband who also works long hours and sometimes away from home, it is a challenge to sometimes keep all of the plates spinning!* However, she goes on, this experience has meant *a huge sense of fulfilment, greater confidence, greater understanding of policy and legislation … an increased professional approach and attitude, sense of worth and recognition for personal strengths.* The higher education experience has allowed Louise to *make informed decisions and to introduce ideas and concepts confidently through having a sound base to support my contributions.*

Louise believes: *I am now a far more confident and professional practitioner since embarking on my studies. I am far more confident in my interactions with other professionals and feel on a more equal footing with them. I have taken on an increasingly responsible role. I also have a great deal more self-belief and confidence in my role … rather than just a 'job'.*

Commentary on Louise

Louise's journey has meant that she has become open to a new way of learning. She has put aside her negative experiences of further education, and reflected upon her new journey. The educational experiences Louise took with her have been eradicated within her transformative learning process. This has been aided by her own reflective qualities in being open to change, because of her determination and passion for quality care and education of children. She has shown that her confidence has improved her knowledge and understanding, as well as her interaction and communication skills with others. She highlighted that part of her success was due to the support of her family who had to adjust to her newly found identity. She also talks of good tutor support in helping her to adjust and Illeris (2014) defines the role of the teacher in supporting any student in the transformative learning process, through careful mentoring and coaching skills. The tutor needs to understand the student's previous educational experience in order to move forward and transform existing perception. The tutor's role is then to encourage the student to critically reflect upon debate and discussion through their writing, their attitude to others, including personal relationships within the educational context, and becoming self-aware if emotional issues try to overtake the learning process (Goleman, 1996).

Extended thinking

Think about your personal journey as a student.

» *Are there any historical educational experiences that cause you to doubt your abilities as a learner?*

» *What are these and how do you think these may be overcome?*

Being effectively mentored and coached through the learning process

Megginson and Clutterbuck (1995) posit how the role of the mentor has often been linked to Greek mythology, whereby the Greek god Ulysses entrusted the care of his son Telemachus to his friend Mentor, and how this raises the question of whether definitions of the mentor role have become distorted. Brockbank and Mcgill (2006) go on to identify the view of Megginson and Garvey (2004), who define mentoring as *a relationship between two people with learning and development as its purpose* (p 2). Brockbank and McGill (2006) further highlight that changing definitions of coaching suggest much more than the mentoring concept and include counselling, something which Rogers (2008) agrees with.

Gravells and Wallace (2012) use their perspectives on the arts to help us to understand and critically evaluate the mentoring process. In doing so they make some poignant points about how the mentor within a particular example (eg film, TV or literature) is able to support the transformation of the identity of the mentee or character within their chosen topic. For example, they highlight the 'storytelling' of the mentor character of Ninny Threadgood (Jessica Tandy) in the film *Fried Green Tomatoes at the Whistle-stop Café* (p 1), which inspires the mentee character Evelyn Couch (Kathy Bates) to reflect upon herself and discover she was not happy with what she saw, and set out to change. I have watched this film many times and can identify with the metaphor as both a mentor and a mentee. Stories, from my mentors, have inspired me to read a book or take action on a specific issue in practice. Stories that I have repeated have had the same effects on my students, in terms of their vocational and academic practice, because I have been in the same situation that they are in. Gravells and Wallace also allude to the story of *Educating Rita* (p 69) and how the character Susan (Julie Walters) sets out on a personal journey to discover her new identity (Rita) supported by her mentor Frank (Michael Caine). Gravells and Wallace point out that, as Rita's confidence grew, Frank, with his own issues of lack of self-worth as a tutor, was also supported by Rita and the mentoring progression became dialogic, a two-way process.

When thinking about the coaching process, Brockbank and McGill (2006) identify preferred methods or models that the coach may use. They evaluate the use of the GROW model (developed by Whitmore, 1996) in terms of its basic functionalist approach, as the client works towards set goals or SMART targets. This model is rebuked by many, including Megginson and Clutterbuck (2009) in terms of its rigid structure, stating that this model is very often used by inexperienced mentors or coaches.

The FLOW model as developed by Flaherty (1999; cited in Brockbank and McGill 2006), highlights its evolutionary coaching methods and suggest this may work well for the external or life coach, but warn that this model may restrict itself when students are constrained to educational objectives.

Turnbull (2009) identifies the CARE model in supporting the student and in particular high-lights their social and emotional needs (as also discussed in Chapter 7), therefore careful communication channels are needed to ensure continuous support of the mentee. This can be time-consuming, so needs careful consideration and dedication on the part of the mentor or coach.

Sieler discusses the *transformative power of ontological coaching* (2009, p 49) which he says gets into the heart of the issues that a student may face as a human being. He suggests that by being resourceful as coaches, tutors can help the student to reflect on past issues and help them to overcome future problems. He highlights a poignant point from Senge (2006), which suggests:

> *real learning gets to the heart of what it means to be human. Through learning we recreate ourselves.*
> (Peter Senge, 2006, *The Fifth Discipline*, cited in Sieler, 2009, p 49)

So let us reflect upon this. How can we recreate ourselves as academic, vocational profes-sionals? Is this possible?

Personal Reflection and discussion point

CASE STUDY 4

Julie

Julie has been a nursery manager for a number of years and she has undertaken her foun-dation degree in early childhood studies. She is currently in her final top-up year to achieve her BA (Hons) in Education which will enable her to go on to undertake her EYT status. She states: *If I am being totally honest the foundation degree (in early childhood studies) was sold to me on the premise that I had to do it because I was a manager of an early years setting. This was my initial reason for starting the course but I have to say, I have learned so much, and made so many friends that, regardless of all the hard work and sleepless nights, I have loved it, which is why I am in the middle of my top-up!*

Julie remembers some of the difficulties and tells us: *When I started the foundation degree I found it very difficult as I was completely unsure of what to expect and what to do. Once the first assignment was completed, and I had passed it, subsequent assignments became a little easier to complete and understand. I still find it difficult to juggle work, life, family and assignment time, but feel the rewards of future professional development will outweigh this ... There does not seem to be enough hours in the day!* She continues: *children and staff are benefiting from my knowledge ... but .... you need to be committed, have the time and be ready for disappointment, I mean, not everyone can get a first, and whatever you do, as long as you pass and enjoy it!*

In Julie's role she tells us: *I have taken the nursery from satisfactory to outstanding and made so many changes to benefit the children and staff.* Julie tells us, however, that although she has extremely high confidence in the workplace her *academic confidence is still low.* She says *This is silly because I keep getting firsts! Maybe when I have finished the BA I might change my mind.* She recommends: *If you have the time, energy and commitment it is definitely worthwhile!*

Commentary on Julie

Julie has recreated herself although, as yet, she does not recognise it from an academic stance, but professionally she has taken her team and the children to new heights. She has used the support from her family and friends, as well as her academic mentors and coaches, to develop her new identity. She recognises that as a professional you need to commit to higher education, and does not give us a false sense of security that it is easy. She is also starting to develop her academic skills now in such a way that she is gaining firsts. This in itself can be an academic pressure. Julie is determined. You may also get the feeling here that she has something to prove, not to the staff, or the children, or even the parents for that matter, she has done that already, but to prove to herself that she can do this and she can do it well!

Extended thinking

Consider Julie's journey and her thoughts on her academic success.

» *Why do you think Julie still doubts her abilities despite her obvious successes in achieving first-grade assignments?*

» *Have any of your educational experiences led you to doubt your abilities? What were these?*

» *Have they hindered your progression or made you more determined to succeed?*

Chapter reflections

This chapter has demonstrated that taking the transitional step from vocational practice to higher education is not an easy one, and one which takes considerable thought. We need to ensure we are not 'bullied' into undertaking this step; the purpose of this chapter has been to allow you to see the advantages and disadvantages of this process. We have also learned that we need to consider the risks, and there is no denying that the transition into higher education can carry risk (Morgan, 2013; Baxter and Britton, 2001). However, there are also many benefits, and you need to carefully balance these benefits against the risks. We need to reflect upon our identity (Wright, 1982; Craib, 1998; Illeris, 2014; Cavallaro-Johnson and Watson, 2004; Willians and Seary, 2011), ie who we are, and look in the mirror to see if we are happy with the practitioner we see staring back at us. We need to disregard those that 'pigeonhole' us, and need to make the step forward for reflective change. We need to consider the difference we can make to our lives and the lives of the children and families in our care, by improving our knowledge. We need to understand that there is support out there, and identify that we are not alone in making those first steps. We know now that we need to be inspired as Rita was, and we need to find the right coach or mentor in supporting us in this process.

When reflecting on how this chapter started we must remember Rita's wine. Did it matter that Rita brought the wrong wine? No. What did matter was that Rita was able to reflect upon her actions in not going to Frank's party and say, 'Hey! I don't want to sing the "same old song" that my mother sings, I want to aspire to sing a better song, and a song that will make a difference!'

Extended reflections

» *So now considering this chapter think about your song. Do you want to aspire to sing a different song? A better song? How might you find that better song to sing?*

Further reading

Warwick-Booth, L (2013) *Social Inequality*. London: Sage.

This book is a well-defined text to allow students to understand the dynamics of contemporary social inequality within a global context. The book explores the social divisions of class, gender and ethnicity and attempts to define the difficult, political and complex concept of the social policy environment.

References

ATL (2003) Right from the Start: Early Years Education Policy and Practice. Available from: www.atl.org.uk/Images/Right%20from%20the%20start.pdf (accessed 4 October 2013).

Basit, N and Tomlinson, S (eds) (2012) *Social Inclusion and Higher Education*. Bristol: Policy Press.

Baxter, A and Britton, C (2001) Risk, Identity and Change: Becoming a Mature Student. *International Studies in Sociology of Education*, 11(1): 87–104.

Brine, J and Waller, R (2004) Working-class Women on an Access Course: Risk, Opportunity and (Re)constructing Identities. *Gender and Education*, 16(1): 97–113.

Britton, C and Baxter, A (1999) Becoming a Mature Student: Gender Narratives of the Self. *Gender and Education*, 11(2): 179–93.

Brockbank, A and McGill, I (2006) *Facilitating Reflective Learning through Mentoring and Coaching*. London: Kogan Page.

Cameron C, (2006) Men in Nursery Revisited: Issues of Male Workers and Professionalism. *Contemporary Issues in Early Childhood*, 7(1): 68–79.

Cameron C, Moss P, Owen C (1999) Men in the Nursery Gender and Caring Work. London: SAGE.

Cavallaro-Johnson, G and Watson, G (2004) 'Oh Gawd, How Am I Going to Fit into This?': Producing [Mature] First Year Student Identity. *Language and Education*, 18(6): 474–87.

Challis, R (2006) The Experience of Mature Students. *Studies in Higher Education*, 1(2): 209–22.

Christie, H L, Tett, V E, Cree, J, Hounsell, V and McCune, V (2008) A Real Rollercoaster of Confidence and Emotions: Learning to Be a University Student. *Studies in Higher Education*, 33(5): 567–81.

Clayton, M (2012) On Widening Participation in Higher Education through Positive Discrimination. *Journal of Philosophy of Education,* 46(3): 414–31.

Craib, I (1998) *Experiencing Identity*. London: Sage.

Dearing Report (1997) The National Committee of Enquiry into Higher Education. Available from: www.leeds.ac.uk/educol/ncihe/ (accessed 4 October 2013).

DfE (2012) Statutory Framework for the Early Years Foundation Stage (2012 review, DfE). Available from: www.foundationyears.org.uk/early-years-foundation-stage-2012/ (accessed 4 October 2013).

DfE (2013a) Department of Education, Education Terms: Childcare (Children's Services). Available from: www.education.gov.uk/vocabularies/educationtermsandtags/1402 (accessed 4 October 2013).

DfE (2013b) Evaluation of the Graduate Leader Fund – Final Report. Available from: www.education.gov.uk/publications/standard/publicationDetail/Page1/DFE-RR144 (accessed 23 April 2013).

DfE (2013c) Graduate Leaders in Early Years: Early Years Professional Status. Available from: www.education.gov.uk/childrenandyoungpeople/earlylearningandchildcare/h00201345/graduate-leaders/eyps (accessed 23 April 2013).

DfE (2016) Early Years Initial Teacher Training and Supporting Advice. NCTL London: Crown Copyright (2016). Available from: www.gov.uk/government/uploads/system/uploads/attachment_data/file/537731/EYITT_Requirements_Supporting_Advice_2017_to_2018.pdf (accessed 20 November 2016).

DfEE (1998) *Meeting the Childcare Challenge – A Framework and Consultation Document*. London: DfEE. Available from: http://webarchive.nationalarchives.gov.uk/20130401151715/https://www.education.gov.uk/publications/standard/Childrensworkforce/Page5/Cm%203959 (accessed 4 October 2013).

DfES (2000) *Foundation Stage Curriculum Framework*. London: DfES.

DfES (2003) *Birth to Three Matters: A Framework to Support Children and Families in Their Earliest Years*. London: DfES.

DfES (2006) *Childcare Act*. London: DfES.

DfES (2007) *Early Years Foundation Stage*. London: DfES.

Goleman, D (1996) *Working with Emotional Intelligence*. London: Bloomsbury Publishing.

Gravells, J and Wallace, S (2012) *Dial M for Mentor: Critical Reflections on Mentoring for Coaches, Educators and Trainers*. Northwich: Critical Publishing.

Her Majesty's Stationery Office (HMSO) (1963) The Robbins Report: Higher Education Report of the Committee Appointed by the Prime Minister under the Chairmanship of Lord Robbins. Available from: www.educationengland.org.uk/documents/robbins/robbins1963.html (accessed 4 October 2013).

HMSO (1997) *White Paper: Excellence in Schools*. London: HMSO. Available from www.educationeng-land.org.uk/documents/wp1997/excellence-in-schools.html (accessed 4 October 2013).

HM Treasury (Her Majesty's Stationary Office) (2006) *Prosperity for All in the Global Economy: World Class Skills: Final Report (Leitch Review of Skills)*. London: HMSO.

Illeris, K (2014) *Transformative Learning and Identity*. Oxon: Sage.

Khan, O (2007) Race, Equality and Community Cohesion, in Wetherell, M, Lafleche, M and Berkeley, R (eds), *Identity, Ethnic Diversity and Community Cohesion*. London: Sage.

Megginson, D and Clutterbuck, D (1995) *Mentoring in Action*. London: Kogan Page.

Megginson, D and Clutterbuck, D (2009) *Further Techniques in Coaching and Mentoring*. Oxford: Elsevier.

Megginson, D and Garvey, B (2004) Odysseus, Telemachus and Mentor: Stumbling into Searching for and Signposting the Road to Desire. *International Journal of Mentoring and Coaching*, 2(1): 16–40.

Modood, T (2012) Capitals, Ethnicity and Higher Education, in Basit, N and Tomlinson, S (eds), *Social Inclusion and Higher Education*. Bristol: Policy Press.

Morgan, J (2013) Foundation Degree to Honours Degree: The Transition Experiences of Students on an Early Years Programme. *Journal of Further and Higher Education*, 1–19. DOI:10.1080/03 09877X.2013.817005.

Mytton, G and Rumbold, P (2011) Enhancing Transition from a Foundation Degree to the Third Year of an Undergraduate Degree. *Innovations in Education and Teaching International*, 48(3): 251–61.

Nutbrown, C (2012) *Foundations for Quality: The Independent Review of Early Education and Child Care Qualifications*. Runcorn: Crown.

Rogers, C (1969) *Freedom to Learn*. Columbus, OH: Charles E Merrill.

Rogers, J (2008) *Coaching Skills*. Maidenhead: Open University Press.

Rushforth C (2010) Vanessa George Case Review Lessons to be Learned. *Nursery World*. Available from: www.nurseryworld.co.uk/nursery-world/news/1095440/vanessa-george-review-lessons-learned (accessed 20 November 2016).

Schön, D A (1987) *Educating the Reflective Practitioner*. San Francisco: Jossey-Bass.

Senge, P M (2006) *The Fifth Discipline: The Art and Practice of the Learning Organisation*. London: Random House.

Sieler, A (2009) The Transformative Power of Ontological Coaching, in Megginson, D and Clutterbuck, D, *Further Techniques in Coaching and Mentoring*. Oxford: Elsevier.

Sullivan, A (2002) Bourdieu and Education: How Useful Is Bourdieu's Theory for Researchers? *Netherlands Journal of Social Sciences*, 38(2): 144–66.

Turnbull, J (2009) *Coaching for Learning*. London: Continuum Books.

UK childcare (2013) Policy and Legislation: The National Childcare Strategy. Available from: www.ukchildcare.ca/policy/strategy.shtml (accessed 4 October 2013).

United Nations (2007) *Millennium Development Goals Report*. New York: United Nations.

Warwick-Booth, L (2013) *Social Inequality*. London: Sage.

Whitmore, J (1996) *Coaching for Performance*. London: Nicholas Brealey Publishing.

Willians, J and Seary, K (2011) I Feel Like I'm Being Hit from All Directions: Enduring the Bombardment as a Mature-Age Learner Returning to Formal Learning. *Australian Journal of Adult Learning*, 51(1): 120–42.

Wright, H R (2013a) Choosing to Compromise: Women Studying in Childcare. *Gender and Education*, 25(2): 206–19.

Wright, H R (2013b) In Search of Stability: Women Studying in Childcare in an English Further Education College. *Journal of Further and Higher Education*, 37(1): 89–108.

Wright, J (1982) *Learning to Learn in Higher Education*. London: Croom Helm Ltd.

6 Reflection informed by observation and assessment

CAROL HAYES

In *A Scandal in Bohemia*, Holmes instructs Watson on the difference between *seeing* and *observing*:

> '*When I hear you give your reasons,*' *I remarked,* '*the thing always appears to me to be so ridiculously simple that I could easily do it myself, though at each successive instance of your reasoning, I am baffled until you explain your process. And yet I believe that my eyes are as good as yours.*'

> '*Quite so,*' *he answered, lighting a cigarette, and throwing himself down into an armchair.* '*You see, but you do not observe. The distinction is clear. For example, you have frequently seen the steps which lead up from the hall to this room.*'

> '*Frequently.*'

> '*How often?*'

> '*Well, some hundreds of times.*'

> '*Then how many are there?*'

> '*How many? I don't know.*'

> '*Quite so! You have not observed. And yet you have seen. That is just my point. Now, I know that there are seventeen steps, because I have both seen and observed.*'
>
> (Arthur Conan Doyle, 1891)

What is observation?

A clear definition of observation is really difficult. After all, as Sherlock Holmes suggested, we nearly all have eyes to see and the rapidly changing visual stimulation that we inflict our brain with every waking moment is clearly immense. Your eyes may be the window to your world but you need to make sense of the thousands of images that invade your brain every day. What Sherlock Holmes was saying was that there is a difference between seeing and observing although, to observe, you clearly need to have seen something. The term observation, as we use it in an early years context, has more depth of meaning and carries greater importance and significance than just watching and listening.

> *Observation means more than watching and listening; it is a process by which educators can understand and give meaning to what they see and hear, drawing on their own knowledge and experience as well as on the evidence of their senses.*
>
> (Drummond, Rouse and Pugh, 1992, p 424)

Observation is also:

> *the process through which data are gathered about a child's overall development, learning styles, interests, attitudes and behaviours.*
>
> (Vaclavik, Wolanski and Wannamaker, 2001, p 10)

However, to be effective, an observation needs to have a clear intention and be a well-organised way of looking at and recording children's development and behaviour. In the first instance it needs to focus upon what a child *can* do rather than concern itself with what they *cannot* do, and only when this is fully established can you move to the process of reflection upon the observation, to theorising upon the content and how this can assist you to plan for what the child *needs* to know.

Observation therefore is a very specialised tool with which to reflect upon the child, their families and their lives in context.

> *By observing what children do, we understand their development and the way in which they behave and react within certain situations and contexts. This reflection informs not only our early years practice but is also an important channel of communication for the children's families.*
>
> (Palaiologou, 2016, p 42)

Observation is one of the best ways to learn about a child and can offer you important information about that child, especially the very youngest children. This information is often not available elsewhere, but simply watching the child is not enough. There is little point in taking time and effort to record what you have seen and then stick it in a file to forget about it, secure in the knowledge that you have exercised your lawful duty under the Early Years Foundation Stage requirements. This valuable information needs the close, critical reflection and consideration that only someone who has a sound knowledge and understanding of child development and behaviour can give it. The observer needs to be able to reflect analytically, evaluatively and honestly upon what has been seen within the perspective of up to date theory and practical context.

Observation is therefore only the first step within the process of understanding children's lives, needs and interests and it is what is *done* with the information that becomes the key to the whole process.

Observations facilitate professionals' reflective thinking and thus empower them to evaluate their own practice in an attempt to develop effectively.

(Paliaologou, 2012, p 43)

So observation is an ongoing process of collecting information, documenting and recording, critically reflecting on and using the information to support children's learning and development. Observation helps you to find out what a child in your care understands, their interests and their personalities. With this information you can give feedback to the children and their families to plan challenging and enjoyable experiences in the future.

How difficult can it be?

Understanding the importance of observing children is not new and, in the early eighteenth century, the German educator Friedrich Froebel (1782–1852) encouraged early years practitioners in the kindergartens to be *observers of children*. He viewed the adults as *learners of children*. Vygotsky (1896–1934) and Piaget (1896–1980) also focused their theories on how to observe the ways in which children perceive and make sense of their world. These eminent researchers used their observations of children to identify ways in which children behave and, by reflecting on these, became conscious of what that might mean for their learning and education in general. Interestingly, while the whole concept of 'play' has differed throughout this time, it continues to be the major focus of naturalistic observation.

No other assessment technique can offer such instantaneous feedback and response to the practitioner as an observation, and you can make instant revisions to activities and language, depending upon what has been observed. However, to observe without sensitivity and interpretation is empty and frequently useless. Clearly this is a powerful technique but there are both strengths and challenges to the process (see Table 6.1).

Reflective activity

»   *Reflect upon how you currently collect information about children's learning and development in your setting.*

»   *What do you do with this information?*

»   *Could the information be used more effectively to inform planning or develop better understanding of the child's context and background?*

»   *Do you share this information with the children in any way? How could you do this and does it have value?*

»   *How often do you share this information with the parents in your setting?*

»   *How could you involve parents more in this data-gathering exercise? How useful would this be?*

Table 6.1 *Strengths and challenges of observing*

Strengths of observing	Challenges of observing
Observations can be spontaneous or carefully planned.	Remaining objective throughout the observation.
Can take just a few seconds or minutes.	Can involve prolonged periods of time and considerable effort to organise.
Provides valuable information about the context of learning.	Observers must have the appropriate skills training to recognise and record the key pieces of information.
Provides immediate information about children's learning and development.	Observers must have a sound knowledge of normative child development and up-to-date research information, to be aware of what information s/he is looking for and how it influences the observation.
Helps to identify children with learning delays or difficulties, including Specific Learning Difficulties (SpLD).	Liable to misinterpretation of the data, bias and stereotyping.
Can provide a lasting account of children's work to indicate progress and share with appropriate other professionals.	It needs to be developed over a period of time if young children are going to be given the opportunity to show their skills and understanding.
Provides information about activities which interest children.	Observers need good listening skills and an awareness of potential cultural differences.
Enables future planning dovetailed to a child's own interests and developmental needs.	Can be difficult to observe large groups at the same time.
Enables the creation of a supportive environment suited to a child's unique abilities and talents.	Informed consent at the appropriate level of maturity can be difficult to obtain.
Can capture unexpected incidents.	It may be difficult to ensure that all children are observed at the most appropriate time.
Can provide rich data focusing upon the holistic child not just a particular behaviour.	A key issue is knowing how to choose the most important data and eliminating any unnecessary information.

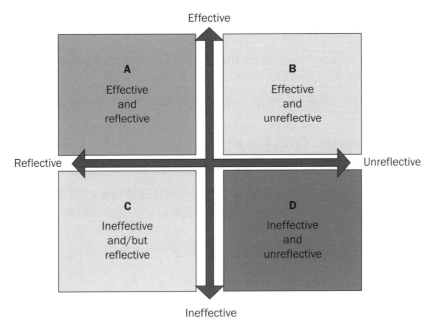

Figure 6.1 *Reflection and effectiveness (Atherton, 2010)*

Extended thinking

Figure 6.1 first conceived by Atherton (2010) perhaps offers an alternative view to a much 'taken for granted' concept that reflection is always good. Examine the diagram with a colleague and try to answer the following questions:

» *Is it possible that A on the diagram is always good and D is always bad?*

» *Are B and C even conceivable?*

» *How often do you think that C occurs in your practice?*

» *Is it possible for B to occur?*

» *Is D only about Ignorance?*

Before undertaking an observation there are some fundamental points to reflect upon, or ten steps to quality observations.

1. Have you reflected upon why an observation needs to be done?

2. Have you clearly defined the aims of your observation and what you hope to see?

3. Have you and your team considered how to set aside time for observations throughout the day?

4. Who will be involved in the evaluation of this observation: the child, families, other professionals, or perhaps all of these?

5. Have you reflected upon how all partners in the observation process can share observations and feed into the assessment process?

6. Do you respect parental contributions to the observation process and how do you demonstrate this?

7. How will you document the evidence?

8. How do you share all this information and with whom and when?

9. Does your learning environment support the observation process with opportunities for participant observation and opportunities to stand back and allow the children to take control?

10. How have you discussed this with the children?

What do I observe, why and how?

Many observations are unplanned and spontaneous, happening during everyday routines, events and activities in the setting. These can provide you with valuable information and should not be disregarded as insignificant or unscientific.

> *Initially this may be an alarming experience since it strips the observer of the usual competencies which protect us from being taken unaware. The observer has no idea what he or she will see and therefore is exposed to a whole new level of perception of human relationship. This is both disturbing and exciting.*
>
> (Reid, 1997, p 1)

However, planned observations can add more detail about what and how the child is learning and developing. So what we observe could be as broad as 'everything that the child does for a limited period of time' or could be a focus of a particular activity or behaviour. Clearly this will be largely determined by the aims and objectives of the observation, and the reasons for undertaking the observation, whether for assessment, planning or information. Whatever the rationale for the observation it has to have an outcome and, without this, it ceases to be worthwhile or purposeful. There has to be a clear relationship between the process and the outcome to form the basis of any discussion about that child and their development. The Warnock Report (DES, 1978), the Education Act (DES 1981) and the later updated Code of Practice (DfE/DoH, 2015) emphasised the importance of ongoing assessment of children with special needs and understood the importance of early identification of children's needs to ensure that the appropriate programmes were in place for each child. Clearly observations are the basis of such assessment (see Figure 6.2).

Figure 6.2 *Rationale for observation*

Observations in early years settings are usually naturalistic with the child in their home, school, nursery setting, etc. Whilst the child will be at their most relaxed and in a normative state, it does introduce a wide range of additional variables of context. This can influence the interpretation, analysis and evaluation of the behaviour observed and could skew the findings of the observation, thereby offering an unrealistic view of the 'real' child. The child could be doing the same activity in different contexts and behave differently, for example, a child dressed as Batman in a playground with lots of space could be very physically active, racing around, jumping, pouncing and play fighting. The same child dressed as Batman inside the nursery could be engaged with a sedentary activity of drawing Batman saving the world. Drummond, Rouse and Pugh (1992) discuss the importance of SOUL:

Silence: Remain silent until you know what the children are doing.

Observation: Observe as children work, this will enable you to better understand their actions and interactions.

Understanding: Think about what you see children doing to fully understand what is happening.

Listening: Listen to what children are saying so that you know what is important to them.

This is an approach used as part of the HighScope programme (HighScope Educational Research Foundation, 2013) and they believe that it reduces the risk of interrupting play, allowing the children to initiate play, giving the observer more time to be sensitive to their needs in a naturalistic context.

Alternatively, observations can be undertaken under controlled circumstances, ensuring that each child observed experiences a similar environment and thereby controlling more variables and potentially ensuring a more reliable outcome. This more scientific approach to observations is often favoured by psychologists, and perhaps the most well-known observation under such experimental conditions was Mary Ainsworth's 'strange situations test' to assess children's security of attachment. This was described originally by Ainsworth and Wittig (1969) where a child was left in a room first with the mother, then with the mother and a stranger, then alone with the stranger and finally completely alone for a few minutes. When the child was reunited with the mother and the stranger, Ainsworth observed the child's reactions and was able to classify three distinct types of attachment to be applied to other children and their attachment behaviour: Secure Attachment, Anxious-avoidant Attachment and Anxious-resistant Attachment. Whilst this method of observation has great advantages by limiting the variables, which may influence the results of the observation, it may not account for the possibility that the child will behave differently in unaccustomed and unfamiliar environments, its ecological validity or the individuality and unique qualities of the human mind.

The power of observation

The real power of observations is in their ability to improve the education and learning environments for young children and, during that process, all our senses are engaged; looking, listening and feeling. Maria Montessori is attributed with saying:

> *We cannot create observers by saying 'observe', but by giving them the power and the means for this observation, and these means are procured through education of the senses.*

> (Dr Maria Montessori)

Now imagine that you were being tailed by a private detective. You would want to know why and for what reason and to what purpose the information gained was to be used, especially as certain judgements and evaluations will be made, based on the investigator's own moral values and beliefs, about you, your lifestyle and behaviour which could influence your life in the future. Most of us would justifiably feel affronted by this invasion of our private lives. In the same way adults always have ultimate power over children, they are bigger, louder, more experienced and knowledgeable about the world, but this potentially places the child in a vulnerable position. The United Nations Convention on the Rights of the Child (UNCRC) places in law the right for children to have their opinions on matters that affect them taken into account in accordance with their maturity and a right to privacy (United Nations, 1989). Article 16 of the UNCRC states that children should be seen as developing adults and as 'active citizens'. Article 12 demands that children have the right to be consulted about activities and their feelings and interests taken account of and for these views to be respected and taken seriously. Just like adults, children have the right to information about the observations to be conducted and what use will be made of them. In other words children DO have the right to privacy and by letting children decide what is important to them we have the basis of a joint analysis based on a single, more equal, power relationship.

To do this you must ensure that, before observations take place, every child understands what you are doing and that they have the right to refuse, in other words you are offering them informed consent. This is clearly challenging particularly when working with the very youngest children, but seeking the child's informed consent must be embedded in all early years practice.

> *Practitioners should treat babies and toddlers with sensitivity, being aware and responding to behaviours that indicate that they do not wish to participate.*
>
> (Palaiologou, 2012, p 101)

This requires you to understand the inherent power relationship that exists between you and the children that you care for and to recognise that a child may be too fearful to say 'no'. Clearly parental consent also needs to be obtained before observations on vulnerable children can take place, but you have to understand ways of 'hearing' what the child is saying through their reactions, posture, movement, gesture, facial expression, eye contact and general body language, which may supersede what they are articulating. There is never an excuse to observe children or adults when the act of observation makes them feel upset or uncomfortable in any way.

Children have implicit trust in the adults who care for them and you need to reciprocate that trust by maintaining confidentiality and, where appropriate, anonymity, being sensitive to their individual and holistic needs. You need to be very clear why a planned observation is necessary, so clearly defined aims and objectives need to be identified prior to the observation commencing. You need to consider who will benefit from undertaking the observation. Is it, for example, simply to ensure that Ofsted requirements are being seen to be satisfied, or will the emerging picture of the child really help you to plan more appropriately for their learning and development? The child needs to be at the centre of all observations and reflections and you need to consider the following before undertaking any observation.

- Always ask the child in language appropriate to their age and understanding whether it is acceptable to observe.

- Where oral language is not age-appropriate, pictures, 'smiley faces', role play or story time may be used to aid communication.

- Check that the child understands what is being done.

- Support the child in their right to say 'no' even to a more powerful adult.

- Observe and respect the child's body language and external signs for any reluctance to continue.

- Never exert pressure upon a child to undertake an activity purely for the purpose of observation; they may be tired, unwell or upset.

- Check with the child before sharing information, quotations or extracts from that observation.

- Consider how the child can become more involved in their own assessment.

- In the evaluation and analysis consult with the child, taking account of their own perspective.

- Ensure the security of information and data and that it is only used for the purposes intended and agreed.

- Ensure that children understand that you have a legal obligation to share information when there are issues of child protection and safeguarding.

- Always take account of feelings of tiredness, inclusion and cultural contexts.

Parental involvement and consent is enshrined within the UNCRC article 5 and is also a requirement of the Early Years Foundation Stage (DfE, 2014). Parents are entitled to a clear understanding of what they are signing when they complete a consent form, and it is important that they understand that they have a legal right of access to their child's records at any time, or to withdraw their consent with no obligation to say why. Palaiologou (2012) argues that such ethical considerations should not only be about consent but about involvement of all engaged with the observation: parents, children, the early years team members and possibly even outside agencies such as Ofsted.

Reflective activity

Reflect upon the following questions and try to discuss them with other practitioners who have more and less experience than yourself.

» *How much of a young child's life is private?*

» *How much should be private?*

» *Do we have the right to intrude upon a child's life in this way?*

» *Reflect upon the levels of parental involvement in your setting. Do you believe that parents are aware of the observation and assessment policy?*

» *How could you involve parents further and is this what they want?*

» *Is there any other way to ensure that a young child is able to offer informed consent?*

Extended thinking

Every setting knows about the multiple requests each year from students and outside researchers to observe their children. This brings into question ethical considerations of the purpose of observations. Observations conducted by practitioners within the setting for assessment, planning and programme development are clearly undertaken to benefit the child, but what about observations undertaken for the benefit of the practitioner, student or researcher?

Consider the following questions.

» *How does this alter the dynamics of the ethical arguments?*

» *Would your responses change if the student/researcher was also a parent of a child in the setting?*

» *Settings usually require parents to sign permission slips to allow observations to be conducted with their children in the setting, but should there be additional safeguards in place to protect confidentiality and anonymity when students/ researchers are removing the observations from the setting and outside bodies such as tutors and fellow researchers are going to view them?*

» *Is the observation necessary and justifiable?*

According to Bentley et al (2016) if a child is under 16 years they cannot legally give consent; this has to be done by a parent or guardian. So to fully engage children with the observation process they need to be informed in such as way that they understand their right to privacy and whether they want to participate. To do this you need to be sensitive to their feelings, emotions and behaviour and not betray the trust that they give you as their carer. This goes far beyond the formal permission given by parents, managers and outside bodies and puts in place support for children to understand their right to say 'no'. This is not a one-off 'permission slip' but an understanding that today s/he may feel tired, uncomfortable or excluded, and continues for as many times as you observe.

So the sort of conversation that might take place with a child who is of an age to understand the language might be:

> *Would you mind if I watch you today doing that jigsaw and write down on my paper what you are doing? I will be able to see how well you are getting on and we can see whether it is too easy for you and whether I should get the larger jigsaws out of the cupboard tomorrow. You can tell me whether you would rather that I did not watch or that I stop, and no one will be cross with you. We can have a chat about how you are getting on and I will not share this with anyone else unless you tell me something that could be harmful to you in any way.*

> *You can talk about this with your mummy if you want and I can show her how well you have been doing.*

The planning cycle

A few years ago, prior to the government interventions that we are familiar with today, working with young children often meant turning up in the morning and deciding what the children would do for the day depending upon the whim of the practitioner. Today you have legal obligations to the children and families in your care to ensure that they are learning, progressing and developing in a way that is acceptable to society's view of early years practice. You are bound by the vagaries of Ofsted and inspection agencies, by governmental pressure and parental expectation, to ensure that you are planning your sessions to meet the individual needs of the children in your care. The only way to really understand what those needs might be is to observe; observation then becomes the most important tool that you possess as you begin to reflect upon and understand the whole ethos of the setting. In fact the whole philosophy and character of the setting hangs on the observations that you do, the activities that you plan and the enabling environments that you create for the children. The Early Years Foundation Stage Statutory Framework clearly states that observation:

involves practitioners observing children to understand their level of interests and learning styles and then shape learning experiences for each child, reflecting on these observations.

(DfE, 2014, p 10)

The planning cycle diagram (Figure 6.3) shows how this process is ongoing, with each section feeding into the next and round again. If the ultimate and overarching aim of observation is to enable you to plan an appropriate environment for the children to learn and develop, then the observation is only the first stage of the process, and what is done with the information next is what will impact most on the children's learning. This observation-led planning should stretch the children beyond their current skills and knowledge, but not impose unrealistic expectations upon them.

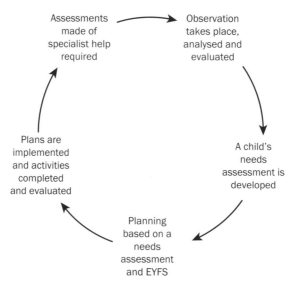

Figure 6.3 *The planning cycle*

Through observing children and the learning environment you can revise plans, make changes to the education and improve provision. Reflection and further observations will then be needed to inform further planning so that the process is a continuous cycle.

When do we observe?

Working with young children is a busy task and you will be constantly on the move and dealing with more than one thing at a time. This makes it hard to find the time to observe. It really requires a rethinking of your role, and an understanding of the vital place that observation needs to take in your day-to-day activities to ensure the enabling environment. Becoming a skilled participant observer is one way forward, but you may need to create areas in the setting which do not directly involve the adults but where you can see and hear what is happening. This will allow you to observe at the same time as supervising the children, and the areas can be targeted to particular aspects of development that you want to evaluate. *The Teachers' Standards for Early Years* (National College for Teaching and Leadership, 2013) emphasise that observations should not detract from the day-to-day interactions with the children and should not involve 'excessive paperwork'.

Observations start from the moment that the child comes into your care. This will provide vital entry data and a baseline for all further assessments. This will also involve discussions with the family, and needs to take into account possible cultural and home background differences between the children. This first observation is a 'snapshot' of the child and you will need to undertake ongoing observations to build a full profile for assessment.

One of the difficulties with the observational process is recording accurately what you have seen, when the activity observed has taken place in a fraction of a second. Unless you film the activity, which is often very intrusive and can change the behaviour of the children observed, it is not possible to relive that moment again and to 'rewind' the behaviour. Even a photograph does not capture the whole of the experience with the antecedents and the contextual experiences. Some say that the 'camera never lies', but when observing children this stance may not be so easy to defend.

Reflective activity

Look briefly at the photograph of a child on a rocking horse (on page 112) and put it to one side. Now write down what you saw.

» *Compare this with someone else's description, are they the same?*

» *If not, in what way are they different?*

» *How accurate do you think they are?*

As we noted in Chapter 1, all models of reflective practice begin with accurate description, which is to recount accurately what you see or saw. At this stage of an observation when the only thing that you can say about this picture is descriptive, your writing should have been factual and accurate. Perhaps it looked something like this:

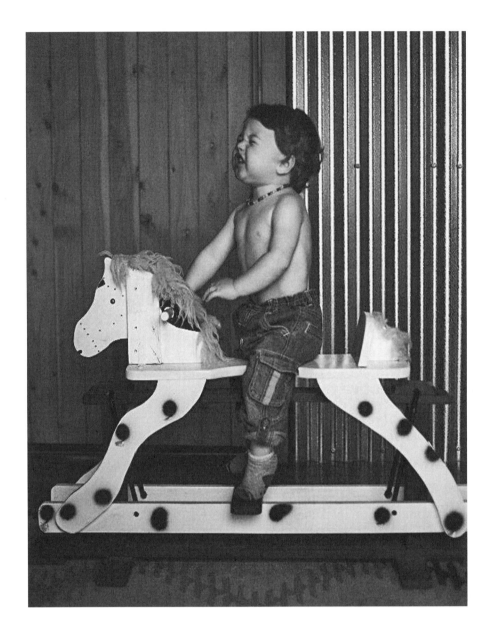

a)   *A child sitting on a rocking horse.*

This is factual, accurate and descriptive but does not really tell us very much. This description is only the 'what' and does not indicate the 'how'.

Did your observation look more like this:

b)   *A white child sitting on a white spotted conventional rocking horse, holding the handles with his right hand, the left hand free. He is balanced and his feet just reach the cross bar to maintain that balance. He is wearing trousers and shoes but no top. He is wearing a necklace of beads. He has medium length dark curly hair. The child has his mouth open, revealing his teeth and his eyes are screwed up tight. There are no other toys in sight and no adult supporting him.*

If your observation does look like this, give yourself a pat on the back as this is a clear, accurate description of what you can see.

Now look at the following observations of the same picture:

c)   *A little girl sitting on a rocking horse crying and feeling very unhappy.*

d)   *A little boy laughing excitedly on the rocking horse.*

e)   *A boy playing cowboys and the rodeo on a rocking horse.*

f)   *A child made to sit on a rocking horse by an adult.*

What can you see in these observations that were not there in the first descriptions?

In the observations c, d, e and f the observers have tried to give an explanation for the behaviour, but this is purely supposition and opinion, probably based on their own values and attitudes, which may not be shared by everyone who sees that picture. It can be seen that the observers cannot agree upon something as basic as the gender of the child or even whether the child is enjoying the experience or not. The danger is that such observers will be tempted to go one step further and to make additional inferences from these judgements and these may be:

* *The little girl is unhappy because she has been told to come off the rocking horse; clearly she cannot share the toys.*

* *The little boy is unhappy because he cannot make it go; his physical development skills are below norm.*

* *The child is unhappy so needs to be comforted and have a cuddle.*

* *The child has really good imaginative skills as he can play creatively and interpret roles.*

* *The child has been forced to sit on the rocking horse to calm down because he is refusing to wear his shirt.*

* *The child is really happy and independent, managing to rock the rocking horse on their own for the first time.*

You can see how many of these there might be, and how erroneous they might be. Such interpretations and explanations are intensely subjective and could potentially lead to quite incorrect planning for this child, and be a damaging stereotype which could lead to unhelpful scheduling for him/her in the future. There is also a serious danger that, when a group of practitioners that communicate frequently come together, this subjectivity can be compounded and taken for granted, thereby reinforcing this opinion of the child. It is then accepted as a truism which might live with him/her for many years to come, seriously influencing his/her learning and development and the expectations of those around them. It is therefore important to record what you can see and not what you think you can see, or hope that you can see.

> *There can be several filters along the route, as information about an event speeds towards the human brain. Good qualitative analysis of classroom behavior involves rigorous scrutiny of these barriers to accurate perception.*
>
> (Wragg, 2012, p 51)

Extended thinking

The debate between what is objective and what is subjective has raged in science and philosophy for a very long time. They are often treated as being diametrically opposed: objectivity is good, subjectivity is bad. However perhaps it is not as clean cut as this and more like two ends of a spectrum.

Certainly when observing children objectivity is preferable, but there may be occasions when an element of subjectivity is allowable.

The statement 'The child is 3 years 2 months old', is objective and verifiable. However, 'Natasha enjoys playing football' is perhaps influenced by opinion and prior knowledge.

The degree to which absolute objectivity can be achieved is certainly debatable and often one morphs into another, particularly when observing the 'unobservable' such as feelings, emotions and opinion.

» *How achievable do you believe total objectivity is when observing children?*

Reflective activity

» *Imagine that you are attempting to describe to an intelligent Martian what you have seen, avoiding all ambiguity and obscurity. Now look at the second photograph showing Luke using the hammer and briefly record what you see.*

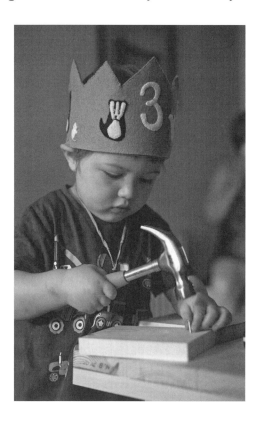

» Look at the following list of words and separate them into those which you think are objective and those which are subjective and based on opinion. The first few have been done for you:

good	writing	poor
sitting	reading	pincer grip
blinking	happy	standing
naughty	effective	deviant

Objective	Subjective	Why?
	good	What one person sees as 'good' another finds annoying or insufficient. This is largely dependent upon your own experiences, training and upbringing.
	reading	It is not possible to <u>see</u> someone read ... what you see is a child looking at text. It is only possible to know whether reading has taken place by testing or asking the child what s/he has read about.
sitting		This is clearly observable and would be undisputable by whoever was observing the child at the time.

Extended thinking

Reflection is a good intention frequently found to have fallen on hard times. There is nothing to distinguish it from 'thinking' which is a quintessentially human activity. What is important is the quality of thought.

(Harvey and Knight, 1996, p 161)

» Consider the quotation from Harvey and Knight (1996). How far do you agree/ disagree with this statement?

Once you have clear and unambiguous observations to work with, some element of evaluation and interpretation needs to be made. This does not however, necessarily mean that this will be made by the original observer, and clear and explicit observations are useful to all professionals who work with the children, and even to parents who may wish to gain an understanding of how their child reacts/responds in the setting. These observations can go on to form the basis of evidence for the diagnosis and identification of special or particular needs, and to instigate expensive intervention programmes and planning for that child.

Who should observe and share?

Involving parents in the observation process enables a more holistic view of the child to be made; the parent is the 'expert' in *that* child, and is likely to have a more rounded view of the social and cultural life of the child than the practitioner can ever hope to have. The child may well exhibit behaviours at home which you may not have observed in the setting and vice versa. This could be down to unfamiliarity of the environment, separation anxiety, a lack of emotional confidence or there may be cultural, language or family issues which may cause them to display differing reactions to different environments.

> *Understand that parents and carers are partners who have the lead role and responsibility for children and young people. Involving them in decisions affecting their child can have a positive effect on supporting their children to achieve positive outcomes.*
>
> (Children's Workforce Development Council/DfE, 2010, p 9)

This partnership approach is reiterated in the Early Years Foundation Stage (DfE 2014) documentation. One of the key findings of the iconic piece of early years research, Effective Provision for Pre-school Education Project (Taggart et al, 2003) was the importance of parental involvement to the establishment of high-quality settings with shared educational aims. To enable this genuine sharing of care and education of a child, formative feedback needs to be regularly shared with the parents.

Sometimes it is hard to remember that the daycare setting in which you observe the child is only a very small part of a child's life and children are constantly engaged with learning and developing, not only in the setting with the practitioners. The child regularly engages with outside environments such as shops, parks, relatives, sometimes different homes and different family relationships, but if parents are to keep you informed and abreast of the child's most recent environment the relationship between you and the parent must be based on a mutual trust, respect and a level of honesty which may at times be difficult to maintain. Most parents will not actively seek out this sort of relationship, perhaps remembering the relationship between their families and schools and nurseries in years gone by, which was often one of antagonism, possessiveness and an attitude that the professional was the expert, not to be questioned. Therefore you will need to engage with the parents and convince them that you value and respect their reflections on their child. To do this you will need to make time and perhaps even create the physical spaces to enable you to listen to parents and shape continuous, regular dialogue, keeping them fully informed about the progress of the assessment profile. Technology can be part of this communication highway and become part of the co-construction of planning and strategies to support learning and development. Parents are deeply emotionally involved with their own children and in most cases, according to Reid (1997), this can deepen their empathy with both the helplessness and capabilities of their children. However, at times they may find themselves emotionally overwhelmed by the experience and a defensive system emerges, and this may pervert their own thinking about the child. For this reason parental involvement should be a choice for parents to make, and they should at all times retain the right to withdraw their participation if they feel that their involvement is too stressful or not mutually beneficial.

The children can also become a valuable part of the reflective process if you provide the time and opportunity for them to discuss their learning and development with their peers, practitioners, parents and other significant people in their lives. However, you need to ensure that children feel that their views and ideas are valued and respected by demonstrating that they too can be co-constructors of their next steps and planning. This can be done by allowing them to take ownership of their own learning journey, through them asking questions, making comments and sharing their own judgements about their development. You need to see that every interaction with the child is an opportunity to learn more about them in a two-way flow of information (see Figure 6.4).

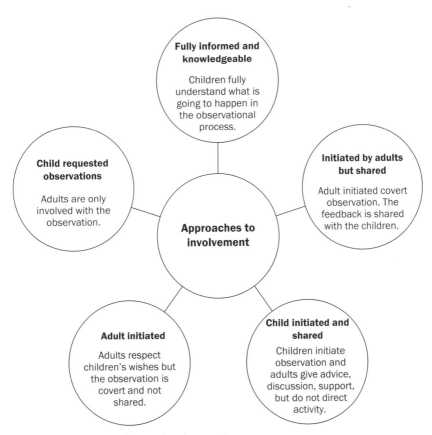

Figure 6.4 *Alternative approaches to involvement*

The Common Assessment Framework (CAF) for children and young people referred to in the code of practice (DfE, 2015) requires you to liaise and communicate with a range of outside agencies. This whole framework is designed to enable the sharing of information between all parties interested in the safety and well-being of the child. To enable such a systematic assessment to take place you will need to gather data about the child for whom concerns have been raised and an essential tool for this type of data-gathering process will be naturalistic observation. However, to enable this data to be shared across a range of different professionals and agencies (for example, health, education, social work, psychology or universal services), it needs to be gathered and recorded in a pro-fessionally recognised manner and then documented in a way which all involved with the child can recognise as valid and reliable data. This suggests a role for early years practitioners that has not been considered in the past, and highlights the importance of open and honest inter-professional communication and collaboration. This view of the early years practitioner as having an equal but distinctively different role to play in the observation and understanding of the child, is challenging and may require a relaxation of professional boundaries and a willingness to, on occasions, lead across those profes-sional boundaries. This difficulty is possibly compounded by the Nutbrown Review (2012) and the report by the DfE (2013) which both suggest that that there may be a culture in early years settings that direct work with very young children is seen in the UK as low status.

Reflective activity

» *Reflect on the implications of this shift in the role of the early years practitioner and consider the impact this may have on your contract of employment.*

» *What future professional development do you think will be required for early years practitioners to feel confident to fulfill these roles?*

» *Share your ideas with a colleague.*

Extended thinking

… qualifications are closely linked to career progression. In any sector, an individual seeks additional qualifications and training so that they can take on new roles and responsibilities. They also, not unreasonably, expect to be rewarded in line with this, including through pay, status, working conditions and job satisfaction.

(Nutbrown, 2012, p 44: 4.1)

» *How far do you agree with this statement by Nutbrown?*

» *How achievable do you think this is?*

» *Explain whether you think that a rise in qualification status, such as that suggested by Nutbrown (2012), would impact upon a practitioner's confidence to engage with other professionals to the benefit of the child.*

Interpretation and links to the EYFS

Observing children goes far beyond recording what you see children doing and it is a more extensive and profound process, involving analysis, evaluation and communication and it helps us to understand why certain human behaviour occurs and how to improve our own practice at planning for and dealing with it. It is highly probable that it is not possible to achieve a clear, valid and reliable picture of the holistic development of the child on the strength of one observation, so it is important to gather a range of observations, using differing methods and different observers for analysis before making conclusions. This is unlikely to be a 'one-man job' but a whole-team event probably including professionals from other spheres. It must also be remembered that observing children is a bit like looking at an iceberg. What we know about an iceberg is that most of the ice is below the waterline and not visible to view. It can be a shock for you to discover how little you really see in real situations; you see the surface behaviour but not the deeper level of human interaction and communication.

Figure 6.5 *The iceberg theory*

So it is with much of the behaviour that you see exhibited in children; what you see on the surface, what you can observe objectively and impartially, is often not the whole story and, however objective and evidence based you strive to be in your observations, there has to be an element of subjective 'guessing' or hypothesising in the interpretation of what you see.

It is important though to proceed with the analysis as soon as possible after the observations have been completed as memory fades very quickly. Your analysis and evaluation should compare your data with what you would expect a child to be able to do at this stage using reliable and up-to-date sources of secondary evidence, research and study. It is, however, vital that any interpretation is made on the strength of the evidence based on the observation and not on the perceived, personal, prior knowledge of the child. You need to start by considering what the observation tells you about the child's development, progress, interests and skills and how this compares with your understanding of child development, research and theory and consider why the child behaved in the way that they did, or said what they said.

All children develop at different rates, this is part of their unique make-up, but there is a distinctive pattern and sequence to that development that all children experience. We call these the developmental norms or developmental milestones. The children that you observe can be tracked against these to allow for assessment of their stage of development. Not all children will develop at the same rate and there will be periods of enhanced development as well as periods of delay, peaks and troughs, so not all children will reach the same end point or will reach it at different times in their lives. Indeed, children may be developing to norm in certain areas of their lives but not in others so, while development can be said to be a continuous process, it does not necessarily progress smoothly or routinely. It is also clear that there is a dynamic interaction between the two influences of the genetic make-up of the child, and the environmental forces leading to the gene expression, an epigenetic reaction.

Observation and reflection at this level can be emotionally and intellectually exhausting and could not be sustained throughout life and it is possible that everyday events do not bear up to close scrutiny. Reid (1997) likens observation to looking at human relationships through a microscope and this can result in focusing upon minute details rather than the broader picture. However, through this close observation you have the chance to see the links between the areas of development, for example, between emotion and cognition, or language and physical development. Gradually you will see patterns emerging and you will see these in different contexts and through different perspectives. Your role is to see the similarities and differences between the patterns and indicate important areas for further observation. This becomes like a complex 3D jigsaw puzzle demonstrating the links and relationships.

Your reflection upon the activities that you observe enables the jigsaw pieces to be gathered together and to gradually build as much of the picture of this child as is possible with the pieces available. Carr (2001) calls this the credit-based model of assessment where you take pedagogical decisions based upon your reflections to ascertain the child's competencies, perspectives and meanings, set within their own unique cultural and social context. Observations offer you an evidence base for such decisions and, from professional conversations, they can be engaged with to ensure a holistic approach to the support of the child and their enabling environments. This is only possible if you have detailed knowledge of normative child development and the Early Years Foundation Stage requirements, and you are up to date with child development research and thinking.

One of the features of the observational experience is that it brings us into close contact not only with the common elements of human growth and development but also with the rich and infinitely variable differences which make up each individual human being.

(Ellis, cited in Reid, 1997, p 56)

One of the headings of the Common Core of Skills and Knowledge (Children's Workforce Development Council/DfE 2010) is observation and judgement. There is a clear intention that those working in early years should be able to observe, record, reflect and report children's behaviour and development. The Early Years Foundation Stage Profile is a statutory document requiring you to record each child's developmental needs at the end of the Early Years Foundation Stage. It is based entirely upon observations and assessments made by skilled, reflective practitioners. It is clearly stated that:

Most evidence for the EYFS profile judgments will come from practitioners observing a pupil's self-initiated activities

(DfE, 2017, p 13)

Observational assessment is the most reliable way of building up an accurate picture of a pupil's development and learning. This is especially true when the attainment is not dependent on overt adult support. Observational assessment is central to understanding what pupils really know and can do

(DfE, 2017, p 11)

The profile must reflect the ongoing observations produced when assessing the child against the Early Learning Goals. So this profile report, which must accompany each child into Year 1 of their primary school, must be founded on the observations completed by you. The government expectation of proficiency is also reflected in the standards for the new Early Years Teacher (National College for Teaching and Leadership, 2013).

Reflective activity

»   *How has the evaluation and analysis of observation(s) that you have done in the past influenced your understanding of a particular child?*

»   *Has your response to that child changed as a result of the observation or series of observations?*

»   *Were you able to share this information with appropriate others?*

»   *Reflect upon how this may have influenced their understanding of the child.*

Extended thinking

Communication and establishing a sound community of practice is an issue that occurs in any debate on sharing observations and reflections.

» *Reflect for a moment upon whether your setting has a successful community of practice, with design and organisational structures in place that recognise the importance of participation and communication.*

» *How has your setting developed methods to link diverse communities through shared dialogue and co-ordination of different professionals and practices?*

Whatever you do with the findings of your observations they must be used to improve the existing situation for that child and the feedback needs to enable adaptive measures to be taken to advance that child's learning and development.

Chapter reflections

From what you have seen in this chapter observations can be more complicated and more time-consuming than any other form of assessment, but the benefits derived from rigorous and impartial observations can make it worthwhile in the end. This chapter has demonstrated the importance of ensuring that observation and reflection is an integral part of every day within your setting. The whole process of observation, evaluation and assessment is an extraordinarily rich and complex one, but it is a method of learning about a child that is rigorous and exacting and at times creates a moment of wonderful discovery.

This chapter started with an examination of the difference between watching and observing. Observation clearly involves watching but watching is not the same as observation. The difference between watching and observing is that observation is watching with knowledge and reflection. The chapter closes by reflecting upon the best way to share these observations and their importance not only to the all-round development and safety of the child but also to fulfilling the government's initiatives on early years, integrating your knowledge and understanding of child development into your planning, philosophy and teaching .

Extended reflections

Observing children is arguably the most important task that you perform as a practitioner yet often it is regarded as difficult and too time consuming. In the light of what you have read in this chapter, how would you now respond to this?

Further reading

Palaiologou, I (2016) *Child Observation: A Guide for Students and Early Childhood* (3rd edn). London: Sage.

This is a really useful updated text for those studying at higher education level who have limited experience and understanding of the process of observation. Palaiologou takes the reader through the practical skills of observation and the theoretical and underpinning background to child observation. This is a really practice-based text which highlights the central importance of your knowledge of child development and observation to the planning of a high quality setting.

References

Ainsworth, M and Wittig, B (1969) Attachment and Exploratory Behaviour of One Year Olds in a Strange Situation, in Foss, B (ed), *Determinants of Infant Behavior* 4. London: Methuen.

Atherton, J (2010) *Reflection: An Idea Whose Time is Past*. (Seminar, University of Lincoln, Feb 2010.) [online] Available from: www.doceo.co.uk/heterodoxy/reflection.htm (accessed 20 March 2016).

Bentley, H, O'Hagan, O, Raff, A and Bhatti, I (2016) *How Safe Are Our Children*? [online] Available from: www.nspcc.org.uk/globalassets/documents/research-reports/how-safe-children-2016-report.pdf (accessed 25 February 2017).

Carr, M (2001) *Assessment in Early Childhood Settings: Learning Stories*. London: Paul Chapman Publishing.

Children's Workforce Development Council/DfE (2010) *Common Core of Skills and Knowledge: At the Heart of What You Do*. Leeds: CWDC.

Conan Doyle, A (1891) *A Scandal in Bohemia* (2nd edn). London: Penguin.

DES (1978) *The Warnock Report*. London: Crown.

DES (1981) *The Education Act 1981*. London: Crown.

DfE (2013) *More Great Childcare: Raising Quality and Giving Parents More Choice*. London: Crown.

DfE (2014) *Statutory Framework for the Early Years Foundation Stage: Setting the Standards for Learning, Development and Care for Children from Birth to Five*. London: Crown.

DfE (2015) *Working together to Safeguard Children: A guide to inter-agency working to safeguard and promote the welfare of children*. London: Crown.

DfE (2017) *Early Years Foundation Stage Profile 2017 Handbook*. London: Crown.

DfE and DoH (2015) *The Special Educational Needs and Disability Code of Practice*. London: Crown.

Drummond, M, Rouse, D and Pugh, G (1992) *Making Assessment Work*. Nottingham: NES Arnold/National Children's Bureau.

Elfer, P and Dearnley, K (2007) Nurseries and Emotional Well-Being: Evaluating an Emotionally Containing Model of Professional Development. *Early Years*, 27(3): 267–79.

Harvey, L and Knight, P T (1996) *Transforming Higher Education*. Buckingham, Society for Research in Higher Education and Open University Press.

HighScope Educational Research Foundation (2013) HighScope Inspiring Educators and Inspiring Children. [online] Available from: www.highscope.org (accessed 20 March 2016).

National College for Teaching and Leadership (2013) *Teachers' Standards, Early Years* (from Sept 2013), London: Crown. [online] Available from: www.gov.uk/government publications (accessed 20 March 2016).

Nutbrown, C (2012) *Foundation for Quality: Independent Review of Early Education and Childcare Qualifications*. Cheshire: DfE/Crown.

Palaiologou, I (2016) *Child Observation: A Guide for Students of Early Childhood*, (3rd edn). Exeter: Learning Matters.

Reid, S (ed) (1997) *Developments in Infant Observation: The Tavistock Model*. Hove: Routledge.

Taggart, B, Sammons, P, Sylva, K, Melhuish, H, Siraj-Blatchford, I, Elliot, K and Walker-Hall, J (2003) *Effective Provision for Pre-school Education Project*. London: Institute for Education, University of London.

United Nations (1989) *The Convention on the Rights of the Child*. Defence International and the United Nations Children's Fund: Geneva. [online] Available from: www.unicef.org/crc/ (accessed 20 March 2016).

Vaclavik, M, Wolanski, A and Wannamaker, N (2001) *Observation: A Focus on Evaluation, Planning and Growth for the Kindergarten Learning*. Toronto: Elementary Teachers Federation of Ontario.

Wragg, E C (2012) *An Introduction to Classroom Observation*. Oxon: Routledge.

7 Reflecting on emotionally enabled practice

RUTH GILL

'Pooh, promise you won't forget about me, ever. Not even when I'm a hundred.'

Pooh thought for a while.
'How old shall I be then?'

'Ninety-Nine.'

Pooh nodded.
'I promise,' he said.

Still with his eyes on the world Christopher Robin put out a hand and felt for Pooh's paw.
'Pooh,' said Christopher Robin earnestly, 'if I – if I'm not quite –' he stopped and tried again - 'Pooh, whatever happens, you will understand, won't you?'

'Understand what?'

'Oh, nothing.' He laughed and jumped to his feet. 'Come on!'

'Where?' said Pooh.

'Anywhere,' said Christopher Robin.

(A A Milne, 1928, p 248–9)

Introduction

The love between a boy and his bear is enduring and something that will forever be present even as time goes by. This is a 'love' you share with the children in your care, and one that touches all of us in the sector. Caring for children and 'love' are often mentioned in the same sentence by those working in the profession. You often hear early years practitioners saying 'I love working with children'. Working with children conjures up images of a predominantly female workforce leading to the assumption that the profession must therefore be a 'caring' one. Yes, there is no doubt that you do 'care' about the children you look after. However, there is sometimes a reluctance to acknowledge that love is a significant feature of caring for children; there is a difference between caring for children and loving children and this chapter will consider how you try to reconcile your professional responsibility to 'care' for children and your own emotional attachments to children and the developing 'love' that occurs when you work with young children. Attention will be given to the key person approach and how parents feature in the relationship triangle with you and their child.

Choosing to work with children

Mock interviews of early childhood students at levels 2 and 3 revealed that when asked, *Why have you applied for this post?* they all replied *I love children* or *I love working with children*. The intentions of those seeking to join the profession are bound by a 'love' of what working with children can bring. What is not apparent to some young adults joining the workforce are the incredible demands emotionally and physically that you are faced with when employed as an early years professional. However, the motivation to work with children does start with our 'love' of what childhood and children bring to us as people. Not everyone has the same motivation to work with children. It is vital to increase your understanding of your own motivations to work in this sector which needs careful reflection to appreciate why you made this choice and continue to work in the profession. Goleman (2004) explores emotional intelligence and 'self-awareness', which involves attending to your own internal states to gain a greater understanding of yourself.

Reflective activity

» *Reflect upon what motivated you to work with children. Was it something you had always wanted from a very young age or was it the only career choice you had? What is your earliest memory in a caring role and what feelings do you recall were associated with that memory?*

» *Write a short narrative to explore your motivations to work with children and what continues to motivate you. How often do the words 'care' or 'love' feature in your writing?*

Extended thinking

Reflect on how others you work with share the same caring values as you.

» *Do you connect as professionals on your shared understanding of the love and care children need?*

» *Conflicting values on care and love can create a difficult working environment when your values are not shared by other adults.*

Whatever your motivations are for working with children there has to be a degree of emotional availability on your behalf to be able to emotionally connect with fellow professionals, parents and children. This emotion in caring is a direct result of the attachments you make with children in your care.

Attachments with children, for children and ourselves

John Bowlby (1979, 1988) defines the difference between attachment behaviour and the enduring attachment featured in consistent care with a few significant others in a child's life. There is a subtle difference between the attachments to significant others and attachment behaviour shown to a variety of individuals a child may come into contact with.

> *Briefly put, attachment behaviour is conceived as any form of behaviour that results in a person attaining or retaining proximity to some other differentiated and preferred individual, who is usually conceived as stronger and/or wiser.*
>
> (Bowlby, 1979, p 129)

Attachment behaviour shows a dependency of the child when in the setting and allows the child to feel secure. Bowlby indicates that this available attachment figure, who is responsive to the child, creates a relationship whereby the child feels secure and able to value the relationship and continue it (Bowlby, 1988). This would suggest that, without the security, value and trust in the relationship, children would not 'attach' to you. However, it is the continued proximity to children that enables you to begin to build those close relationships; attachment is gradual. Rutter (1981) explores attachment, further asserting that attachments are multiple and vary in strength of bond, and that the strongest of bonds are not always with the mother. As family situations change and parents decide to return to work, attachments will alter and new bonds have the potential to form.

Your practice involves the child's dependence on you for their every need; they search for you when you are not there and can become anxious if they do not understand where you have gone. The nature of your role in the setting creates a relationship opportunity and determines the extent to which your interactions with children foster attachment behaviour. The strength of your bond with a child depends on many facets.

Reflective activity

Consider your interactions with a child.

» *How much time do you spend together?*

» *What do they need from you or ask you to do for them?*

» *How eager are they to interact with you on entering the setting?*

» *Do you explain to the child if you have to leave the room?*

» *How accepting is the child of your other relationships with children?*

» *If the child is unwell are you concerned and do you 'worry' about their recovery?*

» *When the child is absent from the setting do you think about him/her?*

Your answers will draw attention to the significance of the time you spend together and the extent of your attachment to the child.

Attachments can form unknowingly and often the strength of your attachment is only apparent when the child is absent or feeling unwell and you begin to wonder how they are and what they are doing. Often the attachment is expressed in the joy you both experience in your daily inter-actions. Laughing together is another indication of a shared thinking and feeling in your bond with a child. A sense of wellness and contentment accompanies this experience. Shared joy is an indication that emotionally you have both invested trust and respect in each other. Sharing moments such as this encourages children to seek further experiences with you where you laugh together, share stories and build further emotional connections. As these experiences grow, you and the child allow yourselves to be emotionally available to each other. Brooker (2010, p 183) confirms this interaction, *a reciprocal bond develops which is mutually satisfying and mutually reinforcing*. The sense of well-being you both feel is something that is unique in the 'caring' pro-fession and perhaps something that motivates you to continue in your role.

Extended thinking

»   *Does the closeness of relationships with children give rise to judgmental thoughts about how others interact with the child?*

»   *Keep a record of the times when you felt the need to 'defend' the actions of a child towards others. Was this justified?*

»   *Is there such a thing as becoming too close to the children you work with?*

Writing these occurrences will help you reflect on a series of events for careful consideration. Love and professionalism can work well together but when professional judgment becomes subjective you need to think carefully about the relationships you have formed.

ABC of well-being

Roberts (2010) proposes a model of well-being which underpins your daily practice and is consistent over time given the optimum conditions. The ABC of well-being, like Maslow's hier-archy of needs, considers four elements that contain the notion of well-being and will help you to understand the conditions needed to optimise well-being in the setting.

*   Agency

*   Belonging

*   Communication

*   Physical Development

Roberts (2010) explores the notion of well-being and how the model can attend to the child's holistic development. She considers that 'Agency' and 'Belonging and boundaries' are the feeling part of well-being and this is how children and adults begin to identify themselves as individuals interacting with each other and feeling at ease with each other. The Communication aspect is the 'process' and children's well-being is determined by this process (Roberts, 2010). This model is underpinned by 'Physical development' which encompasses an indi-vidual's health and development in relation to well-being. As Roberts suggests this founda-tion includes the external environment, of which you are a significant part, when considering your involvement in a child's life. When children are in your setting consistently the physical foundations change; you become an integral part of their world and life. You provide the optimum conditions for well-being to flourish. Not all children experience positive foundations and interactions; this model can be undermined if you or the child are experiencing difficulties. A child in difficulty will be supported due to the strength of attachment and the secure base they have formed in your relationship. Complexities arise when the one in difficulty is you and not the child. When you feel unwell or under pressure your emotional mood changes and unknowingly your whole emotional state has changed. Goleman (2004, p 54) refers to this as *unconscious emotions* that alter your usual positive emotional state, undermining your own well-being.

Reflective activity

Recall a work-based situation where you feel that your well-being was undermined by your emotional state.

» *What was the trigger for this and how did it influence your behaviour?*

» *Did work colleagues notice the change in your behaviour?*

» *How did you manage your emotional state or did others offer support?*

» *How do you feel your emotional state changed your practice?*

In daily lives it is often termed as 'one of those days' where nothing seems to go right and you cannot wait for the day to be over. In the childcare sector it is often your work colleagues that offer the support you need when your emotional state is negative. Just as children attach to you for support, you need attachments with work colleagues to support you through difficult times.

Attachment through the key person approach

The key person approach is described by Elfer et al as a way of working in a nursery which supports close attachments between children and staff.

The key person approach is an involvement, an individual and reciprocal commitment between a member of staff and a family. It is an approach that has clear benefits for all involved.

(Elfer et al, 2003, p 18)

There is, however, still reference in some settings to the key worker system. Goldschmied and Jackson (1994) refer to a key worker as a social work practitioner with sole responsibility for a client or family. It can be seen from both the views of Elfer, on what the key person approach is, and what Goldschmied and Jackson refer to as a key worker system why some confusion between the approaches still exists. Although saying that if you look deeper into the meaning of a key person the differences become more apparent.

Elfer et al (2003) compare the differences between a key person and a key worker. In terms of a nursery setting they suggest that a key worker describes how staff work to ensure the smooth running of the organisation and keep records up to date. This system is devoid of any importance on the relationship side of the care of children and interactions with significant others in children's lives. Elfer et al (2003, p 19) go on to say that the key person approach

[handwritten: Mayes, C et al 2017 Pg 130]

[handwritten: Close links with significant carers can provide you with an insight that enables you to provide meaningful care + education based on the child's individual needs.]

is ... itional strategy. This approach is evident in ... g at attachments through to love and care of ...

... *nasises the importance of a continuing* ... *ns/key practitioners who care for, play* ... *e their homes in close association with* ... *m home.*

(Selleck, 2001, pp 82–3)

... in engaging children and significant others – ... ship between all parties involved to facilitate ... s, the significant attachment figures children ... king the home environment to the setting. The ... environment, along with the child's primary carers, has an impact on how children ... d behave either at home or in the setting. Close links with the significant carers can provide you with an insight that enables you to provide meaningful care and education based on the child's individual needs. Selleck continues to say that messages from research are clear:

> *Children above all else need continuity of experiences with significant close adults who stay alongside children and engage with them in these three years.*
> (Selleck, 2001, p 84)

The interpretation therefore of this approach is essential to ensure the youngest, most impressionable and vulnerable children are cared for in an appropriate manner according to their individual needs and preferences based on home experiences and that of the setting. Selleck (2001) claims that these attachments made in the first three years have long-term consequences.

The unique relationship between the carer and the child has gained attention in research as more and more children experience day care as parents return to work. Lee (2006) ponders that there has been much emphasis on the child/mother and child/teacher relationship and research is needed to discover the relationships between child and practitioner. She also suggests that studies which have researched into the attachment relationship between child and practitioner *show a narrow focus* (Lee, 2006, p 135). Elfer et al (2003) had already begun to highlight this relationship through the key person approach but according to Lee (2006, p 135) academics should *take into account all aspects of the infant–caregiver relationship as much as possible, broadening the focus beyond attachment.* It is notable that emotion is gaining more attention with studies into relationships extending original attachment theory and this is becoming an integral part of higher education training.

The attachment relationship has always been viewed seriously and in previous years Goldschmied and Jackson (1994, p 36) asserted that *The denial of close personal relationships is a serious flaw in most group day care.* The key person approach as highlighted by Elfer et al (2003) considers its implications for children, parents and practitioners which, as Lee (2006) would suggest, is more than just attachment. Attachments and emotion in caring *[handwritten notes overlaid on page:]* Developing as a reflective early years professional — A Thematic Approach — 2017 second edition — Carol Hayes, Jayne Daly, mandy Duncan, Ruth Gill + Ann whitehouse — pg 131 — States ...

[handwritten notes overlaid on page:] ... setting + solve the issuer surrounding training. Staff illness + shift patterns. X

involve ...   ...unique relationship structure: parent/
child; ...   ...ey person approach is for all those
involved   ...r

Key p...

Babies an...   ...arers, often the parents, are
secure, co...   ...eir parent is close by. When
a young chi...   ...dings, adults and other children create...   ...s the child has to cope with
their significa...   ...nied and Jackson describe
the feelings o...   ...). They suggest, to lessen
this anxiety, th...   ...nate way. The key person
approach can c...   the parent.

Babies and your...   ...y, according to Gillespie-
Edwards (2002),...   ...ons and are able to build
a relationship with...   ...that a second key person
or backup person is...   ...will enable the child to
have at least one sp...   ...the issues surrounding training, staff illne...   ...ot be disadvantaged
because you are away thro...   ...ain their secure base
and attachment and le...   ...r adults they have a
weaker attachment to.

Research into brain deve...   ...sts that the growth
of connections between n...   ...nd if a child is not
stimulated can result in a...   ...t al (2003) highlight the work of Shore (19...   ...al conditions are
significant for brain develo...   ...nt age as when
attachment behaviour is stil...   ...on the research
and suggests that although...   ...llenge current
practices. These theories and...   ...ugh to ensure
that practice is changed beca...   ...ractice not to
change. Examination of practi...   ...en are to be
cared for to the best of your ab...

All too often, due to how busy t...   ...ren are cared for by a number of adults
who all carry out intimate care ro...es, such as nappy changing. This could mean that you
are not able to care for all the child's needs. Elfer et al (2003) assert that this generalised
care is not in tune with the individual child's needs. This also creates a confusing situation for the child and undermines the ability to form secure attachments. Manning-Morton
claims:

> *children do not thrive if they do not also receive loving attention, so perfunctory
> attention to children's physical needs alone is not sufficient.*
>
> (Manning-Morton, 2006, p 45)

Therefore, attention to physical needs, routines and the key person approach can be met by two practitioners who can tune in to the individual baby or child, creating a secure environment and relationship which will allow the child to feel attached, secure and special.

Reflective activity

Consider your work setting and how the key person approach is managed.

» *Are there two key persons per child that effectively cover the hours the child is in the setting?*

» *Do the key persons attend to the child's needs exclusively?*

» *What difficulties are experienced in this approach?*

» *Is the approach supported by all practitioners?*

Often interpretations of the approach are different and what practitioners say they 'do' and what they 'do' in practice can be very different.

» *Ask the practitioners in your setting what their understanding of the approach is. How do their responses differ? Is there a common theme?*

A key person role is rewarding yet exhausting both physically and emotionally. Investing your time to research and understand this approach is possible through becoming aware of the benefits to the child, building the foundations for their future.

Extended thinking

» *Planning for transitions is important. These can be daily from the arrival of the child to saying farewell at the end of the day. You will need to be sensitive to parents' needs and help them to feel part of the relationship you both share with the child. Observation is key here and your interpretation of the verbal and non-verbal signals from parents can indicate what support the parent may need. Sensitive interactions with parents are fundamental and your well-timed support will be greatly appreciated after their time away from their child. Consider a range of verbal and non-verbal signals you might see at the start of the day and what they might indicate.*

Key person approach for parents

As previously mentioned increasing numbers of parents are returning to work after maternity leave to continue in the quest to provide food and shelter for their family in an ever-changing fragile economic climate. The difficulty for parents is then in part coping emotionally and physically with the demands of raising a family and often working long hours. Elfer et al (2003, p 1) describe the balancing act parents face and the *emotional transactions to be negotiated*. The decision to place a child in anyone's care is a huge emotional task and parents feel anxious about the quality of care their children will receive. However, there are positive benefits for all in choosing good quality childcare, including a better standard of living if both parents work.

And children may end up with the best of both worlds – the love and uniqueness of private family life, and being a part of a nursery community of adults and other children.

(Elfer et al, 2003, p 2)

This is how Elfer et al (2003) propose the key person system is instrumental in joining up the two worlds a child will have at home and in a day care setting. However, they do not claim that the nursery relationship is the same as the relationship a child experiences at home.

Swick's view on parental involvement is viewed as essential for the child's future education.

The nurturance of an 'involvement process' where parents are a significant partner in their children's education and development is key to empowering everyone in the child's life.

(Swick, 2007, p 100)

Parents as partners is something that is embedded into day care. However, not all partnerships are positive. Understandably, parents can feel emotional stress as their child builds up a relationship with another care giver. Elfer et al (2003) suggest parents may feel threatened by this relationship and jealous of you as the child's key person. This situation needs careful consideration to enable parents to see that the settings are by no means a replacement parent for their child. So although the assumption is perhaps that the key person approach is for the child, you would be misguided to think this way. It is vital for you as the key person to have a strong bond with the parent if you are both to successfully care for the child. Tensions need to be minimised and a greater understanding of each other needs to develop.

Parental involvement is essential if you are to understand the depths of a child's character and how family values impact on that child. Parents want to feel that in their absence their child is seen as special by someone else. Parents with sound relationships with a key person can benefit from finding out what other things their child likes, what friends they have made and feel included in their child's day. The parent/practitioner relationship is viewed by day care staff in one setting as *someone the parents can have a bond with, a special relationship.*

Gillespie-Edwards (2002) confirms that forming a positive relationship with a child's parent can build trust between you and the parent. It also helps to deepen both your and the parent's knowledge of the child in the nursery and home setting. Elfer et al (2003) suggest parents with a positive relationship with the key person can share some of the stresses and strains of everyday family life with that key person. As one practitioner suggests:

They've got someone to talk to.

Your relationship with the parent can be rewarding due to the realisation of a shared goal of the child's well-being and developmental progress. This relationship-based practice is described by Benson-McMullen and Dixon as a critical element in working with children and their families.

There seems to be growing consensus among the diversity of professionals who work with children birth to three and their families across the global community that to be effective practitioners, we must attend thoughtfully, purposefully – mindfully – to relationships.

(Benson-McMullen and Dixon, 2006, p 50)

The key person approach needs to incorporate your relationship with the parent as a fundamental element in a child's care and education.

Key person approach for practitioners

The formation of the Birth to Three Matters framework (BTTM, DfES 2003) confirmed to those of you working with 0–3s the significance of early attachments and emphasised the relationships between you and the children as an important feature for them to flourish (David et al, 2003). This research report highlights the responsiveness and sensitivity of the child's closest relationships. Attachments and key person relationships have continued to be a feature in early years curriculum documents (Early Years Foundation Stage (EYFS), DfES, 2007; DfE, 2012). Many settings state in their policies that a key person approach is embedded in the care children receive. It is an expectation from an organisational perspective that parents have come to expect this from you in your role. Elfer (2012) considers that such an expectation needs to be managed carefully to allow practitioners the opportunity to talk through the emotional demands involved in forming close relationships.

You may feel undervalued in the sector through lack of financial recognition, intense working conditions and, for female workers, a general feeling from society that childcare work is an easy career option for some women after they have had their own family. The stereotypical view of childcare practitioners is echoed by Moylett and Djemli (2005, p 64), suggesting that working with children is either an 'Aaaah' or an 'Oh No!' factor. Goldstein (1998, p 244), too, considers the 'gentle smiles and warm hugs' view of caring in this sector.

Yarrow (2015) considers the emotional work in early childhood and the well-being of staff. He further explores 'emotional capital' of early childhood educators and suggests this capital is an ongoing feature in everyday practice; managing our own emotions when working in the sector can help to support positive well-being for ourselves and others. Attending to the management of your own emotional capital can help to mitigate some negative assumptions made about the role that you do in being emotionally available.

Reflective activity

» *How do others outside of the sector view your profession?*

» *How often do you feel you have to defend your profession to increase understanding of your role and value in the workforce?*

» *How is your professional contribution viewed by parents of the children you care for?*

» *What needs to change in the sector to gain the value and status equivalent to that of teachers?*

Extended thinking

Once you are secure in your management of emotional capital others may need support to help manage their own. You can do this in a number of ways:

» *Have end-of-day informal conversations about the emotions experienced. You may have to share your own thoughts and feelings first to show others they are 'safe and secure' to do the same.*

» *Informally observe staff to help identify when their emotional capital is not secure. You are in a position to offer them some time out to share their experiences and together understand what they and the children need in terms of emotional support.*

Regardless of your professional status in the setting everyone needs to understand the importance of emotional capital management so with other like-minded staff you can provide a consistent and united approach that others will benefit from.

Your reflections may reveal the difference between the emotional and physical care involved in day care and that of formal education by teachers in school settings. The status of the former is highlighted by Elfer and Dearnley:

> *Direct work with children, particular babies and very young children, may be seen as lower status, particular as it involves much physical care such as nappy changing.*
> (Elfer and Dearnley, 2007, p 268)

Regardless of profession or status it is about nurturing the child, and being available and a facilitator of their development. In day care or formal school settings the people that work with children need to exhibit the ability to genuinely 'care' for a child's well-being and educational progression. There is an element of care and education within all settings and the key person approach can embrace the care element and the individual developmental needs of the child. Children in day care settings develop and progress through the environment and their interactions with you but they still require emotional care, not just physical care. Therefore, self-awareness of your ability to 'care' well is essential.

> *Without 'caring' we could never realise our full human potential. Our sense of self is enriched when we care. Whether we call it loving or 'tending' or by other terms, caring equips us to live more fully. It empowers us to develop a sense of worth that becomes our self-respect.*
> (Swick, 2007, pp 97–8)

Dowling (2005) also refers to the feeling a child has of being special through placement in day care and subsequent relationships with you as a result of the attachment process through the key person approach.

Goldstein (1998) considers the work of Noddings and conducted her own research into the care practitioners give to the 'cared-for' in settings. She considers that while most situations involve enjoyable moments there were situations that required the practitioner to be firm and manage difficult child behaviours. Goldstein (1998) describes these as caring encounters that involve conflict between you and the child. It is through caring that firm boundaries are placed to enable children to socially grow and develop. As parents experience, setting firm boundaries is not easy, and your attachment to a child will raise similar emotional reactions whereby it is unpleasant to enforce boundaries that a child dislikes. Manning-Morton and Thorp (2003) imply that certain children will provoke a particular set of feelings in an adult. Regardless of those positive or negative feelings provoked, the emotional demands on you can sometimes be too demanding.

An initial fear experienced by practitioners in forming close relationships with children and their families is one concerning child protection issues. Elfer and Dearnley (2007) confirm that, due to this, practitioners are reluctant to form close relationships with children that involve close contact. Whilst this may be true in some settings the majority of you are knowledgeable enough to justify providing for children's emotional needs through cuddles and being close to one another. Further training, as highlighted by Elfer and Dearnley (2007), would clarify the issue of child protection and the key person approach and therefore enable practitioners to feel justified in their interactions. Setting support through Continuous Professional Development (CPD) would also address these concerns and give you and others the confidence to act on child protection issues and justify the emotional ties formed with children. You need to feel confident that, should you need it, support will be available from other practitioners in the setting.

> *Support is indeed at the core of what we do in early childhood education. Three dimensions of support are critical: (1) bonding with the families we serve, (2) linking families to the resources they need, and (3) creating possibilities where families have a mutually responsive relationship with us.*
>
> (Swick, 2007, p 100)

Practitioners need to feel the setting is supportive and can provide relevant resources to assist them in carrying out their roles and responsibilities. It goes without saying that the most important resource a setting can have is its staff. Without quality staff who are qualified, the childcare setting can only perform at a basic level to provide the essential care children and parents require.

Caring and love: what does this mean in early years?

Noddings considers the relationship status of the carer and the 'cared for'.

> *Natural caring is clearly emotion-based. We have some neurologically based capacity for reading the emotional state, needs and intentions of others, and with appropriate guidance, we can bring our empathic capacity to a high level.*
>
> (Noddings, 2010, p 170)

She raised in her earlier work that caring is associated with wants and needs and that the response to those wants and needs is attentive and appropriate care (Noddings, 2002). Reflecting on your own emotional state and that of those you care for can heighten your capacity to care and become empathic but it is also associated with how you understand the wants and needs of children and respond appropriately. The response to a child from you and from those you work with can be significantly different and this is determined by your own emotional frame of mind.

The interviews and extracts that follow confirm the care and 'love' experienced in day care and childminding practice. Part of this also considers how the parent views close relationships formed between their child and practitioners.

CASE STUDY

Interview extract

Here is a senior practitioner in a day nursery reflecting on her emotional ties to the children in her care.

My daughter attended the same nursery I worked in and she always called me 'Mummy' in front of her peers, why wouldn't she? She was only one at the time. Another little girl the same age also started calling me Mummy and this went on for another three years. At first I was a bit embarrassed, after all I wasn't her mum and how did her own mum feel about it? I'm certain her mother was a little bit upset at first but then over the years we would laugh about it and I would be the 'nursery mummy'. I must admit that I loved it when she called me Mummy, I felt quite honoured and although I knew she was only mimicking my own daughter it still was very special to be called this by another child. Eventually this little girl went on to school. I remember the day she left as I was out on my lunch break and I didn't get to say goodbye; I was really sad but thankful as I think I might have shed a tear in front of her, that wouldn't be fair as perhaps my attachment to her was stronger than hers to me. If she saw me upset I would feel that I hadn't cared for her responsibly.

Reflective activity

»   On reflection should this practitioner have allowed the child to continue to call her 'Mummy' or was this unprofessional?

»   Should the practitioner have remained less emotionally involved?

»   What might the child gain from having a 'nursery mummy' and if the care is different how is this fair for the other children in attendance?

Extended thinking

»   Does the case study demonstrate favouritism of some children over others? Individual children either seek or avoid emotional bonds for a variety of reasons. Consider how your own emotional state 'imprints' on the children in your care.

»   How different are the child's emotional needs from yours? Management of your emotional capital (Yarrow 2015) will allow children to choose the moments they need emotional support from you; they 'know' you are emotionally available for them when they need it.

This interview extract demonstrates how consistent care and attachments over time influence how you 'feel' about the children you care for. You cannot be an effective practitioner if you remain emotionally 'closed' to the attachments children seek from you. Goldschmied and Jackson (1994) describe the apprehension felt by practitioners at becoming involved in a relationship with a child that is not their own, asserting further that practitioners suffer during the parting of the relationship with a child they have grown to love. Perhaps the reluctance to form such close relationships relates to the perceived anxiety that separation will cause when the child leaves your care; anxiety for the child and for you.

CASE STUDY

A nursery manager's reflection on attachment and 'love'

I asked one parent who I had known for a few years why she chose a day nursery rather than a childminder for her three children. She replied 'I didn't want them to have a close relationship with just one carer, that's my role as a mum ... but I know that you all love my children but not in the way a mother loves her children.'

Commentary

This demonstrates one parent's perspective on how she can maintain her role as the main attachment figure and minimise the replication of their relationship through her child forming another strong carer bond. All too often parents feel guilt at leaving their child but also experience feelings of loss if their child 'loves' another person who takes a caring role. Page (2013) asserts that parents who are practitioners have additional feelings of guilt as they return to work to care for other parents' children. The decision to return to work for any parent is a difficult one.

CASE STUDY

A childminder's perspective

A different parent perspective is reflected in the views of this childminder.

As we offer a 'home-based' care, this is closely associated with the same care parents, grandparents and relatives would give to a child. I can genuinely say 'I love my childminding children' and give them the same love and care I would give my own children, and I feel loved by them. Caring from home, and the low ratio, gives a personal element to the care we are able to offer children and therefore we have formed close attachments with a reciprocal relationship. These close attachments intrinsically motivate me to want the best for each of the children I care for. I want to see them achieve, learn and grow, thus influencing the way I care for them and the experiences I offer. However, I never cross boundaries, I use all opportunities to speak positively with them of their parents, relate to photographs and encourage children to involve parents and family members in discussions/drawings/art and talk about how their parents miss them and think of them all the time.

Commentary

This childminder account gives an insight into 'professional love and care' given to children which allows for new attachments and closeness to be experienced in practice, yet reinforces and maintains the family closeness and love when children are away from their family. This demonstrates how children can be surrounded by 'love' from parents and practitioners. However, not all parents feel comfortable with the close bonds their child forms with practitioners as seen earlier.

It is clear that 'love' features from both the parent and practitioner but it is the extent of that love that could potentially undermine how parents feel leading to deliberate choices of care that will help to maintain the parents' status as the most loved and loving.

Parents and practitioners as co-carers: a shared love?

Working together to share the care of a child can be a fulfilling experience for you and the parents. The ultimate goal, as Selleck suggests, is to ensure the child grows and develops knowing they are loved.

> *Parents and, later, nursery staff, by attending to infants' psychological, and biological and learning needs, can provide children with a secure attachment that will enable them to develop fruitful long-term relationships and a sense of being valued and loveable.*
>
> (Selleck, 2001, p 83)

Sharing the care of a child can be rewarding and a shared view of what a child needs can enhance the care a child receives from home and the nursery setting. As mentioned previously not all parents and practitioners are comfortable with the emotions involved when caring for a child. When questioned, experienced student practitioners expressed the variety of attachment situations they had been involved with.

Parents who have secure attachment to their children are happy and confident about their children being emotionally attached to me and my staff, especially for working parents. Parents often tell me they go off to work knowing that me and my staff will treat their child/ren like their own. I have one parent who refers to me as her son's second Mummy, and she tells me that it's wonderful when her son tells other members of her family that he loves me. However we did have one working parent whose child attended our setting full time every weekday, who removed her daughter because of her very strong emotional attachment to her key worker. This child was then enrolled into a very big nursery with a very busy baby room.

This reflects an element of emotional attachment that has a potential negative impact on all those involved. The expectations of parents are that you will care for their child and ensure they are progressing developmentally; the notion of love is not as explicit in this forming of new relationships. Parents and practitioners need to understand that 'professional love' (Nutbrown and Page, 2008) is acceptable and enhances a child's well-being and lifelong attachments.

Reflective activity

»   *Where in your setting information does it state that practitioners will form an attachment?*

»   *Is there an expectation that 'shared love' can be fostered between families and the setting the child attends?*

For some of you this involves explaining to parents that you will cuddle their child when they fall over or when they are feeling unwell. Parents need to be aware of the 'professional love' that you will demonstrate as part of your role. As seen in the following reflection parents often choose day care based on the potential of practitioners to fully care for their child.

CASE STUDY

Manager reflection

Another visiting parent asked if the staff would cuddle her child. I was a bit taken aback; my natural instinct was to say 'yes' and then I paused thinking, is this a 'trick' question? I told her that I would, being a mum myself how could I not cuddle a child in my care! She was visibly relieved after being told at another day nursery that they would not.

Extended thinking

»   *Consider whether practitioners who are also parents are able to show more empathy towards parents. Does this personal aspect enable you to 'connect' emotionally with parents more effectively as you have an understanding of how they feel?*

Professional love is raised by Arman and Rehnsfeldt (2006) who consider that the profession you choose means choosing to love others. They further explore the idea that love is empathy and the concept of love in a caring profession is likely to be misinterpreted in a negative sense. However, as one practitioner expresses, the love for your own children and others is different.

CASE STUDY

Reflections from a family nanny

I became attached to the children and the children to me and the role of carer and caring for them had grown into a relationship involving love. Although I still considered myself as the family nanny – I wasn't a replacement mother, I could never match or would want to match their mother/child relationship – I consider it is a special relationship to be respected and cherished.

Since having my own children I have recognised the difference in feelings that I experienced towards my own and others' children. It's difficult to articulate as it is complex but for me there is a distinct difference between the two relationships. I could though empathise from the position of the parent how other parents might feel when they left their child with me. I could see the look of anxiety, apprehension and almost despair etched on their faces as they handed over their child to me. Could I be trusted? And how would their child cope without them?

Chapter reflections

Professional love is important for children in your care and for your own sense of self in the lives of others. It is a relationship to cherish but the love you express in professional practice may not be the same as parents feel for their own children. Understanding professional love and relationships with children and their parents within a key person approach enables shared love and positive attachments.

Parents and practitioners can enjoy the shared care and 'love' of a child without the negative feelings as have been considered in some of the sections in this chapter. Considering reflective practice and how you emotionally connect with others is a key aspect of your work with children and their families. Early years professionals and 'love' are essential for children in your care; not to replace the love of their own family but to create another opportunity for children to feel safe and secure with adults who are emotionally capable of nurturing a child's sense of self. Noddings (2010) talks of self-interest in giving to others and perhaps this is true of early years professionals. The joy of receiving unconditional love from young children is probably what continues to motivate you to work in the sector. You may not receive the pay and recognition from government agencies, but the recognition from a child demonstrating that you are special to them is priceless.

Extended reflections

The 'Extended thinking' opportunities within this chapter will help you to become more emotionally aware of yourself and others in your day-to-day interactions. You will begin to look with a critical eye at the love and care you express to and with children and watch them grow and flourish within your shared secure relationship. Love and care are the basic building blocks in a child's life and you have enormous influence and a responsibility to help children experience these positive life-affirming bonds.

Further reading

Roberts, R (2010) *Well-being from Birth*. London: Sage.

This book explores further the ABC of well-being and in Chapter 5 'Everyday well-being' is explained, with examples in practice of how the four As of everyday well-being can be observed.

Yarrow, A (2015) What We Feel and What We Do: Emotional Capital in Early Childhood Work, *Early Years*, 35(4): 351–65.

This journal explores emotional capital and research conducted analyses how this moderates the effects of burnout or low morale leading to a more resilient workforce.

References

Arman, M and Rehnsfeldt, A (2006) The Presence of Love in Ethical Caring. *Nursing Forum*, 41(1): 4–12.

Benson-McMullen, M and Dixon, S (2006) Building on Common Ground: Unifying Practice with Infant/Toddler Specialists through a Mindful, Relationship-Based Approach. *YC Young Children*, 61(4): 46–52.

Bowlby, J (1979) *The Making and Breaking of Affectional Bonds*. London: Tavistock/Routledge.

Bowlby, J (1988) *A Secure Base: Clinical Applications of Attachment Theory*. London: Routledge.

Brooker, L (2010) Constructing the Triangle of Care: Power and Professionalism in Practitioner/Parent Relationships. *British Journal of Educational Studies*, 58(2): 181–96.

David, T, Goouch, K, Powell, S and Abbott, L (2003) *Birth to Three Matters: A Review of the Literature*. Research report 444. Nottingham: DfES.

DfE (2012) *Early Years Foundation Stage*. London: HMSO.

DfES (2003) *Birth to Three Matters*. London: HMSO.

DfES (2007) *Early Years Foundation Stage*. London: HMSO.

Dowling, M (2005) *Young Children's Personal, Social and Emotional Development*. London: Paul Chapman.

Elfer, P (2012) Emotion in Nursery Work: Work Discussion as a Model of Critical Professional Reflection. *Early Years, An International Research Journal*, 32(2): 129–41.

Elfer, P and Dearnley, K (2007) Nurseries and Emotional Well-being: Evaluating and Emotionally Containing Model of Professional Development. *Early Years*, 27(3): 267–79.

Elfer, P, Goldschmied, E and Selleck, D (2003) *Key Persons in the Nursery*. London: David Fulton.

Gillespie-Edwards, A (2002) *Relationships and Learning: Caring for Children from Birth to Three*. London: National Children's Bureau.

Goldschmied, E and Jackson, S (1994) *People under Three: Young Children in Day Care*. London: Routledge.

Goldstein, L S (1998) More than Gentle Smiles and Warm Hugs: Applying the Ethic of Care to Early Childhood Education. *Journal of Research in Childhood Education*, 12(2): 244–61.

Goleman, D (2004) *Emotional Intelligence and Working with Emotional Intelligence*. London: Bloomsbury.

Hannon, P (2003) Developmental Neuroscience: Implications for Early Childhood Intervention and Education. *Current Paediatrics*, 13: 58–63.

Lee, S Y (2006) A Journey to a Close, Secure, and Synchronous Relationship. *Journal of Early Childhood Research*, 4(2): 133–51.

Manning-Morton, J (2006) The Personal Is Professional: Professionalism and the Birth to Threes Practitioner. *Contemporary Issues in Early Childhood*, 7(1): 42–52.

Manning-Morton, J and Thorp, M (2003) *Key Times for Play: The First Three Years*. Maidenhead: Open University Press.

Milne, A A (1928) *Winnie the Pooh: The Complete Collection of Stories and Poems*. London: Egmont Children's Books Ltd.

Moylett, H and Djemli, P (2005) Practitioners Matter, in Abbott, L and Langston, A (eds), *Birth to Three Matters*. Maidenhead: Open University Press.

Noddings, N (2002) *Starting at Home: Caring and Social Policy*. Berkeley, CA: University of California Press.

Noddings, N (2010) *Maternal Factor: Two Paths to Morality*. Berkeley, CA: University of California Press.

Nutbrown, C and Page, J (2008) *Working with Babies and Children from Birth to Three*. London: Sage.

Page, J (2013) Will the 'Good' [Working] Mother Please Stand Up? Professional and Maternal Concerns about Education, Care and Love. *Gender and Education*, 25(5): 548–63.

Roberts, R (2010) *Well-being from Birth*. London: Sage.

Rutter, M (1981) *Maternal Deprivation Reassessed*. London: Penguin Books.

Selleck, D (2001) Being under Three Years of Age: Enhancing Quality Experiences, in Pugh, G (ed), *Contemporary Issues in the Early Years*. London: Paul Chapman.

Swick, K J (2007) Insights on Caring for Early Childhood Professionals and Families. *Early Childhood Education Journal*, 35(2): 97–102.

Yarrow, A (2015) What We Feel and What We Do: Emotional Capital in Early Childhood Work, *Early Years*, 35(4): 351–65.

8 Reflecting on racism in predominantly white settings

MANDY DUNCAN

Six humans trapped by happenstance
In bleak and bitter cold.
Each one possessed a stick of wood
Or so the story's told.

Their dying fire in need of logs
The first man held his back
For of the faces round the fire
He noticed one was black.

The next man looking 'cross the way
Saw one not of his church
And couldn't bring himself to give
The fire his stick of birch.

The third one sat in tattered clothes.
He gave his coat a hitch.
Why should his log be put to use
To warm the idle rich?

The rich man just sat back and thought
Of the wealth he had in store
And how to keep what he had earned
From the lazy shiftless poor.

The black man's face bespoke revenge
As the fire passed from his sight.
For all he saw in his stick of wood
Was a chance to spite the white.

The last man of this forlorn group
Did nought except for gain.
Giving only to those who gave
Was how he played the game.

Their logs held tight in death's still hands
Was proof of human sin.
They didn't die from the cold without
They died from the cold within.

The Cold Within by James Kinney

Introduction

This chapter aims to encourage staff in predominantly white schools and nurseries who may not be faced with racist incidents on a regular basis, to question the assumption that racism does not exist in their setting. According to Tomlinson (2008), children in predominantly white settings are more likely than others to grow up with intolerant attitudes and believe they are superior to those from minority ethnic groups. Early research on the racial attitudes of children has shown that even very young children are aware of racial differences and that both white and black children articulate a white bias (Goodman, 1946; Horowitz and Horowitz, 1938). As a white practitioner with anti-racist convictions who has lived and worked mainly in ethnically diverse areas, my own experience of moving to a predominantly white area and working in an all-white school led me to believe that most staff do not want to appear to be racist or unwittingly perpetuate racist practices. However, there is a need for support for staff who want to challenge racism but lack the knowledge and skills to do so because this often leads to avoidance of the issue altogether or a tokenistic approach. Critics may argue that the reflections of white practitioners will be distilled through a white cultural filter and they will not have the cultural experience or capability to understand the experiences of minority ethnic groups (Troyna, 1998). I would counter this with the argument that they have specifically the cultural tools needed to notice the attitudes and prejudices present in places where minority ethnic groups are not present in large numbers but exist at a distance or as isolated families. In other words, their attempts should be to examine white society not black people *per se*. Each individual belongs to many socially constructed groups and this will inevitably affect their interpretations and ways of seeing events and experiences. It is my hope that this chapter will encourage practitioners, whatever their ethnic background, to critically reflect upon their own assumptions and attitudes and engage with the complexities of anti-racist and multicultural policy and practice in their settings.

Critical reflection on specific issues

Critical reflection now plays a central role in the professional development of teachers and early years practitioners. Each of you will have different knowledge, beliefs, experiences, assumptions, values and attitudes which you bring to your practice. Brookfield (1995) advocates viewing practice through four critical lenses which will enable you to explore the implications of these complex factors with the intention of understanding, questioning and improving your practice. The autobiographical lens helps you to engage in self-reflection in order to understand how your own experiences affect your practice with children. The students' or children's lens encourages you to listen to children and try to view practice from their perspectives in order to highlight issues and inequities. The colleagues' lens encourages you to engage in critical dialogue with peers for feedback, advice and mentoring in order to collaboratively explore alternative ways of thinking about practice. The final lens is the theoretical lens which provides you with an advanced vocabulary with which to understand and discuss practice and provides links between professional dilemmas and broader political and economic processes. Brookfield's model is useful in order to structure reflection on a specific issue or incident from as many different perspectives as possible in order to understand the value of current practice and improve the quality of it. Activities to encourage reflection on race equality issues through each of Brookfield's critical lenses are provided throughout this chapter in order to help you identify and become more aware of prejudices and inequalities that may exist for black and minority ethnic group staff and children.

Andrew Hacker (1992), an American college professor, describes an exercise undertaken with his students to reflect upon the value they place on their white skin. Having asked them whether they think equality exists for black people and having ascertained that many students are convinced that indeed it does, he goes on to ask them whether they would want to change places with an African American. None of them would so he asks them what amount of compensation they feel they would be entitled to if forced to become black. His students see no problem in responding with answers such as $50 million or $1 million per year illustrating that, even though they may not be able to or want to articulate it, they clearly perceive the discrimination and disadvantage faced by black people and feel that the money might help to buy protection from this.

Reflective activity – autobiographical lens

» *If you have white skin, how would you respond to Hacker's questions?*

» *If your skin is not white, reflect on how you would feel if forced to become white.*

» *How might your attitudes affect your practice working with young children?*

The social construction of 'race'

Historically, racism has been based on notions of biological inferiority. Until the latter half of the twentieth century, 'race' was seen as a natural, fixed and unchanging biological condition. Later this view was challenged and it gradually became accepted that 'race', far from being an objective condition, is in fact an illusion, a false consciousness, a socially constructed ideology used to divide and manipulate (Ladson-Billings and Gillborn, 2004). Gaine (1995), Zack (2003), Sarup (1991) and many others question the validity of the term 'race'. The idea that there is an unchanging set of characteristics which is tied inextricably to skin colour is false. Blood groups, for example, do not correlate with skin colour, neither do stereotypical special abilities, states Gaine (1995). *White men*, he says, *can jump*. Cole (2006) agrees and adds that the physical difference itself is irrelevant, what matters is the social significance attached to it. To illustrate this Gaine (1995) uses the example of the disproportionate presence of middle-class white girls in ballet classes. This, he says, has nothing to do with genetically programmed ability and everything to do with social advantage. Both stances, however, have their problems. The idea of 'race' as an objective condition presents the problem of who fits into what classification. Political racial categories, although they have changed over time, still do not reveal individual people's racial self-identities but position everyone in relation to the 'normative' category of whiteness (Gillborn, 1995). The idea of 'race' as an ideological construct, however, ignores the reality of a racialised society.

Much of the current discourse surrounding racism in the education system draws attention to the slippery and highly political issue of terminology (Griffiths, 2003; Gaine, 2005; Richardson and Miles, 2003). According to Ladson-Billings and Gillborn (2004) ideas of 'race' are so complicated that we often cannot put them into words even to ourselves, let alone use them to educate others. The language is ever-changing with 'culture', 'ethnicity' and 'heritage' currently being favoured over 'race' and 'colour'. The power of terminology should not be underestimated and fear of not understanding or of not using the 'correct' language can restrict people to the point of silence (Lawrence, 2006). Parekh (2000) writes that racial and cultural differences are being *written out of the national story*. This has manifested itself in schools and early years settings partly through the colour-blind approach adopted by many staff, particularly in predominantly white settings, based on the idea that refusing to recognise difference ensures equality as everyone is treated the same (Jones, 1999).

Racism

Contemporary racism has been described as multifaceted and containing elements of both biology and culture (Cole, 2006; Ladson-Billings and Gillborn, 2004; Richardson and Miles, 2003). There is a move towards the term 'racisms' which stresses the fact there is not a single type of prejudice but that people experience distrust and hostility in many different forms, including anti-refugee and anti-traveller hostility, Islamophobia and anti-Semitism (Richardson, 2006). 'Street' racism refers to both overt (name calling, physical violence, etc) and covert (eg corridor whispers) acts of racism and usually takes place in public places (Richardson and Miles, 2003). One strand of this has been described as 'playground' racism with this metaphor referring to all spaces in schools where pupils are not directly supervised and, according to Richardson and Miles (2003), a substantial number of acts of street racism are carried out by school-age children.

It is important to distinguish between institutional and individual or personal racisms, a point driven home by the Stephen Lawrence Inquiry Report (Macpherson, 1999). Richardson and Miles (2003) describe institutional racism as the way in which an institution treats its members regardless of individual intentions so that racism can persist as part of the characteristic spirit of the institution unless action is taken to recognise and remove it. Tackling racism in schools and early years settings therefore could well start with a critical review of staffroom attitudes and assumptions.

Institutional procedures may intentionally or unintentionally contribute to racialisation; the process by which a group of people come to be seen as a 'race' and attitudes towards them become absorbed into the 'common sense' of a nation (Cole, 2006). This becomes a powerful way in which to categorise people based on their colour or ethnicity and with which to legitimise inequalities (Raby, 2004). In Britain refugees, asylum seekers and Muslims are the most commonly racialised groups at the time of writing but, in the post-Second World War period, labour migration from the Indian subcontinent began the racialisation in Britain of Asians as a group. Racialisation therefore is specific to history, geography and politics.

Reflecting on your family's immigrant background

All of us come from immigrant backgrounds. Figure 8.1 shows the original migration routes of early humans.

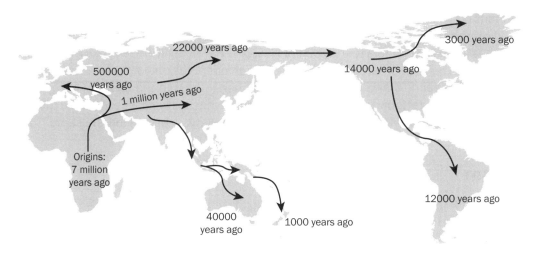

Figure 8.1 *Human migration from Africa*
Source: Adapted from Diamond (1999, p 37)

Many European countries today are home to large numbers of people descended from their former colonies. The UK, for example, hosts significant numbers of descendants from India, Pakistan and Africa.

Reflective activity – autobiographical lens

» *Research human migration to the UK from prehistoric to modern times. Where does your family fit into this picture?*

» *Do you know when the first member of your family arrived in the British Isles?*

» *What part of the world did your family come from?*

» *For what reasons did they come to the UK?*

» *Is there a story to tell about your family's immigrant background?*

Extended thinking

» *Critically reflect on the difference between the terms 'similarity' and 'difference'.*

» *What do these really mean and how can an understanding of these be applied to your practice?*

Ignoring racist incidents

The Stephen Lawrence Inquiry Report (Macpherson, 1999) defines a racist incident as *any incident which is perceived to be racist by the victim or any other person*. Ensuing investigations, it is important to note, should assess the evidence as objectively as possible. Racist incidents, such as telling racist jokes, often happen without the presence of a victim, but should be treated just the same. Schools and early years settings have a duty to record all racist incidents and report them to the parents of the pupils concerned, school governors and LEAs (Hill and Cole, 2001).

King (2004) describes the problem of dysconscious racism. This is where the cultural 'norms' of white domination and privilege are accepted uncritically among the same people that express strong disapproval towards racial discrimination and prejudice. By so doing they are avoiding having to rethink fundamentally their status and identities as white people in society and the resultant possibility of having to instigate institutional change. According to Raby (2004), 'white' is often not considered as a category of race at all and consequently holds the powerful position of representing the 'norm' in society. Along with this status comes structural and material advantage and as a result whites do not typically think much about their colour in their everyday lives.

It is almost inevitable therefore in schools and early years settings where there are no or few minority ethnic pupils that practitioners and parents will prioritise race equality issues very differently from settings in which maybe half the children are from minority groups (Gaine, 2005). 'Race' as an issue is present in white areas but not in everyday life, more at a distance, and therefore people are unsure and even embarrassed about how much to notice it, let alone how to react to incidents of racism. This is one factor that contributes to institutional racism because the political and social significance of 'race' can generate so much anxiety among staff that the issue is either denied existence altogether or avoided in the belief that talking about it will create problems that are not there.

One definition of racism is that of 'prejudice plus power' (Sarup, 1991). Although this might be considered a rather simplistic description, it is useful to see that when a multitude of white practices and assumptions are combined with economic power and sheer weight of numbers, racism results. One school, cited in Gaine (1987), included the following statement in its race equality policy:

> Racism equals prejudice plus power. Given the balance of numbers in this school, it is not possible for whites to be the victims of racism. This does not give free hand to black students to be offensive, but staff should be aware of the inequality.
>
> (p 134)

Many would say, therefore, that it is not enough for schools to challenge racism on a personal or individual level, it must also be challenged at cultural and institutional levels. At a cultural level this might involve challenging shared assumptions and hostility or resistance to change. At an institutional level this might involve legal compliance, changes to managerial style and identification of racist practices in curriculum delivery, recruitment and selection processes.

Kwhali (2006) cites the need for continued dialogue if the anxiety, confusion and inertia that accompany raising the issue of racism in white schools and settings is to be tackled. Staff often have a good will but need support if they are to deal with their own fears and prejudices. According to Gaine (1987), however, it can be very difficult to change entrenched attitudes and practices as people may feel that they are being attacked and accused of being racist and may become defensive or begin to feel guilty as a result. Human growth techniques, which allow people to wallow in self-indulgent acceptance of their guilty feelings about 'race' before going home feeling cleansed, are unlikely to result in action. Behaviour, however, can often be changed without initially changing minds by reviewing and changing rules, procedures, monitoring curriculum and recruitment practices but this implies a willing and able head teacher or senior management team. Without support from above, attempting to change minds via pressure groups, or perhaps with only one or two close allies, may be the only viable initial action.

The present political and legal climate and media coverage of perceived racist attacks, such as the shooting of Mark Duggan by armed police officers which sparked the riots of 2011, mean that it is important to people in British culture that they are not seen to be racist. This means that there is some openness towards information which will help people to under-stand the nature of and begin to recognise racisms, enable them to learn the terminology that allows them to engage in discussion around the subject and subsequently develop strategies to challenge racism in everyday life. There is a need therefore for staff training and this should not only be for teachers and early years practitioners but for support staff as well.

Kapasi (2006) criticises courses which rely on lectures and giving out lists of acceptable and unacceptable words as these do not encourage practitioners to become independent in their thinking and able to come up with their own answers. However, initially at least, this may be what is needed in order to kick-start real discussion on the subject as many people are genuinely worried about causing offence. Likewise, staff may need to be given definite strategies for dealing with incidents otherwise they may resort to ignoring the incident or classifying it along with other forms of bullying simply because they are uncertain about how to handle it (Richardson and Miles, 2003). Gaine (2005) develops this issue further by describing what he calls the *paradox of anti-racism*. This is where the notion that 'race' or colour should not matter leads to staff adopting a colour-blind approach whereby, in the quest to treat all children equally, colour and ethnicity are played down or ignored com-pletely. Children are treated as 'white by proxy' resulting in their colour, ethnicity, religion, language and history, indeed their very identity being denied (Jones, 1999). This, however, is self-deceiving. 'Race' does matter in people's lives and, in order to address the inequali-ties inherent in British society, more attention needs to be paid to it in order that eventually 'race' may matter less. In other words, as recommended in the Parekh Report (2000), we may need to discriminate between people in order to ensure that we do not discriminate against them.

Critical race theory

Critical race theory (CRT) stresses the importance of voice and has its origins in legal schol-arship where litigation, driven by the experiences of ordinary people, results in the formalisa-tion of their stories in legislation and legal discourse. It begins with the premise that racism is a natural condition that is entrenched in society and provides a means to analyse it in its various guises. Its use has become increasingly popular in education where naming your reality with stories serves two important functions; it can act to preserve psychological well-being in those telling their stories and can jolt dysconscious racism by forcing members of the dominant group to confront ways in which their privilege is maintained and perpetuated. The importance of situation is stressed, for example, this is true only for this person, at this time, in this context and on this basis CRT uses individual stories as interpretive structures.

Ladson-Billings and Gillborn (2004) point to some key areas within education where CRT is used to analyse inequalities. The curriculum, for example, is seen to be a cultural artifact designed to perpetuate white supremacy through the legitimation of elitist, white, middle-class knowledge and the marginalisation and misrepresentation of other perspectives. Teaching and assessment strategies are seen to adopt a deficit model, so that when the general techniques assumed to work for all children do not achieve expected results, the children rather than the strategies are seen to be inadequate and corrective action in the form of remedial classes or groups is taken. CRT argues that inequalities in education are the result of institutional and structural racism: the laws, policies and practices that society and its institutions create which intentionally or unintentionally benefit white people and disadvantage minority ethnic groups. One way in which this works is to perpetuate cycles of low expectations, aspirations and underachievement which is illustrated clearly in a Department for Education report on pupil exclusions in England which published the following statement:

> The rate of exclusions was highest for Traveller of Irish Heritage, Black Caribbean and Gypsy/Roma ethnic groups. Black Caribbean pupils were nearly four times more likely to receive a permanent exclusion than the school population as a whole and were twice as likely to receive a fixed period exclusion.
>
> (Department for Education, 2012, p ii)

According to Ladson-Billings (2001), culturally relevant pedagogy should enable children to experience academic success whatever their cultural background and relate their educational experiences to their individual cultural contexts. In the cultural context of a predominantly white setting, where notions of white superiority may consciously or unconsciously exist, practitioners have a responsibility to ensure that they and the children they care for *develop a critical consciousness through which they challenge the status quo of the current social order* (p 143).

Reflecting on practice through a critical race theory lens

Reflective activity

In 2008 Glasgow City Council became the first in Scotland to introduce an anti-racist curriculum for young children which aims to teach children, parents and practitioners how to recognise and challenge racism.

» *Reflect upon the following statements which are taken from this curriculum. What evidence can you provide from your own practice that you are addressing the issue of racism? Complete the following table.*

Statement	Evidence
Develop anti-racist attitudes in young children through the concepts of belonging, celebrating and contributing.	
Provide young children with knowledge and skills so that they may develop positive attitudes to allow them to take action against unfairness.	
Impact positively on children's ability to challenge racism and inequality.	
Develop parents'/carers' awareness of racism and its negative effect on society.	
Enable parents to support their children to develop anti-racist attitudes and practices.	
Develop staff skills in supporting an anti-racist curriculum for early years.	
Empower staff to deal with racism on a day-to-day basis.	
Be reflective about the impact of racism on children and parents/carers.	
Provide support materials for staff.	

Adapted from: Glasgow City Council, Anti-Racist Curriculum for Glasgow – An Approach for Early Years Centres, 2008

Multicultural versus anti-racist education

The Swann Report (Department for Education and Science, 1985) was significant in its acknowledgment that racism impacted on the educational experiences of children in Britain. It recommended multicultural education in schools regardless of ethnicity and location, thereby recognising that racism was an issue in predominantly white schools, settings and areas as well as those with significant numbers of minority ethnic people. Multicultural education, however, has been criticised for its superficial and tokenistic nature which teaches children about the music, food and clothes of various countries but nothing about structural and institutional inequalities which many believe are the real issues (Cole, 2006; Gaine, 2005). Richardson (2006) argues that there has been too much emphasis on 'multi' and not enough on 'common' culture and the resultant 'exoticisation' of minority pupils, far from addressing the prejudices of white pupils, actually serves to draw a line even more firmly between 'them' and 'us'. The only people multicultural education actually benefits, he says, are white practitioners who can believe that they are doing something positive.

The criticisms levelled at multiculturalism gave rise to a greater stress on institutional racism and the need for practitioners to use strategies which include personal examinations of racism and an approach which is more oppositional in nature (Cole, 2006). Anti-racist education was seen by many to provide the answer as it addressed white supremacy and recognised and criticised racialised inequalities (Raby, 2004). It attempted to place minority ethnic groups in a central and active role encouraging them to *lead* by articulating their experiences, as opposed to multicultural education which typically *responded* to the experiences of minority pupils (Ladson-Billings and Gillborn, 2004). Anti-racism education, however, was not without its critics. Cole (2006) cites the accusation faced by some schools that teaching strategies started from the assumption that all white pupils were racist and therefore did not create an inclusive approach to tackling racism. Another criticism was that the multiple and complex forms of racism were not recognised. The multicultural/anti-racist debate became so confused that Jones (1999), in his study of the experiences of beginning teachers in white areas, identified a 'typology of disappearance' whereby issues of ethnicity were being erased from the classroom in large part due to the lack of a clear, agreed and authoritative direction on how to deal with race issues. Multicultural education, although designed to encourage the reconstruction of society, does not encourage pupils to think deeply about and address the inequalities faced by non-white pupils and, on its own, may only confirm stereotypes. Although multicultural education is important in terms of developing positive and open attitudes towards others, many people believe that identifying where racism exists should be the real starting point (Selleck, 2006).

Cultural bag activity – children's lens

This activity draws on the principles of both multicultural and anti-racist education. It encourages all children to name their reality by telling their own stories but also helps them to learn about the cultures of others. It can be adapted for use with adults and children of all ages. It encourages participants to first learn about and reflect upon their own culture, which is an important prerequisite to being able to understand and value the cultures of others.

Reflective activity

» *In preparation, ask each member of your work setting, the group or class to research and gather the contents of their own cultural bag. Items that could be placed in the cultural bag could relate to the following:*

   – *your ethnic or cultural background;*

   – *traditions or customs that you follow;*

   – *any particular religion that you follow;*

   – *the kind of family that you live in;*

   – *what you do during your leisure time and holidays;*

   – *any special days and celebrations that you practice;*

   – *family stories to share about your cultural background.*

» *Organise participants into small groups with as much diversity as possible among participants and ask them in turn to share and discuss the contents of their cultural bag. It would be useful for you to model this first by discussing your own cultural bag.*

Adapted from Wong (2002)

Extended thinking

» *Following this team activity reflect personally upon one item from each bag. Consider why YOU think that that particular member of staff selected that one for their cultural bag.*

Few issues are shrouded in such bitter controversy as the multicultural and/or anti-racist debate. Multicultural education puts emphasis on learning about other cultures in order that stereotypes are dismantled and tolerance promoted. It is often seen as a 'soft' liberal or social democratic stance and critics argue that it does not challenge economic structures and political processes, thereby ignoring the reality of discrimination that black people face regarding access to resources, housing, education and employment (Sarup, 1991). Gillborn (2004) presents the left-wing view that multicultural education is nothing more than a tokenistic gesture designed purely to pacify minority ethnic pupils while at the same time protecting the official and politically generated core of knowledge presented by the national curriculum. One response to these criticisms is the liberal concept of improving life chances through 'equal opportunities', but again this is criticised for the fact that it makes no inherent changes in the structure of society (Sarup, 1991). Anti-racist education recognises the importance of understanding racism on a personal or individual level but goes further and examines how racism is manifested in institutions such as the medical, legal and teaching professions. On a fundamental level anti-racism is about restructuring social and economic relations and thereby redistributing power.

Hill (2001) suggests that the national curriculum, far from increasing equal opportunities, actually perpetuates economic, social and educational inequalities. He describes the national curriculum as *the embodiment of a Conservative vision of a national culture* (p 98). It is criticised for being elitist, with its formal testing procedures resulting in disadvantage for certain groups of people, including working-class and many ethnic minorities. It is seen to perpetuate white, middle-class, heterosexual, male values, seeking to assimilate all to this favoured *national culture*. Delpit (2004) discusses what she calls the *culture of power* within which those with least power are often acutely aware of its existence yet those with the most are either least aware of it or refuse to acknowledge that it exists. She cites the power held by those who develop the curriculum, and those who present it, to determine other people's levels of intelligence and 'normality' and how the results of this education affect the types of jobs people get and therefore their economic status, which is closely related to power. The reality is, she states, that people who are successful in institutions such as schools achieve this largely because they have assimilated the culture of those in power. Hill (2001) discusses the *hidden curriculum*, further stating that its formation was symbolically violent in the way it enforced legally a 'preferred' set of cultural symbols and that this could happen largely because people did not recognise that it was happening. He goes on to state that the programmes of study included in the curriculum are in no way random but designed to impose elite 'ruling-class' knowledge and culture over working-class and other cultural knowledge.

Many anti-racists believe that the focus of multiculturalism on the individual rather than social and cultural aspects of racism reinforces the notion that people from minority ethnic groups have shortfalls that need compensating. However, the effort to encourage wider political considerations in the debate around race equality has left anti-racism open to the criticism that it does not acknowledge the importance of ethnic culture in ethnic identity (Gillborn, 2004). Selleck (2006) agrees and stresses that children need to be taught to be confident of and articulate self-assuredly whatever ethnic heritage or racial identity they have in whatever way they choose. Another major criticism of anti-racism is that it ignores the concept of class. Hill (2001) states that the links between 'race' and social class must be recognised with many minority ethnic groups being disproportionately represented in the working class and therefore unequally affected by low incomes and reduced economic power. This particular strand of anti-racism was highlighted in the inquiry into the death of the 13-year-old Bangladeshi schoolboy Ahmed Ullah, who was murdered in the playground of Burnage High School in Manchester by a white peer in 1986 (Macdonald et al, 1989). The ensuing report was highly critical of the 'symbolic' type of anti-racism practised at the school in which all white pupils were perceived to be racists and all black pupils victims with no regard for the complicated nature of teenage relationships, including issues of class, gender and size (Gillborn, 2004). According to Sarup (1991) this practice has led to resentment among white people with some burying their racism rather than changing their attitudes and many feeling unable to engage in free speech around the 'race' issue.

For this and other reasons anti-racist education is sometimes believed by teachers to be extremist and politically inflammatory. They might argue that Eurocentric curricula are not necessarily examples of institutional racism but simply the result of narrow outlooks or ignorance. They might argue that as most black people are working-class then they are bound to congregate in lower educational sets and streams as are all working-class people. This is countered though with Sarup's (1991) argument that this is typical of multiculturalists who do not see that their own liberal apolitical stance is in actual fact deeply political whether they like it or not.

Schools and early years settings play a significant role in perpetuating and validating the dominant culture in society. By the same token they have the power to invalidate and disregard other cultures (Hill, 2001). The Crick Report on Education for Citizenship and the Teaching of Democracy in Schools (Qualifications and Curriculum Authority, 1998) goes some way towards striking a balance between the principles of multicultural and anti-racist education. It allows for representation of other cultures through community involvement thereby attempting at least to address issues of tokenism and 'exoticisation'. It also attempts to develop skills of critical reflection in children by introducing concepts of social and moral responsibility and the development of political literacy. However, it remains for schools to decide how much emphasis to place on this and as yet has not developed a specific model of good practice to assist delivery.

Curricula, policies and procedures

The Equality Act (2010) places a duty on all public bodies, including Local Education Authorities (LEAs), to eliminate unlawful discrimination, advance equality of opportunity and foster good relations between different ethnic groups. It requires all schools, children's centres and nurseries which are maintained or run by LEAs to produce and implement a written statement detailing how race equality will be promoted and discrimination removed in their setting and to prepare at least one specific and measurable equality objective.

Gaine talks of a *pernicious conspiracy of inaction* (1987, p 12) when referring to raising the issue of racism in predominantly white settings. He states that teachers and practitioners may be anxious about controversy and genuinely unaware of racist attitudes, citing the integration of minority ethnic pupils into school life as evidence that there is 'no problem here'. Jones (1999) describes a 'typology of disappearance' whereby staff 'erase' issues of ethnicity from the classroom using a range of strategies including the belief that the presence of an equal opportunities policy levels the playing field and therefore places responsibility firmly on the shoulders of those from minority ethnic backgrounds to fall into line with this process and to become invisible in order to succeed in the system. Lund (2006) agrees that barriers are erected by the deliberate avoidance of contentious topics and the almost unwitting denial that racialised divides exist which favour certain players over others on the field. According to Osler and Morrison (2000), Ofsted may be endorsing this trend by effectively ignoring racism as a feature of school life in white schools, in part at least, by accepting the presence of race equality and equal opportunities policies as evidence that the school has embedded an anti-racist ethos. On the other hand maybe the Ofsted inspectors, many of whom are white and middle class, are simply not equipped with the cultural tools needed to see what is happening. They like policies largely because they aid measurement and visibility rather than because they actually help schools and early years settings to engage with issues of equality. Gaine (2001) discusses the practice of schools and early years settings hastily putting together policies immediately prior to inspection purely in order to satisfy Ofsted requirements. Jones (1999) states that where policies exist they are likely to have limited effect if their formulation and implementation do not involve all staff members in tackling issues. However, the formation of race equality policies and objectives may be useful in that they put the subject firmly on the settings agenda, set out how to deal with racist incidents, prompt discussion among staff and help ensure time for curriculum development and training.

Gaine (1995) states that policies and objectives are useful for legitimising the work of activists and help protect them from scepticism and criticism. Many white pupils, he points out, are confused, misinformed and hostile about 'race' and schools and early years settings have a duty to confront this. The process of policy formation invites discussion and deliberation among staff which can be valuable in itself, resulting in a greater sense of clarity. Additionally, policy formation and objective setting are sources of internal communication within institutional hierarchies and provide guidance on how to proceed in practice. Hill and Cole (2001), however, write that staff must see the proposed changes as meaningful if actual change is to follow. This may well not be the case in all-white schools in white areas where there is likely to be an absence of pressure from the local community to help drive forward change. In addition, those advocating the change and developing policy may have had months or even years to absorb information about the issue and fully appreciate its meaning. It is unrealistic, therefore, for them to expect other staff members to do this in a matter of days or weeks. This is especially the case if it is attitudes and beliefs that are the subject of change and, if adequate time is not allowed, resistance may be met. In addition to the probability that they will be giving up their own time, teachers and practitioners will need to make an emotional investment if change is to occur. Clarity is also an essential condition and practitioners may need to gain skills and knowledge which might involve in-service training. In short, in order for real change to occur as a result of policy formation there must be a receptive climate and enough available time and resources (Gaine, 2001). However, it should not be assumed that just because the school has taken the time to write down its principles and values, these become automatically translated into the attitudes, beliefs and actions of its staff. Further evidence is needed.

Engaging in critically reflective dialogue – the colleagues' lens

Reflective activity

» *As a team, reflect upon race equality in your setting and develop or update your equality objectives and policy to reflect this. Consider individual, institutional and cultural factors. The Equality and Human Rights Commission (2011) suggests that when developing possible objectives it is useful to reflect upon:*

  – *the proportion of families from different ethnic groups who take up your service, the quality of their experiences and the practical outcomes for them;*

  – *the proportion of people from different ethnic groups who are employed and the quality of their experiences and the practical outcomes for them;*

  – *the frequency of any race-related issues occurring and the harm these may cause to individuals and to groups;*

  – *who it would be useful to talk to in the process of setting objectives.*

The objectives you set should be specific and measurable and explicit about:

• the policy, function or practice they relate to;

• the people that are affected;

• the outcome they seek to achieve;

• why they have been selected;

• how success will be measured and by whom.

A recognised way to set effective objectives is to ensure that they are SMART (Specific, Measurable, Achievable, Realistic and Time-bound).

Extended thinking

» *Before devising your SMART targets, consider what possible barriers or opposition you may encounter from the team and how you will overcome these.*

» *Might there be objections from parents and how would you address these?*

Ofsted have been given a leading role in the implementation of race equality strategies and are responsible for applying the race equality aspect of the inspection framework when reporting on schools and early years settings. Osler and Morrison (2000) researched the quality of Ofsted's reporting and found that inspection reports often deal with race equality issues in a marginal way and that quality of reporting depends on how sensitive individual inspectors are to race equality issues and the degree of importance inspectors attach to them. The research also found that if a school was judged inadequate in its race equality provision this was unlikely to lead to it being placed on special measures. This begs the question of whether a 'snapshot' Ofsted inspection can really make a valid judgement on racial equality, particularly in exclusively white settings, because of the widespread tendency for racism to be seen to be present only in settings where there are pupils from minority ethnic groups (Gaine, 2005; Jones, 1999). In other words, children from minority ethnic groups may be seen to actually cause racism by their very presence. This attitude of 'no problem here' which persists in exclusively white settings means that race equality issues may never be discussed (Gaine, 1995). The problem, Gaine points out, is that the people within them are often very confused about when to notice colour, uncomfortable with the appropriate language and uncertain about how to deal with racism and how to discuss it with parents. He discusses the contradiction between the need to draw attention to 'race' or colour in order to fight racism and the essence of anti-racism which purports that 'race' should not matter (Gaine, 2005). Colour blindness or refusal to recognise ethnicity is insulting. It denies the right to have pride in one's colour. It denies the language, religion and history that are central to one's identity. And to deny colour is also to deny whiteness and all the privilege and advantage that this may bring, thereby contributing to institutional racism. Critical race theory points to the high visibility of the colour-blind approach in the way in which black and Asian leaders and activists are presented in the curriculum presuming *a homogenised 'we' in a celebration of diversity* (Ladson-Billings and Gillborn, 2004). So political activist Martin Luther King Jr, a man whose visions of social justice challenged America on issues of aggression and economic injustice in Southeast Asia, is reduced to a *sanitised folk hero* supported by good Americans everywhere. Thus, the curriculum could be viewed as a culturally specific tool designed to perpetuate notions of white supremacy by silencing multiple perspectives.

The Crick Report on Education for Citizenship and the Teaching of Democracy in Schools (Qualifications and Curriculum Authority, 1998) attempted to address this problem and influenced the development of compulsory citizenship education in secondary schools including three main strands: social and moral responsibility; community involvement; and political literacy. In primary schools, citizenship remains a non-statutory programme of study at Key Stages 1 and 2 which, if followed, builds on the statutory early learning goals for Personal, Social and Emotional Development within the Early Years Foundation Stage. Citizenship education has been criticised for its failure to recognise that individuals have multiple identities and may identify themselves as both British and of a particular ethnic grouping (Osler and Morrison, 2000). It does, however, place emphasis on notions of identity and diversity and provide teachers and early years practitioners with curriculum space and scope for the exploration of issues connected with racism, but it remains to schools and individual practitioners to decide how much emphasis to put on this.

Radicalisation in childhood: an emerging early years issue

Section 26 of the Counter-Terrorism and Security Act (2015) places a duty on schools and registered early years childcare providers to have due regard for ...*the need to prevent people from being drawn into terrorism*. In an article for *Nursery World* in 2014, Hannah Crown suggested that early years practitioners were now expected to join the frontline in the war against terror by becoming the spotters of tomorrow's terrorists. Crown was referring to the Prevent duty, which is part of the government's counter-terrorism strategy under which early years practitioners have a duty to protect children from the risk of radicalisation as part of their safeguarding duties. According to HM Government (2015), terrorist organisations in Iraq and Syria, those associated with Al Qa'ida and those associated with the extreme right currently pose the biggest threats to security and safety in the UK. Radicalisation is the process whereby individuals come to adopt extreme political or religious views. The Prevent guidance (HM Government, 2015) defines extremism as: ... *vocal or active opposition to fundamental British values, including democracy, the rule of law, individual liberty and mutual respect and tolerance of different faiths and beliefs*.

This narrative has been increasingly adopted by successive UK governments since the 9/11 attacks of 2001. However, according to Kundnani (2015), policies which have this account of extremism embedded within them are simplistic and can be counterproductive as there is very little evidence that supports the idea that holding a set of extreme beliefs leads inexorably to acts of terrorism.According to Stanley and Guru (2015), the Prevent policy has resulted in Muslim families being singled out by professionals and subjected to intensified surveillance as a precautionary measure. Many groups, including the National Union of Teachers (NUT) and the National Union of Students (NUS) have publically rejected the Prevent strategy, stating that it creates suspicion and perpetuates stereotypes. Some Muslim groups such as the Waltham Forest Council of Mosques have gone further and condemned the policy as a racist attack on the Muslim community (Taylor, 2015). An article in *The Independent* reported a significant increase in both verbal and physical racist attacks on British Muslim schoolchildren since the Paris attacks of 2015, with Muslim children increasingly being taunted with name-calling such as *terrorist, immigrant* and *paedophile*.

Adults and children who are thought to be at risk of radicalisation can be referred to Channel, which is part of the Prevent strategy. Channel consists of a multi-agency panel of representatives, chaired by the local authority with the aim of creating a tailored plan of support for the individual concerned in order to prevent them from being drawn into terrorist activity. Coppock and McGovern (2014) point out that Prevent's justification for the intensified surveillance of children and their families is provided by psychological profiling and screening work which seeks to identify 'vulnerable' individuals who may be at risk of radicalisation. However, according to Stanley and Guru (2015), this ignores the structural and socio-economic causes of terrorism which might particularly affect disillusioned youth who have few opportunities for employment or who feel alienated from mainstream society and therefore may be particularly at risk of adopting extremist ideologies. The Prevent policy sees these issues as peripheral to the psychological deficits of the radicalised individual which require treatment and normalisation.

Early years practitioners are thought to be in a strong position to recognise when the parents of very young children might pose a risk to them through travel to conflict zones such as Syria and Iraq, or to the dangers of them being educated at home into extremist ideologies. This can pose a considerable dilemma for practitioners when making decisions about whether parents who hold a particular set of extreme beliefs constitute a child protection risk. There are undoubtedly children in the UK who are living at home with parents or older siblings who have convictions for terrorist-related offences and these children might reasonably be thought to be at higher risk of encouragement towards extreme views. However, Stanley and Guru (2015) point out that radicalisation should not necessarily be defined as a child protection issue and more debate is needed lest practitioners find themselves pawns in an *...ideologically driven moral panic* (p 354). Having one's thoughts policed is anti-democratic and violates human rights to freedom of speech and there is a danger that political activity of any type could be conflated by practitioners to pose a child protection risk.

Kundnani (2015) argues that criminalising or restricting radical views does not prevent terrorism and the focus should instead be on those where there is reasonable suspicion of an intention to engage in acts of terrorism. Prevent alienates large sections of the Muslim community in Britain who feel that they are held responsible for the crimes committed by an extreme minority. Indeed, there could be unintended effects of constructing families as a risk to their own children and subjecting them to intensified surveillance and social conditioning, such as a higher number of decisions to leave the UK to conflict zones. Kundnani (2015) calls for an end to the Prevent policy, which he says suppresses civil rights, alienates and subjugates Muslims and ultimately makes Britain less rather than more safe.

Reflective activity: colleagues' lens

As a team, discuss the Prevent strategy and reflect on your new statutory duty to have due regard for the need to prevent people from being drawn into terrorism:

» *Do you feel you have adequate training to take on this role?*

» *What are the particular risks of radicalisation to children in your area? Very young children may be at particular risk of radicalisation from older family members.*

» *Do you think that radicalisation should be defined as a child protection issue?*

» *Does your setting have a clear procedure for protecting children at risk of radicalisation?*

» *What do you think about accusations that the Prevent policy is a racist attack on Muslims?*

» *What could be the impact of Prevent on Muslim families who live in predominantly white areas?*

Chapter reflections

Racism is not just about the unenlightened mental prejudices of a few white people. It is about the effects of structural inequalities in society caused by unequal power relations between white and black people which result in domination and economic exploitation (Sarup, 1991). However, it should be acknowledged that, although there is a distinct relationship between 'race' and class, and efforts should rightly be directed towards addressing social and economic disadvantage, the reality is that at every class level people from minority ethnic groups have less status than and do less well than white people of the same class and level. Therefore, even if the problems of economic and social disadvantage were removed, racism fuelled by false beliefs about 'race' and culture would probably persist (Zack, 2003).

The Parekh Report into the Future of Multi-Ethnic Britain (Parekh, 2000) recognises this and has provided the ideological backlash to The Stephen Lawrence Inquiry Report (Macpherson, 1999) and its long struggle to gain acceptance of the existence and effects of institutional racism. Parekh writes that Britain is not just a political state but also an 'imagined society' and as such needs to re-imagine itself as a multicultural society refocusing the struggle against racism onto the need for culture and identity once again. Whether Britain really is a multicultural society is debated by Gaine (2005), who draws attention to the fact that only 7.9 per cent of the population are non-white and that this has very uneven distribution. Indeed, in many areas of the country it would be misleading to talk of minority ethnic communities as they do not really exist and instead many families live in isolation.

If education is to be effective as a remedy for racism, multiculturalism should, I believe, continue to play a part. Its content in the curriculum can support the success of minority ethnic pupils by helping to dismantle stereotypes and by affirming identities both individually and as part of an ethnic group. This, however, is said with reservations and the acknowledgement that identification with an ethnic group may not always be as important as multiculturalists might believe and, in fact, some people might welcome the chance to forget where one comes from (Zack, 2003, p 267), but this is often not possible as other people may identify us with and see us as members of a particular group.

Multicultural education is often said to reflect a white, homogenous view of black cultures and ignore the issue of racism altogether. Relatively little is being done currently to educate children about false concepts of biological racial taxonomy, particularly in primary schools, and this needs to be addressed since many racist attitudes derive from notions of biological inferiority. The Crick Report (Qualifications and Curriculum Authority, 1998) attempts to address this issue and influence the development of citizenship education with a focus on social and moral responsibility, community involvement and political literacy. It remains to schools and individual teachers, however, to decide how much emphasis to put on this which means that its delivery will be affected by individual and institutional racism where this occurs. Also, as Sarup (1991) points out, equipping pupils with reasoned intellectual arguments is not enough on its own as many racist attitudes are based on deeply irrational moral judgements encompassing feelings of hate and blame towards those deemed to be different or inferior.

Although many schools and early years settings make attempts to help children learn about the cultures of others, taking steps to address and prevent racism is fundamental to the whole issue of race equality and should not be seen as an optional extra (Richardson, 2006). Children should be given the opportunity to learn about the racism of their own culture so that they can recognise it and fight it. This idea is central to critical race theory (CRT), which begins with the concept that racism is a normal and natural condition embedded deeply in society and therefore the problem first is to identify and expose it in its various forms. CRT incorporates the experiential knowledge and shared history of 'otherness' of its advocates. It also stresses the importance of 'naming your reality', which is considered important in the preservation of marginalised groups. The process of telling one's story leads to the realisation of how oppression occurs and the ability to stop inflicting stereotypical brutality, which is absorbed from the majority society. It can also jolt dysconscious racism by forcing oppressors or the dominant group to confront ways in which their privilege is maintained and perpetuated (Ladson-Billings and Gillborn, 2004). In other words, it is important that we keep in our minds that other people are the experts on their own lives and that the role of educators is, as always, to facilitate and encourage debate, to question, to listen, to empathise and to be non-judgemental in the weighing up of evidence.

Osler and Morrison (2000) point to the need for training not only for early years and school staff but also for Ofsted inspectors, who are in a crucial position for promoting race equality. Although policies may sometimes come into being purely to satisfy legal requirements, their formation may at the very least invite deliberation and provide legitimacy for those committed to change. A transparent and specific model of training is needed for all staff in educational settings which is backed up by serious commitment to race equality issues in the form of resources and time.

Although most people will have both good and bad experiences of education, 'race' still matters and it continues to impact on the educational experiences and lives of children in the UK. There still exists a significant degree of discomfort, confusion and even fear in white schools and settings around the discussion of race equality issues. It is, however, the height of naïvety to think that if we don't discuss it and reflect deeply upon it, it will go away.

Extended reflections

» What do you see as the relationship between 'race' and class and how could this affect your practice in the early years setting?

» Why do you think that some early years staff may have 'discomfort, confusion and even fear' of even discussing these issues?

Further reading

Gaine, C (2005) *We're All White, Thanks. The Persisting Myth about White Schools*. Stoke-on-Trent: Trentham Books.

Chris Gaine believes that racism, far from being just an issue for multi-ethnic inner-city schools, exists in pernicious form in predominantly white communities and schools and that this issue needs addressing and prioritising.

Jones, R (1999) *Teaching Racism or Tackling It? Multicultural Stories from White Beginning Teachers*. Stoke-on-Trent: Trentham Books.

Russell Jones highlights the experiences of some initial teacher training students on placements in primary schools which exposed the denial and confusion demonstrated by many staff in the face of even overt racism. He makes recommendations for how schools and universities can tackle racism and promote diversity in positive ways.

References

Brookfield, S (1995) *Becoming a Critically Reflective Teacher*. San Francisco, CA: Jossey-Bass.

Cole, M (ed) (2006) *Education, Equality and Human Rights. Issues of Gender, 'Race', Sexuality, Disability and Social Class*. Abingdon: Routledge.

Coppock, V and McGovern, M (2014) Dangerous Minds? Deconstructing Counter-Terrorism Discourse, Radicalisation and the 'Psychological Vulnerability' of Muslim Children and Young People in Britain. *Children & Society*, 28: 242–56.

Crown, H (2014) Terrorism Bill Means Nurseries 'Must Understand Risk of Radicalisation'. Available from: www.nurseryworld.co.uk/nursery-world/news/1148935/terrorism-means-nurseries-understand-risk-radicalisation (accessed 28 November 2016).

Delpit, L (2004) The Silenced Dialogue. Power and Pedagogy in Educating Other People's Children, in Ladson-Billings, G and Gillborn, D (eds), *The RoutledgeFalmer Reader in Multicultural Education*. Abingdon: RoutledgeFalmer.

DfE (2012) *A Profile of Pupil Exclusions in England*. London: HMSO.

Department for Education and Science (DfES) (1985) *Education for All (The Swann Report)*. London: HMSO.

Diamond, J (1999) *Guns, Germs and Steel: The Fates of Human Societies*. New York: W W Norton.

Equality and Human Rights Commission (2011) *Objectives and the Equality Duty: A Guide for Public Authorities*. Manchester: Equality and Human Rights Commission.

Gaine, C (1987) *No Problem Here: A Practical Approach to Education and 'Race' in White Schools*. London: Hutchinson Education.

Gaine, C (1995) *Still No Problem Here*. Stoke-on-Trent: Trentham Books.

Gaine, G (2001) Promoting Equality and Equal Opportunities: School Policies, in Hill, D and Cole, M (eds), *Schooling and Equality: Fact, Concept and Policy*. Abingdon: RoutledgeFalmer.

Gaine, C (2005) *We're All White, Thanks: The Persisting Myth about White Schools*. Stoke-on-Trent: Trentham Books.

Gillborn, D (1995) *Racism and Antiracism in Real Schools*. Buckingham: Open University Press.

Gillborn, D (1998) Racism and the Politics of Qualitative Research: Learning from Controversy and Critique, in Connolly, P and Troyna, B (eds), *Researching Racism in Education: Politics, Theory and Practice*. Buckingham: Open University Press.

Gillborn, D (2004) Anti-Racism: From Policy to Practice, in Ladson-Billings, G and Gillborn, D (eds), *The RoutledgeFalmer Reader in Multicultural Education*. Abingdon: RoutledgeFalmer.

Goodman, M (1946) Evidence Concerning the Genesis of Interracial Attitudes. *American Anthropologist*, 48: 624–30.

Griffiths, M (2003) *Action for Social Justice in Education. Fairly Different*. Maidenhead: Open University Press.

Hacker, A (1992) *Two Nations: Black and White, Separate, Hostile, Unequal*. New York: Ballantine Books.

Hill, D (2001) The National Curriculum, the Hidden Curriculum and Equality, in Hill, D and Cole, M (eds), *Schooling and Equality. Fact, Concept and Policy*. Abingdon: RoutledgeFalmer.

Hill, D and Cole, M (2001) *Schooling and Equality. Fact, Concept and Policy*. Abingdon: RoutledgeFalmer.

HM Government (2015) Revised Prevent Duty Guidance for England and Wales. Available from: www.gov.uk/government/publications/prevent-duty-guidance (accessed 28 November 2016).

Horowitz, E and Horowitz, R (1938) Development of Social Attitudes in Children. *Sociometry*, 1: 301–38.

Jones, R (1999) *Teaching Racism or Tackling It? Multicultural Stories from White Beginning Teachers*. Stoke-on-Trent: Trentham Books.

Kapasi, H (2006) Race Equality Training in Early Years. *Race Equality Teaching*, Spring.

King, R (2004) *Race, Culture and the Intellectuals*. Baltimore, CO: Johns Hopkins University Press.

Kundnani, A (2015) A Decade Lost. Rethinking Radicalisation and Extremism. London. Claystone.

Kwhali, J (2006) Colour Neutral: The Absence of Black Voices in Early Years. *Race Equality Teaching*, Spring.

Ladson-Billings, G (2001) *Crossing over to Canaan: The Journey of New Teachers in Diverse Classrooms*. San Francisco, CA Jossey-Bass.

Ladson-Billings, G and Gillborn, D (2004) *The RoutledgeFalmer Reader in Multicultural Education*. Abingdon: RoutledgeFalmer.

Lawrence, P (2006) Lost for Words? Thinking about Terminology. *Race Equality Teaching*, 24(2).

Lund, D (2006) Rocking the Racism Boat: School-Based Activists Speak Out on Denial and Avoidance. *Race, Ethnicity and Education*, 9(2): 203–21.

Macdonald, I, Bhavnani, R, Kahn, L and John, G (1989) *Murder in the Playground: The Report of the Macdonald Inquiry into Racism and Racial Violence in Manchester Schools*. London: Longsight.

Macpherson, W (1999) *The Stephen Lawrence Inquiry. Report of an Inquiry by Sir William Macpherson of Cluny*. London: Home Office.

Osler, A and Morrison, M (2000) *Inspecting Schools for Race Equality. Ofsted's Strengths and Weaknesses. A Report for the Commission for Racial Equality*. Stoke-on-Trent: Trentham Books.

Parekh, B (2000) *The Future of Multi-Ethnic Britain: The Parekh Report*. London: Profile Books.

Qualifications and Curriculum Authority (1998) The Crick Report on Education for Citizenship and the Teaching of Democracy in Schools. London: QCA.

Raby, R (2004) 'There's No Racism at My School, It's Just Joking Around': Ramifications for Anti-Racist Education. *Race, Ethnicity and Education*, 7(4): 367–83.

Richardson, R. (2006) Classrooms and Corridors: The New DfES Advice on Racist Bullying in Schools – Messages from Us to Us. *Race Equality Teaching*, 24(3): 31–5.

Richardson, R and Miles, B (2003) *Equality Stories. Recognition, Respect and Raising Achievement.* Stoke-on-Trent: Trentham Books.

Sarup, M (1991) *Education and the Ideologies of Racism*. Stoke-on-Trent: Trentham Books.

Selleck, S (2006) Being Included – Being 'Brown', Being Me! Beginning at the Beginning. *Race Equality Teaching*, 24(2): 33–7.

Stanley, T and Guru, S (2015) Childhood Radicalisation Risk: An Emerging Practice Issue. *Practice: Social Work in Action*, 27(5): 353–66.

Taylor, D (2015) Society of Mosques to Boycott 'Racist' Anti-terror Prevent Programme. *The Guardian*. Available from: www.theguardian.com/world/2015/dec/17/society-of-mosques-to-boycott-anti-terror-prevent-programme (accessed 28 November 2016).

Tomlinson, S (2008) *Race and Education: Policy and Politics in Britain*. Maidenhead: Open University Press.

Troyna, B (1998) 'The Whites of My Eyes, Nose, Ears...': A Reflexive Account of 'Whiteness' in Race-Related Research, in Connolly, P and Troyna, B (eds), *Researching Racism in Education: Politics, Theory and Practice*. Buckingham: Open University Press.

Wong, E (2002) *The Anti-Racism Toolkit. Educational Activities for Use in Workshops and Classrooms*. West Vancouver: First Nations Education Steering Committee.

Zack, N (2003) Race and Racial Discrimination, in Lafollette, H (ed), *The Oxford Handbook of Practical Ethics*, Oxford: Oxford University Press.

9 Reflecting on global childhood poverty

MANDY DUNCAN

Like slavery and apartheid, poverty is not natural. It is man-made and it can be overcome and eradicated by the actions of human beings ... Overcoming poverty is not a gesture of charity. It is an act of justice. It is the protection of a fundamental human right, the right to dignity and a decent life. While poverty persists, there is no true freedom.

Nelson Mandela, Trafalgar Square Speech (2005)

Introduction

Globally, poverty is the biggest killer of children today. According to the World Bank (2013), 1.2 billion people worldwide, one third of whom are children under 12, live in extreme poverty, severely deprived of food, shelter, safe drinking water, health and education. Every day 19,000 children under five years of age die from poverty-related causes across the world (UNICEF, 2012a, 2012b). That equates to 13 children every minute and the actual number may be far greater with an estimated 51 million children unregistered at birth (UNICEF, 2009).

Children living in poverty experience deprivation of the material, spiritual, and emotional resources needed to survive, develop and thrive, leaving them unable to enjoy their rights, achieve their full potential or participate as full and equal members of society.

(UNICEF, 2005)

Helen Penn, in her book *Unequal Childhoods: Young Children's Lives in Poor Countries*, questions the willingness of early childhood practitioners in rich countries and others who advocate for and profess to care about children, to tolerate the vast scale of child poverty in developing countries.

In the North we justifiably value life and the right to life and are shocked by child deaths or abuse in our own country, but overlook the prevalence of those same phenomena in the South.

(Penn, 2005, p 172)

This chapter explores some of the key current debates on child poverty, including the debate about aid donation and the consequences to young humanity of the globalisation of a capitalist economic system. You will be encouraged to reflect upon and question your own assumptions about what is in the best interests of children who live in poverty and explore, through logical reasoned argument, whether you have a moral responsibility to distant vulnerable children. It will encourage you to draw on the writings of contemporary moral philosophers such as Peter Singer, who argues that we should give aid to the point of marginal utility and Garrett Hardin who argued that aiding impoverished and starving people is morally wrong and results in disastrous consequences for humanity. It is hoped that, through this chapter, you will be helped to reflect on your own moral position and improve your thinking on one of the most important global moral issues of our time.

A note on philosophical reflection

Philosophical reflection involves thinking critically about your moral behaviour and attitudes in order to examine your life and your beliefs about life. The aim is to achieve greater understanding and make positive changes to behaviour based on this. Socrates is attributed with the uncompromising claim that the *unexamined life is not worth living* (Longstaff, 2013). He thought that people should seek the truth in order to create fair and just societies. There is of course, in this complex and unsettled world, a certain appeal in not examining too closely and this might well lead to a more pleasant life. Socrates himself paid the ultimate price for challenging the status quo and was sentenced to death for corrupting the youth of Athens. When offered a reprieve if he gave up his questioning of the orthodoxy, he refused; for him, thinking critically about life was his reason to live.

According to Elder (2010), Socrates was concerned with cultivating various intellectual dispositions in order to develop critically reflective thinking. Intellectual humility involves questioning what you actually know about yourself, others and the world around you. It involves identifying your assumptions and any false beliefs you might have and being aware of your potential for prejudice and self-deception. Intellectual empathy is about being aware of and giving due weight to perspectives that are different from your own and involves sympathising with and looking for insights in the views of others. Intellectual integrity involves holding yourself to the same standards you expect from others and examining inconsistencies in what you say and do. It is about questioning your own reasoning and whether you are willing to change your position when a more reasonable one appears. Intellectual autonomy is about taking responsibility for your own thinking and questioning the extent to which you uncritically accept the views of others, and your willingness to stand alone on issues where you do not conform to the established views.

I have attempted to employ these traits during the construction of this chapter on global child poverty by asking clear questions throughout, although I freely admit that my skills of philosophical reflection require much refinement so I hope you will forgive, and of course challenge, any holes in my arguments. This is by no means a fully comprehensive discussion of the topic; it is simply my initial reflections on the issue which I hope will inspire you to think more deeply about it too. At the end I challenge you to construct your own reasoned argument based on what you have learned.

What is poverty?

Poverty is often simply stated as the number of people in the world living on an income of below US $1.90 a day (World Bank, 2015). This measure is based on an attempt to convert national currencies to an amount required to purchase the same goods and services in those countries as US $1.90 would buy in the United States. It represents the average of national poverty lines for the 15 poorest countries in the world and is referred to as the absolute poverty line, below which it is very difficult for a person to survive. Robert McNamara, former President of the World Bank, described absolute poverty as:

> a condition so limited by malnutrition, illiteracy, disease, squalid surroundings, high infant mortality, and low life expectancy as to be beneath any reasonable definition of human decency.
>
> (McNamara, 1973)

Individual countries, however, have differing concepts of poverty. It is difficult to imagine that anyone living in the US or Western Europe could survive adequately on $693.50 per year, which is what the $1.90 a day threshold equates to. Great Britain, therefore, defines poverty in relation to the average income in the country; people living on less than 60 per cent of the median income are said to be living in poverty. According to Child Poverty Action Group (2015), in the period 2014–15, this amount was £393 per week for a couple with two children which, at the time of writing, is equivalent to around US $70 per day and will usually be enough to pay rent and buy food, clothing, electricity and some heating. There will also be access to fresh drinking water and running hot water, an inside toilet and probably items such as a television and telephone. Healthcare and education are free. In contrast, Afghanistan, having suffered many years of war, famine and little foreign investment, defines the poverty line as the amount needed to provide 2,100 calories to each person. Thirty-six per cent of the population lives below the $1.90 global poverty line. These people do not have access to many of the goods and services available to the poor in the UK. Only 53 per cent of the rural population has access to sanitation and safe drinking water and 55 per cent of Afghan children are failing to grow and develop properly due to food scarcity, particularly in the first two years of life (World Bank, 2014). There are clearly problems in comparing poverty between nations although it is broadly accepted that the amount needed to provide a minimum quality of life in developed countries is significantly more than that needed to provide a minimum quality of life in developing countries. Economist Amartya Sen (2009), argues that, instead of trying to make detailed analyses of the cost of consumer goods needed for survival in particular countries, we should look at the capabilities of people to achieve the things that will lead them to live the kind of life they value. This might mean having a job and being able to provide food, shelter, healthcare and education for their children. It might also mean satisfying psychological needs such as for cultural identity, security, belongingness, dignity and respect.

What does child poverty mean in developing nations?

Child poverty is different to poverty experienced in adulthood (Ortiz et al, 2012). It has long-term, permanent, physical, intellectual and socio-emotional consequences. It can stunt children's growth and destroy their opportunities to live fulfilling lives performing the roles expected of them in their societies and communities. Most children who live in extreme poverty today live in sub-Saharan Africa, South and East Asia and Latin America.

Generally speaking, children that live in rural areas experience much higher rates of poverty than those that live in towns and cities. Severe deprivation of shelter and sanitation affects around a third of children in the developing world with 20 per cent of children using unsafe drinking water (Gordon et al, 2003). Fifty-eight million children of primary school age have either never attended school or dropped out without completing their primary education. Girls are more likely to be deprived of education than boys and 70 per cent of the poorest girls in Guinea and Niger have never attended primary school compared to less than 20 per cent of the richest boys (UNESCO, 2015). Minujin and Nandy (2012) argue that, in addition to the accepted multidimensional measures of poverty (household income, health, education etc), there are two extra indicators that should be added when considering child poverty and these are for protection and attachment, which are closely linked. A child who is deprived of parents is often deprived of protection and an estimated 13 million children in developing countries have lost both parents; in many cases due to HIV/AIDS which is prevalent in Africa. Many orphans are forced to live on the streets foraging for food in bins and landfill sites or are forced into prostitution or armed conflict, living their lives in fear and without love, comfort or security. A report by UNICEF (2013) indicates that, globally, 26 per cent of children under five are stunted (low height for age). The damage caused by stunting in the first thousand days of life, from conception to the age of two, is irreversible. It is a slow process indicating that a child has suffered repeated debilitating illnesses, insufficient food and nutrients for growth and inadequate care. It results in short stature and impaired development of the brain which has long-term consequences for a child's cognitive functioning, impacting on school performance, employment prospects and ultimately, where rates of stunting are high, the potential for whole nations to develop. A further 29 million children under five in the developing world are severely wasted (low weight for height), indicating acute under-nutrition usually associated with starvation or chronic disease. The malignant relationship between under-nutrition and disease cannot be overstated. A wasted child is nine times more likely to die from common childhood infections such as diarrhoea: a stunted child is four times more likely to die.

The impact of extreme poverty on children's lives is a violation of their human rights; there can be few greater injustices than robbing infants of their potential to survive and develop fully during their lives (UNICEF, 2013). According to Milanovic (2012), poverty is often thought of as a problem for individual nations since national governments control access to resources such as income, healthcare and education. This, he says, gives a limited two-dimensional perspective of the issue and, in order to get a fuller picture, it must be considered in a global context. This is because globalisation has brought with it a greater dependence on other countries for income generation, while developments in technology have allowed for comparison of lifestyles and a more acute understanding of our own position in the world's hierarchy of wealth. Increasing recognition of the need for a global response to addressing poverty and its associated social issues culminated in the identification, at the United Nations Millennium Summit in 2000, of eight Millennium Development Goals (MDGs) to be achieved by 2015. The goals were inextricably interlinked, in terms of improving outcomes for the world's children, and reflected the world's stated priorities to eradicate extreme poverty and hunger, reduce child mortality, improve maternal health, achieve universal primary education, promote gender equality, combat HIV/AIDS and other diseases, ensure environ-mental sustainability and develop global partnerships. The UN announced in 2010 that one of its primary targets, to halve the proportion of people living in extreme poverty by 2015, was achieved five years ahead of schedule. This is thought to be in large part due to the dramatic economic growth and subsequent progress made by China, where the proportion of the population living in extreme poverty fell from 60 per cent in 1990 to 12 per cent in 2010. The new target is to eradicate extreme poverty by 2030 but this has come under criticism from some who say that poverty reduction is about more than economic growth, and that inequalities in wealth and opportunity are increasing within countries and this is hindering progress towards goals to improve infant and maternal health and increase access to education. Pogge (2012) is sceptical of the UN's announcement that the poverty target was achieved early, pointing out that the number of people in extreme poverty is continually decreasing by around 50,000 deaths each day from poverty-related causes. Ironically, these premature deaths help to improve the poverty count on a daily basis. The MDGs were suc-ceeded in 2015 by 17 Sustainable Development Goals to be reached by 2030 including zero poverty and hunger, gender equality, good health and well being, clean water and sanitation, and quality education for all (United Nations, 2015).

The link between poverty and educational outcomes is crucial for understanding the poten-tial for social mobility and escaping poverty. We have already seen how stunting impairs brain development, making educational achievement more difficult and, even if the family improves its situation later in life, full recovery is not usually possible. Poor health, food scarcity and social problems such as unemployment and unmanageable debt put families under a great deal of stress, which also undermines educational attendance and achieve-ment. Engle and Black (2008) reviewed a range of early childhood intervention programmes in developing countries and found that, with a combination of healthcare, feeding, parent education and attendance at child development centres, it is possible to improve children's readiness for school; that is, their ability to engage with and profit from it. This has important implications for later social mobility, as low or non-engagement with pre-school and primary education is associated with illiteracy, lower rates of secondary education, unemployment and higher rates of imprisonment in adulthood (Minujin and Nandy, 2012).

In a world where there is so much wealth, why do so many children live in poverty?

In order to understand how some people became rich and some people became poor it is necessary to look back in history over the last 500 years to what many see as the beginning of globalisation, ie when the countries of Western Europe began to dominate the rest of the world through exploration and colonisation. Colonialism is the subjugation, exploitation and physical occupation of the territory of one group of people by another for settlement or commercial purposes. Examples of this are the Spanish and Portuguese conquests of the countries of South America from the early sixteenth century, and the establishment of British colonies in India in the early nineteenth century. This process of political and economic domi-nation was often violent, hugely destructive and in many cases included slavery, death and the enforced migration of native people (Canella and Viruru, 2004). It resulted in unequal relation-ships between indigenous populations, who had their land, resources and livelihoods taken from them, and the colonists who, convinced of their own cultural and intellectual superiority, imposed their laws, language, religion, knowledge and values on the local people as well as trade restrictions, taxation and other economically harmful practices which forced many into extreme poverty.

Having gained natural resources and cheap or free labour, the colonists needed to create markets for their products. Colonies were therefore often required to produce a single commodity or crop (eg gold, sugar, coffee) year after year for cheap export to the motherland. As a consequence, farmers were prevented from producing the range of foods needed to feed their families and from making their own tools, clothes and other necessities. Instead, they were forced to buy these from their colonial rulers which transformed millions of people from subsistence farmers into labourers and consumers, dependent on the markets and the goodwill of the mother country (Watts, 2013). The subsequent accumulation of resources in Western Europe and later North America created a huge imbalance, making the countries of the North extremely rich and those in the South increasingly poor.

The impact of colonialism is complex and endures to the present day, decades after many countries have regained their independence. It is one of the main reasons that poor countries remain poor. Although decolonised nations have regained control of the resources they were once plundered for, they find themselves in the context of the global market economy and control of this lies with North America and Europe. These countries are often unable to use their natural resources to solve the hunger and nutrition problems of their people partly because they are still exporting cheap raw products to the rich countries of Europe and North America, who turn them into finished products which they can then export for a far greater profit.

Colonisation of the mind

Reflective activity

The powerful allegory of colonisers arriving with a rifle in one hand and a bible in the other is much cited (eg Crouch and Stokl, 2014).

» *What is meant by this?*

» *What, do you think, were its consequences?*

Extended thinking

» *As human beings we are all bound together either geographically, economically, culturally or any combination of these. Reflect on this statement in the light of the difference and diversity that you have read about in this chapter.*

The psychological consequences of colonialism are well documented (eg Canella and Viruru, 2004) and involved a significant change in mentality, culture and religion for many colonised peoples. The work of church missionaries, for example, to convert all to Christianity can be seen as part of the wider aggressive imposition of culture introduced by the colonisers *in a sea of persistent savagery* (Andrews, 2010, p 665). Concepts of racial and cultural superiority were central to the psyches of the colonisers who viewed indigenous peoples as objects, destined by God to be slaves for the white man. Equality was not tolerated between white and black people and this resulted in the eventual destruction of psychological and spiritual frameworks, loss of language, culture and sense of identity. It created billions of marginalised people who have still not recovered their place in society today. This may all seem far removed from the contemporary issue of child poverty but children do not live their lives isolated from the political, social and economic landscapes around them and are impacted by their legacies just as adults are. It is important to understand that, while inequality and poverty are not the same thing, inequality is a root cause of much child poverty in the world today (Sen, 2009).

What are the links between capitalism and poverty?

From the end of the First World War, the European empires were gradually dismantled as many colonised countries made bids for independence. Many writers, including Diane George, a prominent political and social scientist, in her classic study of world poverty, *How the Other Half Dies: The Real Reasons for World Hunger* (1976), have drawn links between global poverty and the capitalist economic system that the decolonised nations found themselves in. They point to the presence of the same paradox that affected England during the Industrial Revolution and indeed many other countries undergoing industrial development. The paradox was that increasing prosperity was accompanied by rising levels of poverty, only now this existed not only within nations but on a global scale. Capitalism can be defined as private ownership and control of the factors of production (eg land, factories, mines, labour) where sale of the product accrues profits for the owner. Just as control of the factors of production is fundamental to the development of private business, control of the resources of the South is fundamental to development in the North, as we shall see from the case study below.

CASE STUDY

Mali

Mali, an ex-French colony which gained its independence in 1960, is a landlocked country in West Africa and one of the poorest countries in the world. In the 1990s Mali had experienced widespread student and trade union unrest in protest against the corrupt and dictatorial regime of the time. Under this rule strict austerity programmes were implemented in order to satisfy the debt repayment demands of the International Monetary Fund (IMF) and this had resulted in severe hardship for the Malian people.

In 2008 Mali was in a relatively stable period when the global food crisis hit triggering food riots around the world in response to growing hunger. The food crisis hit rich countries as well as poor; the rich countries responded by attempting to buy up agricultural land in many African countries in order to secure food supplies for the future. In Mali, where 75 per cent of people were subsistence farmers, American agricultural developers, in partnership with the Malian government, began drawing up plans for a vast industrial sugar plantation known as the Sosumar sugar project, which it was hoped would stimulate economic development for Mali. The plans meant that thousands of local farmers would lose their land and, as compensation, were offered the opportunity to become contracted sugar cane growers for the Sosumar project. Many of these families had farmed the same land for generations, their lifestyles changing very little over hundreds of years. Government acquisition of the land (in this case to lease to the American developers) is a prerequisite for economic development in a capitalist system. People will usually only be persuaded to sell their labour and work for an employer if they do not have access to land. A market for a product can only fully develop if it is taken out of the context of subsistence farming, where people are only producing enough for themselves and their families, in order to produce excess products that can be sold on the open market. In many developing countries like Mali, the small farmers do not actually own the land; their occupation of it dates back to times of pre-ownership, which leaves them vulnerable to intervention by governments who can simply take the land from them when they decide they need it, ignoring the rights of the people who live there.

In 2006 Mali had adopted food sovereignty as government policy, which is a political concept embracing the idea that a country should produce its own food rather than rely on the world food market. This should have resulted in more investment in small farmers, including giving them land rights, in order to help them produce more and sell more to improve their standard of living. This development plan was thought to be appropriate to Malians and their traditional ways of life. Instead, increasing violence was accompanying the arrival of foreign investors such as those associated with the Sosumar project. If Malians did not give up their land peacefully, it was taken forcibly using violent methods such as tear gas and electric batons, in direct violation of Malian and international human rights laws. In this way many Malians were persuaded to accept the US $600 per year salary offered by the Sosumar project to cultivate sugar cane. The Sosumar project was financed by a number of organisations including the African Development Bank. Release of the money depended on the Malian government adhering to the Bank's guide-lines which eventually ensured that those who were involuntarily displaced and did not want to work for Sosumar were offered land outside of the proposed plantation as compensation. It was hoped that the Sosumar development, which was the biggest investment in Africa at the time, would reduce poverty in Mali and lead to benefits such as improvements in enterprise, development of modern farming methods, the building of hospitals and schools and better employment prospects for young people. The major criticism of the Sosumar project and others like it is that most of the powerful elite in Africa, as in most countries, are far removed from the lives of the common people. They have often been educated in colonial schools and view the Western model of economic development as the only viable option, leaving them open to the accusation that they are imposing economic models that do not fit with African values and culture.

In 2012 a military coup seized power in Mali as a result of political unrest in the north of the country. The banks suspended funding for the Sosumar project and all foreign employees were removed from the project making it unlikely now that it will go ahead. The coup was seen by some to represent a chance to return to food sovereignty policies and meaningful development for Mail, but to others it represented the frustration of dreams to develop global markets resulting in a better quality of life. In 2013 French armed forces intervened in the conflict but the future in Mali remains uncertain and levels of infant mortality and malnutrition remain high, with an estimated one-third of the country's children stunted.

Land Rush – Why Poverty?, an informative documentary about the Sosumar project, can be accessed via the following link: www.youtube.com/watch?v=O_pKnP-2mOQ.

Reflective activity

»   *How have the Malian people been affected by colonisation and the globalisation of a capitalist economy?*

»   *What are the implications for young children?*

Within any developing economy, whether national or global, most of the benefits go to the owners of the means of production which increases inequalities in the population – the rich become richer and the poor become poorer, almost inevitably suffering from the erosion of human rights and loss of political and economic power, as is demonstrated in the case study above. A study by Oxfam reported that the wealth of the richest 85 people in the world amounted to the same as the total wealth of the poorest half of the world's population (Alvaredo et al, 2013). It goes on to say that this astounding statistic is a sobering reminder that growing inequality exists because the wealthy elite have the economic and political power to manipulate the rules of the economic system to their benefit.

As the colonies gained independence, the debts of the colonial powers were transferred to the newly formed governments and the only solution offered by the North was more loans with high interest rates in order to repay the initial debts. This resulted in even higher states of dependency upon the North, who imposed conditions on these loans allowing them to dictate policies on agriculture, infrastructure and trade, and bestow special privileges on foreign corporations by, for example, allowing monopolies over mineral extraction. According to George (1988) many people think that the loans go to developing countries to help people in poverty but the reality is that most of it ends up back in the hands of Western corporations, who make huge profits building infrastructure in those countries. The debts themselves, of course, are not paid by governments but by taxpayers and ensure that millions of people remain in extreme poverty; every child born in these countries is already shouldering a big share of the burden. Developing world debts are a serious barrier to poverty reduction. Recent initiatives such as the Multilateral Debt Relief Initiative (MDRI) have helped to ensure that the debts of qualifying countries are reduced or written off. However, some countries are unable to meet the requirements of debt relief if, for example, they cannot preserve peace and stability due to ongoing political conflict and civil war. Another chief criticism of debt relief initiatives is that debt relief is too slow and debts are not cancelled until structural reforms are implemented in countries, leaving them to struggle with repayments and the cost of reforms at the same time.

The Singer solution to child poverty

Writing in the *New York Times Magazine* (1999), American philosopher Peter Singer argues that the money Americans spend on luxuries, rather than necessities, should be given to help alleviate the suffering of impoverished and starving children in developing countries. He cites the following tale to facilitate thinking about this moral issue.

CASE STUDY

Bob is close to retirement. He has invested most of his savings in a very rare and valuable old car, a Bugatti, which he has not been able to insure. The Bugatti is his pride and joy. In addition to the pleasure he gets from driving and caring for his car, Bob knows that its rising market value means that he will always be able to sell it and live comfortably after retirement. One day when Bob is out for a drive, he parks the Bugatti near the end of a railway siding and goes for a walk up the track. As he does so, he sees that a runaway train, with no one aboard, is running down the railway track. Looking farther down the track, he sees the small figure of a child very likely to be killed by the runaway train. He can't stop the train and the child is too far away to warn of the danger, but he can throw a switch that will divert the train down the siding where his Bugatti is parked. Then nobody will be killed – but the train will destroy his Bugatti. Thinking of his joy in owning the car and the financial security it represents, Bob decides not to throw the switch. The child is killed. For many years to come, Bob enjoys owning his Bugatti and the financial security it represents.

Reflective activity

» *Do you think it was wrong of Bob not to throw the switch? Try to explain your answer as fully as possible.*

Discussion

Most of you will probably think it was wrong of Bob not to throw the switch, but Singer points out that many of us have the opportunity to save a child's life by donating to aid organisations and choose not to. He states that $200 (allowing for the costs of administration, fundraising and delivery) would give a child safe passage through their first five years and drastically increase their chances of survival. If you think it was wrong of Bob not to throw the switch then surely it must follow that it is wrong not to donate $200 that you would otherwise spend on luxuries such as a holiday, meals out in nice restaurants, or new clothes simply because the old ones are out of fashion? You might argue that only Bob can save the child on the track, but millions of people are in a position to afford to give aid. Singer counters this argument with the reasoning that even if all of those millions of people were in exactly the same situation as Bob and chose not to throw the switch in order to protect their cars, this would still not make it right for Bob to do the same. You might ask the question that, even if you gave your $200 and saved the life of a child, there would still be millions of other children whose lives needed saving, so at what point should you stop giving? It is important at this point to understand Singer's utilitarian position which is that we can determine whether acts are morally right or wrong by their consequences. The utilitarian view of morality holds that if we have a choice of how to act, the right choice to make is the one that will result in the most human happiness. Singer deliberately focuses his argument on children, not because he thinks that the life of a child is more valuable than the life of an adult, but because children cannot be said to have caused their own impoverished situations. His argument rests on two basic presuppositions.

1   Suffering and death due to lack of basic needs such as food is bad.

2   If we can prevent this without causing excessive suffering to ourselves, we have a moral obligation to do so.

The logical conclusion to these statements is that we have a moral duty to help the poor and suffering of the world but it is uncertain as to what lengths we should go to in order to do this. At what point is the sacrifice to ourselves too great? Singer argues that we should give to the point of marginal utility; that is the point at which our own basic needs are satisfied and the consumption of more material goods or services is not necessary. The consequence of using your extra money to go out for meals in nice restaurants might mean a slight increase in your happiness but this is not morally as important as the increase in happiness to the child who can live as a result of that money. In other words, unless you value nice meals in restaurants more than the life of a child, you should give that money to aid the child. Perhaps the most important point Singer is trying to make is that giving aid to poor and starving children should be seen as a moral obligation rather than a charitable act.

We will leave Singer's argument for the time being and reflect upon a different point of view. Garrett Hardin, American ecologist and philosopher, argued that aiding impoverished and starving people in distant, overpopulated countries is morally wrong and results in disastrous consequences for humanity (Hardin, 1974a, 1974b).

CASE STUDY

Living on a lifeboat

Hardin uses the metaphor of the lifeboat to make his point that helping poor and needy people in developing nations will risk disaster for everyone. He invites us to imagine that each rich country is a lifeboat full of people and that each poor country is also a lifeboat but these lifeboats are vastly overpopulated, resulting in people continually falling into the water. These people swim about in the water trying to gain entrance to the rich lifeboats which appear to have room for them. The rich lifeboats, however, although not quite at full capacity, have limited room and to let some people on board would compromise the safety margin and make the boats more likely to sink. The rich people have to make a choice. They cannot admit all the people calling out to them in the water. To do so would result in inevitable disaster for the rich boats and all on board them. They could admit maybe 10 per cent of the people in the water but this would compromise the safety principle and would mean constant vigilance to ensure that nobody else was trying to climb aboard. In any case how would they choose which 10 per cent to admit? On what grounds would they discriminate? The cleverest 10 per cent? The closest? The youngest? The other choice, of course, is to preserve the safety margin and admit no more people to the rich lifeboats, ensuring their survival and that of all on board including their immediate families.

Reflective activity

» *You are on a rich lifeboat. What choice would you make? Again try to explain your answers as fully as possible.*

Discussion

Hardin's argument is built on the premise that the population in poor countries is increasing at a much faster rate than the population in rich countries and that overpopulation is a root cause of poverty and hunger (Hardin, 1999). His solution to this problem, as an ecologist, is to do nothing and let nature take its course and effect its own solution to overpopulation in the form of famine and disease. Like Singer's solution to global poverty, Hardin's is also rooted in utilitarianism as he believes that this will ultimately lead to the greater level of human happiness for the greatest number of people. Hardin recognises that some of you might find this solution deplorable and guilt might persuade you to offer your unjustly held place in the lifeboat to someone in the water. This, he says, might alleviate your conscience but it will not alter the lifeboat ethics. The person who takes your place is unlikely to feel guilty about his sudden change in fortune. If he did, he would not get into the boat. You might argue that the developed world has a duty to help those in poor countries as a result of past exploitation and atrocities inflicted during colonisation. Hardin counteracts this by stating that we must think of a way forward from the current situation in order to ensure that we do not leave a world that is overpopulated and devoid of resources for future generations.

In order to give serious consideration to Hardin's argument it is necessary to think a little more deeply about the links between population and poverty. According to Marris (1999), the English cleric Thomas Malthus (1766–1834) was the first to develop the idea that population growth has a negative influence on prosperity. In other words, human beings depend upon food for life and food comes from the land. The amount of land available to grow food is limited and therefore, if the population increases to the extent that the land cannot provide enough food, famine, war, disease and death will be the outcome which will return the population to a more sustainable level. Prosperity will then cause the birth rate to rise and the whole cycle will begin again (Malthus, 1798).

Hans Rosling, a Swedish medical doctor and statistician, discusses this in a modern context refuting the whole idea that the population is exploding out of control and supporting the idea that we should give aid to developing countries. The population is indeed increasing, he says, but this is due to population momentum and will level out by the end of the century (Rosling, 2006). Despite the popular belief that saving the lives of poor children will lead to population growth the reality is very different, as he explained in the BBC2 documentary *This World: Don't Panic – The Truth about Population* (2013). Of the total 7 billion people currently living on our planet, the population is growing fastest among the poorest 2 billion, where child mortality is highest. For the other 5 billion people on Earth, the birth rate is lower and simply replaces the adult population as they die. This means the population has stabilised among this section of the population and has stopped growing. The reasons that the population has stopped growing in much of the world are related to improvements in medicine, meaning that many more children are surviving and people no longer have to compensate for high rates of infant mortality by having lots of babies. The availability of modern contraceptives and improvements in the rights of women to be educated and have control over their own bodies has also been a causative factor. Therefore, if the lives of poor children are saved and the poorest 2 billion people are helped out of poverty, those parents will also decide to have fewer children. Before the population stops growing, however, another 4 billion people will be added to the total population, but this depends on saving the lives of the poorest children now; if we do not, this number will only increase.

Can aid end poverty?

By the late 1960s, most developed countries had created budgets for overseas assistance and development with the overall effort being co-ordinated by the Organization for Economic Co-operation and Development (OECD) and increasingly this aid has been targeted at those living in absolute poverty. Official aid either goes directly to the governments of aid-receiving countries (bilateral aid) or is distributed via organisations such as the World Bank (multilateral aid). There is a United Nations target that wealthy countries should transfer 0.7 per cent of gross national income (GNI) to assist developing nations. Most donor countries have never hit this target. The UK government announced that the target had been hit by them for the first time in 2013. According to the poverty action group, ONE, a person on an income of £25,000 in the UK will pay an average of £5,465 in tax for the year and of that, £52 will go to the overseas aid budget. As we have seen, Singer would advocate that this is not enough and that perhaps we should adopt the Marxist ideal: from each according to his ability to each according to his need. According to Hardin (1968), however, there is a fundamental error in the principle of sharing. Unrestricted access to a limited resource (food) will eventually deplete that resource to the detriment of all because some groups of people will over-exploit it for their own gain and will not fulfill their parallel responsibility to look after and replenish it. Some countries will only make deposits in the 'world food bank' and some will only make withdrawals, resulting in a huge disincentive for developing countries to solve their own food shortage problems.

Very few critics, however, are against all types of aid, particularly short-term humanitarian aid which is given in times of crisis, such as when the recent Typhoon Haiyan struck and devastated much of the Philippines in 2013. That said, in recent years there has been a growing body of criticism towards both official government aid and that given by non-governmental organisations (NGOs) such as Save the Children. One of the most prominent arguments cited against aid is that it does not reach those people who need it most and it is often undermined by corrupt governance. In 2012, for example, many donor countries withheld aid to Uganda after reports that prominent Ugandan government officials had been involved in the long-term theft of huge sums of money donated for humanitarian development purposes, including from primary education and health service funds. Economist Dambisa Moyo argues that aid has had a negative impact on Africa by perpetuating the poverty cycle and hampering economic growth. She uses the example of an African mosquito net producer who was forced out of business by well-meaning aid agencies who were giving out nets for free (Moyo, 2009). Official aid, she says, actually fosters corruption by engendering a culture of dependency, propping up corrupt governments and making those countries unattractive to both domestic and foreign investors, which has a harmful effect on economic growth. Charitable aid agencies are often criticised on the basis that they have high administrative expenses and are driven by the needs and objectives of their own organisations and governments which are not necessarily congruous with the needs of the local populations. According to Marris (1999) there is an upper limit, in the economic development of any country, to the amount of external resources that country can soak up, and inevitably most of the resources must eventually come from within the country itself. Although aid, on its own, is unlikely to produce sustainable development, it cannot, on the other hand, be blamed for the failure of development (Riddell, 2008). Penn (2005) agrees with this, pointing out that we share a global responsibility for the past, present and future state of our planet and the inhabitants of it wherever we live. It is not for the countries of the North to impose their values under the assumption that rich-world industrial living is the norm that all should aspire to. Instead, the focus should be on achieving the lifestyles that people value.

Contemporary German philosopher Thomas Pogge (2001) brings another uncomfortable strand to the discussion and that is the concept of justice. It is one thing, he argues, to do nothing to help impoverished people if you are not contributing to their suffering but it is quite another to do nothing when you are actively contributing to and profiting from their impoverishment. Part of the problem, he states, is that many citizens of the rich countries of Europe and North America do not realise that extreme poverty in developing countries is a condition to which they are actively contributing. Pogge is heavily influenced by seventeenth-century English philosopher John Locke whose theory of natural rights asserts that people in their natural state (without government or sovereign rule) would be entitled to a proportionate share of the Earth's resources (Pogge, 2005). Thus, the basis of any just society should be that the poorest people are at least as well off as they would be in a state of nature. Unlike Singer, who advocates that we have a moral duty to help the poor, Pogge concentrates on the ethical principle of non-maleficence; our moral duty to first do no harm which is rooted in his belief that there is a global institutional order that is shaped by rich countries and imposed on poor countries. This, he states, is giving rise to extensive and severe violation of human rights and causing radical inequalities both between and within nations which could be avoided through institutional change.

The institutions that Pogge refers to are the Washington-based World Bank and the International Monetary Fund (IMF). These organisations are the agents of the richest countries in the world and were set up at the end of the Second World War to rebuild the economies of Europe. They later began to offer loans to poor countries but usually with the conditions attached that they privatise their economies and offer Western corporations access to their raw materials and markets. Consequently, many developing countries became locked in a cycle of debt that they could not escape and this contributed to rising food insecurity and appalling rates of child mortality in these countries. As we have seen, even when debts are cancelled or reduced many countries are still unable to escape poverty as austerity measures alone are not enough to support recovery. They are also subject to institutional control in other ways such as through tied aid (aid that must be spent in the country providing it or a small group of nominated countries) and policies that are dictated by the World Bank and the IMF giving rise to a form of neocolonialism.

There is an underlying assumption by rich countries that it is in the best interests of poor countries for them to integrate into the existing international economic order. In order to do this they need to develop their 'export baskets' which typically contain cheap, raw products (eg iron) and develop the capability to manufacture connected, finished, sophisticated products (eg cars) which will enable economic growth (Felipe et al, 2010). The World Trade Organization (WTO) is an international body that deals with the rules of trade between countries. Part of its mission statement is to ensure a level playing field for all and it has recently pledged to offer more leniency to developing countries and make their needs a priority. Despite this it has been plagued with criticism such as the accusation that it pays large subsidies to rich-world farmers which has created barriers for small farmers who are being forced out of business and into increased levels of poverty. The battle over intellectual property rights has also been well documented with the WTO's decision to protect the rights of the large pharmaceuticals to make profits resulting in the inability of governments in many developing countries to be able to afford or make affordable versions of medicines that would provide lifesaving treatments for their populations. Consequently, the WTO along with the IMF and World Bank are frequently accused of pushing through free market policies that serve the financial interests of their major stakeholders: the USA, Japan and the European countries of Germany, France and the UK, sometimes at great cost to people living in poverty in developing nations (Stiglitz, 2003).

According to George (1976) the world has enough resources to support a much larger population than it has now but:

> Unfortunately for the millions of people who go hungry, the problem is not a technical one ... Whenever and wherever they live, rich people eat first, they eat a disproportionate amount of the food there is and poor ones rarely rise in revolt against this most basic of oppressions.
>
> (George, 1976, p 23)

She cites the example of Goldman Sachs, a US-based global investment banking firm which shared its profits of 2.2 billion dollars among its 161 partners, while Tanzania, a developing country in East Africa, had to share its 2.2 billion dollar gross national product among 25 million people. Even though the figures may now be dated, George maintains that the arguments remain the same.

Bagby (2007) describes how English philosopher Thomas Hobbes, in his book *Leviathan* (1651), considers the life of the human being in his natural state without government or the social contracts that structure civil society and describes such a life as one which is lived in fear of death and danger: *solitary, poor, nasty, brutish and short*, a characterisation that Amartya Sen (2009) attributes to those that live in extreme poverty today. According to Hobbes, in order to avoid this state of being, individuals must sacrifice some rights in order to secure the protection of the sovereign power and subsequently any abuses of this power cannot be resisted. Pogge (2001) agrees with this, stating that people who are preoccupied with the daily struggle for food, in many cases stunted and illiterate, do not have the means to resist their rulers and therefore become subject to oppressive practices which prevent them from changing their situations. The global neoliberal economic system we have now, which is based on free markets, free trade, deregulation and privatisation, is designed by the rich, for the rich. The radical inequalities that now exist are caused and maintained by three main conditions: the legacy of colonisation; the impact of shared institutions which affect the circumstances of poor people through trade, loans, military aid, exports etc; and the widespread exclusion of people from their share of natural resources. Even where countries have corrupt governments in power, their continuing ability to rule often depends on loans provided by the World Bank and IMF in the full knowledge that funds will be diverted to buy the weapons needed to maintain power. In other words, we in the North are causally implicated in the situations of those living in poverty in the South, and therefore have a collective responsibility for these human rights violations. Today, Pogge continues, there is a new chapter in the global book of poverty because today poverty is completely avoidable. Sachs (2005) agrees, believing that global poverty can be eradicated by 2025 if wealthy nations urgently increase the quantity and quality of aid to poor countries. For Pogge, however, eradicating poverty is not a matter of charity; it is a matter of justice, and reform of the global mechanisms and institutions that create and perpetuate inequalities, and oppression is one of the biggest factors needed to achieve this.

Minujin and Nandy (2012) propose the case for a human rights rather than a needs based approach to addressing child poverty not least because human rights frameworks offer internationally agreed standards for living, which the presence of child poverty directly contravenes. Although children's rights are often criticised on the basis that they reflect and promote a global view of childhood from a predominantly liberal Western perspective, the United Nations Convention on the Rights of the Child (UNCRC) has been ratified by all the countries in the world with the exception of the US and Somalia indicating that there are some universal values and a well-defined consensus on what is needed to live a decent and dignified human life. By implication, the Convention places obligations on nation states to examine the relationship between child and state and, by extension, the global economic structures that perpetuate child poverty. It offers the potential for the Convention to be used to hold both governments and key international institutions to account for failing to protect children from the effects of extreme poverty.

Reflective activity

» *What should early childhood practitioners do about child poverty in developing nations?*

» *Try to reflect critically on this question and produce a reasoned response. The following questions may help you to do this:*

– *What assumptions is your argument based on?*

– *What are the strengths and weaknesses of your argument?*

– *How reliable is the information that supports your argument?*

– *What ideas and theories inform your argument and are they consistent with each other?*

– *What are the logical conclusions and implications of your line of reasoning?*

Extended thinking

» Meet with your colleagues and explain to them the logic of your arguments.

» How do you respond to any counter arguments that they may propose?

Chapter reflections

Pogge has convinced me that there has to be a fundamental shift in the institutional structures of our global society if child poverty is to end. I do not accept personal causal responsibility for the many human rights violations inflicted on the countries and peoples of the South because I did not have a choice in the economic system I was born into any more than poverty-stricken children in developing countries did. However, I believe that it is unjust that these children continue to suffer at the hands of an economic system many would say I benefit from (I would not necessarily agree that I benefit from this system, but I will leave this argument for another time) and therefore I have a moral responsibility to try to change it. If Western economies do not respect human rights then we are all at risk of violations, not just those in developing countries. Maybe what is needed is collective action at global level; perhaps a democratically elected world government would at least ensure some co-ordinated working between the nations of the world although, of course, there are many objections to this idea including that it would make the existence of many cultures more difficult and it would be impossible for citizens to leave if they were unhappy. If early childhood practitioners are concerned with protecting children's rights then it is not unreasonable to expect that they should work towards a system of institutional reform. According to Nagel (2005) theories of global justice are still embryonic and therefore perhaps the most useful thing that many early childhood practitioners, policy makers and academics can do is to recognise the importance of the issue of child poverty, keep thinking and talking about it and start trying to alter the perception that alleviating poverty is merely a good cause that they might or might not contribute to.

On the basis that any proper solution to global inequalities is a long way off, I am also convinced that some form of humanitarian assistance is needed in order to help people who are suffering now. I have already countered Hardin's argument with Rosling's view that saving children's lives now will not mean that the population will increase and in fact will ensure that it continues to decrease. In any case, it is difficult to think of any situation where it is morally acceptable to let thousands of children die every day. Singer's argument that we should donate to the point of marginal utility rests on the idea that those who donate will have to take into account that most people will choose not to donate so the amount of money needed to lift people in the developing world out of poverty will have to be raised by relatively few people in affluent countries. If all people with money to spare donated something, nobody would be required to reduce themselves to marginal utility. If this donation was worked into current taxation systems and adjusted according to income level it would involve very little impact on current lifestyles in affluent countries. However, in the absence of effective collective action at a global level it is difficult to see how any donation, which comes with no strings attached and is sensitive to local needs and culture, can do any real harm.

Extended reflections

In the light of the forthcoming Brexit, some people are calling for a discontinuation of Overseas Aid.

» *Reflect on the implications of this to the politics of such a move, and to any potentially harmful effects upon the current recipients of this aid.*

» *Where do you stand on this issue?*

Further reading

Penn, H (2005) *Unequal Childhoods: Young Children's Lives in Poor Countries.* Abingdon: Routledge.

A detailed consideration of child poverty and inequalities in childhood, both within and between nations, with a focus on case studies in four particular countries: Kazakhstan, Swaziland, India and Brazil.

Minujin, A and Nandy, S (2012) *Global Child Poverty and Well-Being. Measurement, Concepts, Policy and Action.* Bristol: Policy Press.

A comprehensive and thoughtful analysis of the issue of child poverty and the way forward, with contributions from many of the key writers in the field.

References

Alvaredo, F, Atkinson, A, Piketty, T and Saez, E (2013) The World Top Incomes Database. Available from: http://topincomes.g-mond.parisschoolofeconomics.eu/ (accessed 12 February 2014).

Andrews, E (2010) Christian Missions and Colonial Empires Reconsidered: A Black Evangelist in West Africa, 1766–1816. *Journal of Church and State*, 51(4): 663–91.

Bagby, L (2007) *Hobbes's Leviathan: Reader's Guide.* New York: Continuum.

Canella, G and Viruru, R (2004) *Childhood and Postcolonization: Power, Education and Contemporary Practice.* London: RoutledgeFalmer.

Child Poverty Action Group (2015) The UK Poverty Line. Available from: www.cpag.org.uk/content/uk-poverty-line (accessed 29 November 2016).

Crouch, C and Stokl, J (eds) (2014) *In the Name of God: The Bible in the Colonial Discourse of Empire.* Leiden, NL: Koninklijke Brill NV.

Elder, L (2010) Reason to Live. *Times Higher Education Supplement,* 18 February.

Engle, P and Black, M (2008) The Effect of Poverty on Child Development and Educational Outcomes. *New York Academy of Sciences*, 1136: 243–56.

Felipe, J, Kumar, U and Abdon, A (2010) How Rich Countries Became Rich and Why Poor Countries Remain Poor: It's the Economic Structure ... Duh! Working Paper 644. New York: Levy Economics Institute.

George, S (1976) *How the Other Half Dies: The Real Reasons for World Hunger*. Harmondsworth: Penguin.

George, S (1988) *A Fate Worse than Debt*. Harmondsworth: Penguin.

Gordon, D, Nandy, S, Pantaziz, C, Pemberton, S and Townsend, P (2003) *Child Poverty in the Developing World*. Bristol: Policy Press.

Hardin, G (1968) The Tragedy of the Commons. *Science*, 169(3859): 1243–1248.

Hardin, G (1974a) Lifeboat Ethics: The Case against Helping the Poor. *Psychology Today*, 8: 38–43.

Hardin, G (1974b) Living on a Lifeboat. *Bioscience*, 24(10): 561–8.

Hardin, G (1999) *The Ostrich Factor: Our Population Myopia*. Oxford: Oxford University Press.

Hilman, D (2013) This World: Don't Panic – The Truth about Population. BBC2, Wingspan Productions [Documentary].

Longstaff, S (2013) The Unexamined Life Is Not Worth Living. *New Philosopher*, 1(1): 3–16.

Malthus, T (1798) *An Essay on the Principle of Population*. Oxford: Oxford World's Classics.

Marris, R (1999) *Ending Poverty*. London: Thames and Hudson.

McNamara, R (1973) World Bank Annual Meeting Speech, 24 September: Nairobi.

Milanovic, B (2012) Global Income Inequality by the Numbers, in History and Now. Policy Research Working Paper 6259, World Bank Development Research Group.

Minujin, A and Nandy, S (2012) *Global Child Poverty and Well-Being: Measurement, Concepts, Policy and Action*. Bristol: Policy Press.

Moyo, D (2009) *Dead Aid: Why Aid Is Not Working and Why There Is a Better Way for Africa*. New York: Farrar, Strauss and Giroux.

Nagel, T (2005) The Problem of Global Justice. *Philosophy and Public Affairs*, 33(2): 1–19.

Ortiz, I, Daniels, L and Engilbertsdóttir, S (2012) *Child Poverty and Inequality: New Perspectives*. New York: UNICEF.

Penn, H (2005) *Unequal Childhoods: Young Children's Lives in Poor Countries*. Abingdon: Routledge.

Pogge, T (2001) Eradicating Systemic Poverty: Brief for a Global Resources Dividend. *Journal of Human Development*, 2(1): 59–77.

Pogge, T (2005) World Poverty and Human Rights. *Ethics and International Affairs*, 19(1): 1–7.

Pogge, T (2012) *Poverty, Human Rights and the Global Order: Framing the Post-2015 Agenda*. Bergen: Comparative Research Programme on Poverty (CROP).

Riddell, R (2008) *Does Foreign Aid Really Work?* Oxford: Oxford University Press.

Rosling, H (2006) *Global Health: An Introductory Textbook*. Lund, Sweden: Studentlitteratur.

Sachs, J (2005) *The End of Poverty: Economic Possibilities for Our Time*. New York: Penguin Books.

Sen, A (2009) *The Idea of Justice*. Cambridge, MA: Belknap Press.

Singer, P (1999) The Singer Solution to World Poverty. *The New York Times*, 5 September.

Stiglitz, J (2003) Democratizing the International Monetary Fund and the World Bank: Governance and Accountability. *Governance: An International Journal of Policy, Administrations and Institutions*, 16(1): 111–39.

UNESCO (2015) *Education for All 2000–2015. Achievements and Challenges*. Paris: UNESCO.

UNICEF (2005) *The State of the World's Children: Childhood under Threat*. New York: UNICEF.

UNICEF (2009) *The State of the World's Children. Celebrating 20 Years of the Convention on the Rights of the Child*. New York: UNICEF.

UNICEF (2012a) *Levels and Trends in Child Mortality*. New York: UNICEF.

UNICEF (2012b) The Progress of Nations 2000. [online] Available from: www.unicef.org/pon00/immu1.htm (accessed 21 December 2013).

UNICEF (2013) *Improving Child Nutrition: The Achievable Imperative for Global Progress*. New York: UNICEF.

United Nations (2015) Sustainable Development Goals. Available from: www.un.org/sustainabledevelopment/sustainable-development-goals/ (accessed 29 November 2016).

Watts, M (2013) *Silent Violence: Food, Famine and Peasantry in Northern Nigeria*. Athens, GA: University of Georgia Press.

World Bank (2013) The State of the Poor: Where Are the Poor, Where Is Extreme Poverty Harder To End, and What Is The Current Profile Of The World's Poor? *Economic Premise*, 125: October.

World Bank (2014) Data, Afghanistan. [online] Available from: http://data.worldbank.org/country/afghanistan (accessed 16 February 2014).

World Bank (2015) Global Poverty Line Update. [online] Available from: www.worldbank.org/en/topic/poverty/brief/global-poverty-line-faq (accessed 29 November 2016).

10 Reflecting upon childhood, creativity and play

JAYNE DALY

She took a step further in – then two or three steps – always expecting to feel the woodwork against the tips of her fingers. But she could not feel it. 'This must be a simply enormous wardrobe!' thought Lucy, going still further in and pushing the soft folds of the coats aside to make room for her. Then she noticed that there was something crunching under her feet. 'I wonder if that's more mothballs,' she thought, stooping down to feel it with her hand. But instead of feeling the hard smooth wood of the floor of the wardrobe, she felt something soft and powdery and extremely cold. 'This is very queer,' she said, and went on a step or two further.

Next moment she found that what was rubbing against her face and hands was no longer soft fur but something hard and rough and even prickly. 'Why, it is just like branches of trees!' exclaimed Lucy. And then she saw that there was a light ahead of her; not a few inches away where the back of the wardrobe ought to have been, but a long way off. Something cold and soft was falling on her. A moment later she found that she was standing in the middle of a wood at night-time with snow under her feet and snowflakes falling through the air.

(C S Lewis, 1950, p 14)

Introduction

I can still remember the anticipation and trepidation in terms of what happens next when my primary school teacher first introduced us to *The Chronicles of Narnia* all those years ago. I sat on the floor cross-legged in the classroom, listening eagerly among my fidgeting classmates, when my teacher suddenly announced, *'Okay children, it's home time; we will pick this up again tomorrow afternoon'*. What? My beloved teacher had let me down! It was like a Saturday morning ABC picture show: *What will happen to Flash Gordon as he is left in a pickle?... Find out next week!* I was devastated. How could I wait until tomorrow afternoon? What was the magical world behind the Wardrobe? I would investigate when I got home.

I only lived across the road from my school, so collection was a very grown-up affair; you could literally see into my house from the school gates. So at home time my mum stood at the bottom of the pathway to our house and watched me cross the road. I gave my mum a fleeting hug and ran past her up to the bedroom I shared with my sisters. In those days, wardrobes were much sturdier and not the *throwaway* flat-packs we see today. It had a lock, and I searched around the bedroom looking for any new hiding places my elder sisters may have put the key. Yes! Found it in a pretty pink glass trinket bowl on the dresser. I nervously unlocked the wardrobe and stepped in among the 1960s coats. They were not fur as Lucy had experienced, but there was a smell of mothballs! I tried to touch the floor as Lucy had done, hoping to feel snow, but no, just the handle of a 1950s discarded handbag and a pair of winkle pickers (a pointy style of shoe popular in the 1950s/60s, worn by male and female British rock and roll fans). What about the back of the wardrobe? I knocked on the wooden panel, as if someone might let me into the new world I had heard about, the world behind the wardrobe, *Narnia*.

The Chronicles of Narnia, particularly *The Lion, the Witch and the Wardrobe* and *The Magician's Nephew* (Lewis, 1950) inspired my imagination as a child – a world full of adventure, secret compartments and doors. When the *Chronicles* became films more recently I realised at an older age that there was a much more frightening aspect to these books, but as a child they inspired my imagination to think outside the doom and gloom of 1960s and 70s post-war Britain. James and Brookfield (2014) explain that in order to advance as human beings, we must firstly develop our imagination and in essence this will nurture our reflective thinking. They suggest:

> *Without the capacity to imagine a different world that is more beautiful than the one in which we live, change is impossible. Why would we strive for something better or different if we didn't have the imagination of a more beautiful way of living?*
> (James and Brookfield, 2014, p 3)

Furthermore, they highlight the importance of the use of the creative imagination and play in learning. Not just for children but for all of us. Singer and Singer wrote in 1990 about the creative and imaginative world of play, suggesting that our childhood memories of play are often special to us.

> *Memories of pretend play are often associated with a special person who encouraged play, told fantastic stories, or modelled play.*
> (Singer and Singer, 1990, p 4)

This chapter explores the imagination, creativity and playfulness of young children. It uses scenario case studies and activities to help you to reflect upon your encounter of children's use of imagination, creativity, play and playfulness in learning and development. It reflects and gives examples of my own experiences of these playful and creative moments both from my childhood and from an adult perspective. It asks whether you encourage or condemn children for this, whether you join in or reprimand and whether you really understand what is meant by creativity and playfulness. In other words, do you understand the importance of play pedagogy?

James and Brookfield amusingly denounce some of the stringent teaching, learning and assessment regimes tutors and supervisors put older students through. As they reflect upon the work of Bohannon (2011) by asking, *Why shouldn't doctoral students dance their PhDs?* (James and Brookfield, 2014, p 3), I ask, why shouldn't your youngest children be allowed and encouraged to jump in puddles, to make snow angels, to make guns, to climb trees, to play superheros, to recreate a piece of architecture out of recycled materials, and actually develop their creative and beautiful minds rather than being stifled? The *beautiful mind* is something which I have reflected upon many times and echo in this chapter. Perhaps it is time to reflect on how you are fostering that beautiful mind in children by supporting them, setting challenges for them, opening up a world of opportunities for them to explore their own creativity and to put that *beautiful mind into action* (De Bono, 2004, p 224).

Reflecting upon creativity

Fisher (2004) asks the question, *What is creativity?* and draws on the work of Gardner (1997), Robinson (2001) and Lucas (2001) with the diverse nature of their definitions of creativity. The challenge here is that all three authors have varying opinions, but the common thread that Fisher (2004, p 8) records is that:

> *Creativity is seen as a property of people (who we are), processes or products (what we make) [but argues that] The processes that underpin creativity also underpin the evolution of life.*
>
> (Fisher, 2004, p 8)

More recently, James and Brookfield (2014) also recognised that there are many definitions of creativity, and attribute this to the context of the discussion; however, they very clearly and cleverly link the word *creativity* to imagination, play and reflection, by suggesting that without reflection you cannot be creative in your vision. Their writing suggests that in order to unravel learning potential, you must be allowed to be put into a position where you are using your imaginative and creative skills in order to foster your own identity. However, we are not considering adults here; we are considering very young children and as Roberts (2006) pointed out, young children haven't quite mastered the concept of taking responsibility for themselves. You therefore tend to protect children, because, as Roberts suggests, *we are the adults and we know best* (p 62). As adults you might be 'wise old owls' in comparison to children (as my son used to call his grandmother when he was small; often being scolded by my mother growling, *Less of the old, young man*), but does being wise make you creative? You may know a lot; you may have experienced a lot, and learnt from your experiences but do those experiences make you more or less creative? Are you more guarded in your creativity because of some of your personal experiences or the experiences of others? Are you turning your children and the next generation into a generation of cotton wool children? Are you becoming overprotective and therefore stifling that beautiful mind in your children? Palmer recognised this in her book *Toxic Childhood*, originally published in 2006 (updated in 2015). In one chapter Palmer (2006) lists a number of things a child should do before they are ten years old. I tested this out on my 27-year-old son and my husband and both were able to tick every item on the list, except my son asked what *Poohsticks* were, and my husband suggested that Palmer had missed *scrumping for apples*! – something which I assured him Palmer would not be encouraging children to do! While Palmer had a good overview, you must consider that not all children are lucky enough to visit the seaside, to bury a friend in sand, or to have a garden to camp out in, as she suggests. However, the concept she has goes back to my point that there are opportunities available for children to be creative, to make a den, to climb a tree, to paint using feet as well as hands, to lie in the snow and make snow angels and to do some of the more contentious things such as superhero or weapon play.

I remember being inspired to write my dissertation for my undergraduate foundation degree following the words and work of Loris Malaguzzi and his *Hundred Languages of Children* (Edwards et al, 1998). My thirst for this creative concept of children's learning and development has lived with me ever since, in terms of the Reggio approach to early years. Malaguzzi recognised the young child as a creative and capable individual learner. He called his concept the *Hundred Languages of Children* as he suggested that a child's capable creative mind opens up a world of possibilities for their learning. Malaguzzi suggested that the *Hundred Languages of Children* was children expressing their thoughts, their feelings and concepts through their creativity. I would also suggest expressing their *beautiful mind*. There are, according to Malaguzzi, occasions when children might also express their frustrations in the same way.

Taking this creative concept back into the workplace, however, was a somewhat disappointing experience at that time, as my colleagues seemed much less enthusiastic about this. I think the problem at the time was that my colleagues and I were at odds in relation to how children were perceived. Today, with the introduction of the *Statutory Framework for the Early Years Foundation Stage* (DfE, 2014), early years practitioners work within the concept that children should be perceived as unique and individual. The Reggio approach fosters that uniqueness in children, understanding that in order to recognise each child's individuality you must show them respect in terms of their competencies. You must listen to them, and recognise that you must encourage their independence and creative mind by allowing them to experience new things. These new things may be risky, they may be contentious, but the independent and unique child needs to become familiar with these things in order to become a resilient, confident and capable young person and adult (Abbott and Nutbrown, 2001; Thornton and Brunton 2014).

Stuck in the messy play time warp

One of the things I encountered when I shared my ideas of the creative Reggio concept was the tendency for other colleagues to support the use of the messy play areas within the setting as the only method of engaging creative minds. I am not suggesting for one minute that these messy play areas were not a good thing; even today Barnardo's (2016) promotes on their website, *Bringing Five to Thrive Alive*, workouts for parents to do with their babies and toddlers, which includes simple creative activities to promote brain development, but I just wanted more for the children, beyond the messy play area or the home corner.

Malaguzzi's image of children was that they were connected to other children and adults. He realised their potential; these strong, commanding and capable young people. He also recognised that as educators you must understand this, and give children the time to research and discuss their ideas with each other and with adults. Time to think, reflect and transform. Time to go beyond the messy play area; to be allowed to be creative in whatever aspect of learning they choose. On her visit to Reggio Emilia, Abbott (2001) reflects upon a recognition that children there were given time to use their creative skills, to co-operate in their projects. She does not suggest that this kind of work was not being undertaken in the UK (in fact, the opposite) but her chapter makes some poignant observations about the value of play and playfulness in play pedagogy, as well as understanding how children use their imagination and creativity.

Abbott (2001) also recognises the bond Reggio children have with their teacher, which supports them in building the strong and resilient personality that Malaguzzi spoke about (Edwards et al, 1998), and the fact that children are supported by the same adults as they progress. On this point, Abbott reflects on the trauma that children in the UK often face in terms of effective transitions from teacher to teacher and setting to setting at such a young age. She recognises that as much as we try, we still don't appear to have got this quite right. I suggest that you, as a reader, might put yourself in the child's position and reflect. If you are anxious about something, does this stifle the creative, imaginative and beautiful mind? Therefore, is this going to have an impact on your learning? Children need to be emotionally ready to learn, as without opportunities for creative play or playfulness when making key environmental transitions, children will not relax into their new surroundings, and therefore it is likely that this will have an impact on their learning.

Have you ever faced a difficult situation, a trauma, a loss, stress at work and a loved one says to you, *Let's get away from all this, let's stop a while to reflect, ready to go again*. The Thomson holiday company TV advertisement from 2014 imitates this situation well as *Simon the Ogre* (Thomson TV advertisement, 2014) gradually turns back into *Simon the adult* as he finds time for creativeness and play with his family. This shows to me the importance of creativity and play for all of us. The creative recreation allows Simon time to forget his work issues and rejoin his family, time to reflect and to reset his timer. Children are no different; as Malaguzzi said, children need time too. Singer and Singer (1990) also wrote about the importance of time in engaging in creative play. They suggested that:

> children may play one game again and again. Each time, mastery of the materials, the language and the plot is enhanced through repeated practice... Children who are deeply in an enchanting game of pretend or a challenging game of skill find little reason to be bored.

> (Singer and Singer, 1990, p 11)

As they suggested, children need time and space to be creative and to be supported in building resilience to disturbance in their lives.

Disturbance or trauma for children in today's world can come in many forms, from that first step of making that transition to leaving parents for the first time to go to nursery, to the extremes of the abused child, the disabled child, the bereaved child, the refugee child. Using the concept of the beautiful and creative mind to encourage children's creativity and play, you can help them to overcome this. You may see examples of this this in hospitals where sick children are supported with play therapies, but you also need to be mindful of this in your settings, particularly in light of the number of transitional difficulties children are likely to face in today's world.

As a student or practitioner you may feel that you want to make a difference to children's lives and learning, but you may not have the confidence to do this alone. When you share your ideas with others they may not have the same vision or understand your thinking or logic. It is possible that you suppress your imaginative and creative thoughts and stay in your 'comfort zone'. Not a good move! This lack of personal reflection can make you stale and your beautiful mind becomes distorted by your worries; hence your creativity is stifled. It is therefore vital that you understand that you have an important part to play in supporting children's creativity, taking them beyond the norm, taking on board their ideas and most importantly recognising when they are ready to make transitions as individuals. Thornton and Brunton (2014) recognise the *powerful image of the child* (p 15) and the importance of adults working alongside them; however, they warn of a tendency to overtake or stifle children's creativity because of a 'we know best' attitude. Observe yes; listen yes; but with a co-creative (but always safe) approach.

CASE STUDY

Scenario 1

Little Smiles nursery is facing an Ofsted inspection in the near future. It has recently appointed a new manager and she has challenged the team to find new and exciting ideas to develop the setting in order to promote children's creativity beyond the *messy play area*. Outdoor play is limited and the budget cannot stretch to much new equipment. Sofia is a newly qualified, newly appointed Early Years Teacher to the setting. As a 'breath of fresh air' she has been put in charge of leading this difficult task. She has a number of personal ideas which are new and exciting and begins the task of sharing these with the team, but the rest of the team are reluctant to get involved and continue to 'play it safe' in the messy play area.

Reflective activity

» List the kind of ideas you might expect Sofia to be suggesting to enhance and encourage children's creative thinking given the limited budget, her qualifications and the points already discussed, particularly in relation to the Reggio approach.

» Why do you think that the team may be reluctant to move beyond the 'norm' and messy play areas in developing creative ideas? List your thoughts.

» Think about times when you have opposed change. Why was this? List your thoughts.

»   *What do you think will be the impact of this situation on the children?*

»   *How might Sofia move forward in her new leadership role to make this task a success in order to benefit the children?*

Extended thinking

Read Chapter 11 of this book.

»   *Sofia is well aware of the important role she has undertaken in making a difference to children's creative and beautiful minds. However, was her approach in motivating the team in this case right?*

»   *How might she improve her team leadership skills for future tasks given the points discussed in Chapter 11?*

»   *What might she consider better next time, in terms of the children?*

Reflecting upon play and playfulness

Hallet (2016) defines play and playfulness as *integral to the ways humans learn and interact across generations, cultures and contexts* (p 65). She makes reference to the work of Wood (2010) and Bruce's (2005) 'Twelve features of play'. Playfulness, Hallet advances, comes in the form of the mood and spirit of play; play can be carried out by anyone (although we often associate this with children) and is often a creative and dynamic action.

Moyles (2010) asks you to reflect throughout her text on your own values and beliefs about play. Moyles defines quality play as *pure* play (p 20) led by the children. She asks you to consider whether you understand the meaning of *play and playful pedagogies* (p 13) and to critically reflect upon the benefits to children. Do you as a practitioner understand how children learn through play? Do you understand its educational value? She makes the poignant point that you often present the statement *children learn through play*. She then continues to observe that often when you reflect upon how much time a child is actually engaging in self-initiated imaginative and creative play, in comparison to adult-led activities, it is relatively limited. Some of the reasons she suggests are based on target setting, compliance, and pressure to get children engaged in formal learning such as reading and writing.

Considering this viewpoint, adults must ponder play and playfulness on a daily basis. You want the best outcomes for your children and for children to reach their maximum individual potential. You therefore need to consider when the children actually do have the opportunity for pure play and playfulness. Sensitively observe and note children's learning, from their self-initiated imaginative and creative experiments within our all-encompassing playful teaching strategies. You must note whether these teaching strategies are as open ended as you can possibly make them to ensure the concept of Moyles' idea of playful pedagogy is being applied (Moyles, 2010).

You must also address the point that if you are making the statement that children are learning through play then you must reflect and demonstrate that you know how this process is happening. You must know how you know. Knowing about knowing is a metacognitive process. Tarrant and Holt (2016) define metacognition as knowledge that *is defined as what we know about ourselves as a thinker and learner* (p 1). They go on to suggest that as educators this process is important, as you can not only use this process yourself; you can also determine how much the children know about their own knowledge and learning. For an adult or child to know how they learn and to be aware of this helps them to become a better learner. Knowing how, or indeed, if, a child is learning from *pure* play and playfulness must not be restricted to a statement. It must be something that is thought about by the adult, reflected upon and used to determine the next steps for individual progress, given the particular need of the child.

Hallet (2016), like Moyles, recognises how you may often have to justify play and playfulness as pedagogy to those that do not consider child-led activities as a learning process. Her poem, 'Are the children *just playing* today?', demonstrates this:

> *So – are the children just playing today?*
> *Through their play, the children learn how to;*
> *Care and love, build, create, imagine, write, read, talk and count.*
> *Understand who they are and who they may become.*
> *They are learning how to communicate and relate to others.*
> *And to understand the everyday world they live in.*
> *Yes, the children are just playing –*
> *And – they are learning today, with their bricks, dolls, paint and clay.*
>
> (Hallet, 2016, p 73)

In 2001 Jenkinson asked readers to look much more closely at play in her publication, the *Genius of Play*. She stressed the importance of people who sanction play; people who understand that play improves the well-being of the child. Further, she noted that through their imagination being stimulated, their cognitive skills will also develop (Jenkinson, 2001). Errors will probably be made; you must show faith in children's abilities and show them tolerance and support for when things do not go as planned in play. I believe that you have the ability to use your beautiful mind to understand the genius of play, to become a play genius through critical reflection, noting how the pure play of children can be enhanced by careful listening, observation and co-construction, and by being tolerant of playfulness. The play genius needs to creatively know when to step in (to keep children safe) and when to take a step back to allow pure play time.

You must understand the diverse nature of children's worlds and their family circumstances, as I have already highlighted earlier in this chapter. Blundell (2016) suggests that you must also consider the space that children use in order to develop their creativity in their play. Singer and Singer (1990) also referred to the environment and play spaces. They considered that having a large house or open space does not guarantee a child will use the space effectively for imaginative or creative play; they proposed that the child needs to be encouraged by the adult in a co-constructive way to use the space effectively to foster playfulness. Blundell (2016) recognises that in today's society, for many children their surrounding environment is often only viewed via the window of a car or some other form of transport as children's *free play has become circumscribed by adult world agendas whether at home, in school or in other organised recreational settings* (Blundell, 2016, p 102). This suggests that the adult often has other agendas, something which differs from the interpretation of Singer and Singer's (1990) proposed ideologies of childhood memories of play and the significance of the adult. This suggests that as a *play genius* you may need to develop your thoughts too about the environment that children are playing within. Children have never been to the seaside? Then bring the 'seaside' to the child!

Reflective activity

» What does being a play genius *mean to you?*

» Do you aspire to be your own interpretation of a play genius?

» How will you need to change in order to achieve this? Make a list.

Extended thinking

» Do you constantly reflect on your day spent with children or how might you improve your reflective practice?

» Do some of the points Hallet and Moyles make with regard to play and playfulness sound familiar? Think about examples from your experience.

» Reflect on your strengths and weaknesses in engaging children in co-constructed play and playfulness. Make a list and develop an action plan for reflective change.

To be or not to be Luke Skywalker or Princess Leia, that is the question!

Another of my earliest memories as a child was that of my days engaged in weapon and superhero play. I was a bit of a tomboy; most of the children in my street were boys so I tended to engage in *their* play. This included many war games; as was typical of the day, not too many years after the Second World War had ended. Popper (2013) recognises the contentious subject of weapon and superhero play, including attitudes towards culture and gender stereotypes. I recognise here, that my own description of this type of play was of a masculine pastime; as a female I was the one that was continually *mown down* as the enemy by an imaginary Tommy gun (a type of machine gun) on a number of occasions! This was typical of the days before the Sexual Discrimination Act 1975 (National Archives, 2016). This was because I was *just a girl* and girls didn't have Tommy guns, oh no, girls had pretty lace dresses and ribbons in their hair. They didn't get engaged in play that concerned *boys' stuff*, did they? Well, I did!

There was nothing stereotypical about me; despite my mother's best efforts. The evidence: the pretty lace from the edge of my Sunday best dress (made with my mother's fair hands) being wrapped around the wheel of our *Tank* (a makeshift go-cart made out of planks of wood and pram wheels). I was scolded for this, yes, but boy, it was worth it. I had such fun! Did this weapon or war play make me want to go out and be aggressive towards someone or shoot someone in later life? No, but in today's society there is some trepidation in terms of allowing children the freedom to play in whatever way they choose; to use their creativity to engage in all kinds of imaginative play.

I must clarify here that I am not suggesting for one minute that we should encourage children to be violent towards one another. Children need to understand boundaries. Popper (2013) considers that they also need to develop a sense of morality and the strength of good over evil. Popper's (2013) book highlights some of the current practices regarding weapon and superhero play and the *zero tolerance approach* (p 10) by some settings. Popper (2013) recognises and properly considers the points taken from literature in terms of childhood aggression, but also notes the balanced view that having a zero tolerance approach is not necessarily the answer, suggesting that understanding the concept of good over evil in children's play can actually support them in *overcoming potential anxieties and in understanding how to negotiate a peaceful solution* (p 10). Moreover the idea that children can develop qualities within their personality that strengthen their ability to be resolute and resilient, by engaging in creative play, can only be a positive in my view.

Palmer (2006) addresses the point that if you are not careful, children will live their lives in fear. She considers that as adults we must support children in putting fear in its place. How will you do this if you do not allow children to understand the concepts of what is real and what is not? As Palmer (2006) suggests:

> very young children don't need encouragement to use their imagination but parents [and I believe some practitioners] need to be discouraged from stopping them.
>
> (Palmer, 2006, p 247)

CASE STUDY

Scenario 2

Cuddles Nursery has a zero tolerance approach in relation to any war, weapon or superhero play. Adam is a new member of the staff team. He is witness to three four-year-old children playing with stickle bricks, and they begin to form these into gun shapes. They get up and start to run around 'shooting' each other. '*Let's play Star Wars*', one of them suggests. '*Yeah, you be Luke Skywalker, I will be Darth Vader and Ellie you be Princess Leia*'. They rush into the dressing up area to complete their look. Adam is watching the children carefully and he is assessing their behaviour in terms of safety. The children are doing nothing wrong but he knows that he should approach them, but he allows them to continue their play. Just then Adam's supervisor notes what is going on. She goes over to the dressing up corner. '*Err children*', she says, '*You know the rule; no guns in nursery*'. She quietly leans over to Adam and asks if she can catch up with him at break. Adam is aware that he will be reprimanded for not dealing with this incident.

Reflective activity

»   *What is your opinion of Adam's actions? Do you feel he was right or wrong to allow the children to engage in playing with 'weapons' and potential superhero play?*

»   *Reflect on the nursery's decision to have this zero tolerance policy in place. Do you think they may have good reason or are they overreacting?*

» *What might be a good compromise moving forward? List suggestions.*

» *What things do you need to consider if you are allowing children to engage in weapon and superhero play? What are the potential benefits, if any?*

Extended thinking

» *Read Popper, S (2013)* Rethinking Superhero and Weapon Play. *Maidenhead, Berkshire: Open University Press.*

» *Consider your answers to the reflective activity after reading Popper (2013). Have any of your viewpoints changed? If so what? Why do you think this is?*

The health and safety minefield

So why are some practitioners and some parents so reluctant to allow children the freedom to develop their self-initiated creative side; to use their imagination as Palmer (2006) suggests? This is an interesting reflective point, as I was reading in the *Guardian* newspaper recently that currently parents of Muslim children are afraid to allow their children to engage in certain types of activities or express their religious views for fear of their child being put on anti-radicalisation programmes or removed from the family. Quinn (2016) informs that one four-year-old's drawing was reported by nursery staff to his mother, suggesting they may have to report to the Prevent Channel initiative programme (HM Government, 2015) as the cucumber he had drawn looked like a *cooker bomb*. When questioned, the four-year-old had no idea what a *cooker bomb* was, but when shown a cucumber (which he had drawn) he said it was a *cuker bum* (Quinn, 2016). The child was merely drawing a picture of his father cutting a cucumber. While this case was not officially reported, there are many more cases that are. It is surprising to know, as Quinn reports, that as many as 300 under-18-year-olds were referred to the programme between June and August 2016. It is understandable that you may be worried; you want to do everything in your power to protect children from such influences (HM Government, 2015) but you must also ask whether you are going back to the point here that, *we are the adults and we know best!* Media images of tragedies and violence put us into a frenzy but that frenzy can sometimes create panic, which has an effect on us promoting children's creative thinking.

This is only one example of how this may happen. This anxious action of parents and practitioners to media and tragedy is not new. In the 1960s when I was growing up in Staffordshire, the A34 murders (Hawkes, 1970) meant that my parents and teachers kept an additional watchful eye over us. At the time, this felt stifling from a childhood perspective, but after being a mother and practitioner myself, I now understand the protective stance that adults take in order to protect the vulnerable. Woods and Hall (2013) recognise the challenges that face the adult in terms of children's playfulness and their desire to take control of the learning environment. After all, as you get older you lose some of your playfulness, as it is replaced by anxieties and tensions in terms of hazard and risk. Woods and Hall (2013) further note that these tensions are additionally exasperated if the child or children in question have additional or complex needs.

Children are precious, a gift, and you are understandably fearful that someone will take that precious gift away. As a practitioner and then manager of a setting, I would often re-evaluate nursery policy based on media-reported tragedies, for example, tying chains on blinds to keep them out of reach, or reviewing the snack policy for choking or allergy risk, and banning mobile phones in playrooms (I am sure if I was still in practice today I would be out there with the best of you protecting the next vulnerable child). When it came to being spontaneous, however, I was the first to allow the children to jump in puddles, make snow angels, build a den out of curtains and wood, make an 'aeroplane' out of lengths of drainpipe or support the children in creating their own seaside adventure using the sand and water tray, by taking them *out* of the messy play area. Yes, it was okay to put the teddy bears from the maths corner into the sand or the stickle bricks from the construction area into the handbags. Yes, it was okay to wear the bunny hat out of the dressing up area all day because it made the child feel secure.

In my early career days as a registered childminder, I hadn't taken the first steps to educate myself about the concepts and theories of child development, and children learning through creative, imaginative play. To me it was just what children did and it was what I did as a child, as I have already outlined. It was natural to me; no one ever did a risk assessment, and I guess I was just lucky that I made it through my playful childhood without too many skirmishes. You now know, however, that today's world is ever changing, and the risk of legal action and litigation are all around us. So what do we do?

As Jenkinson (2001) posited, *The future direction of children's play rests in our hands* (p 140), so you need to reconsider spaces that you are creating for and around the child:

> *Where is the space between repression and freedom? Can we strike a balance between forbidding and permitting?*
>
> (Jenkinson, 2001, p 140)

So can you strike the balance? You probably know what you need to do. You know that children's well-being and safety is your prime concern but surely you can't wrap children in cotton wool (Palmer, 2006; Palmer, 2015)? Blundell's (2016) research recognises that as an adult you are probably *islanding children*, as the only places that children are allowed to go are those that you choose for them as you transport them from play space to play space. Surely children must be allowed to make mistakes and reflect upon these mistakes? They must be allowed to use their imagination, their creativity and take risk, and you need to challenge them to do so. Blundell (2016) reports that children play outside less frequently because of parental anxieties in relation to traffic and stranger danger and highlights some high-profile cases of child abduction to support his points. He then goes on, however, to discuss the freedom that Finnish children have in their country, where it has become the norm for children at the age of seven years to travel independently to places within walking distance. He refers to the work of Gillis (2008, cited in Blundell, 2016, p 112), who reflects sadly on the:

> *stranded children, ever more dependent on adults to transport them from island to island and to keep them on schedule in their increasingly hurried lives.*

So where is the creativity here? Where are the beautiful minds? Where is the time for children? Where is the freedom of children? Where is the choice for children? As the adult and co-constructor you have an important job to do.

CASE STUDY

Scenario 3

Little Daisy's childminding services see a mother and daughter team, Jean and Joanne, undertaking the care of two baby boys under one year and twin girls aged three. Little Daisy's is based in a large house in a quiet cul-de-sac. Jean and Joanne are looking to expand their business in the near future, and have spent a considerable amount of money on toys and equipment in the indoor spaces that are not occupied by the family. The extension/veranda at the side of the house is equipped with child-size furniture and commercial toys. There is a sand pit and water tray and easel for painting and drawing. There is also a quiet area for the children to rest and look at books. The childminders call this the children's safe place and it is indeed well equipped. The veranda leads to a large fenced garden space, which is not overlooked. It has flowers, a herb garden, baby and child-friendly places to sit, a bird table and some swings, with potential space for children to play. There is also an area with junk boxes, sand pit, ball pool and a large outdoor tent with dressing up clothes.

The parents Donna, Elaine and Ranjit drop their children off here at the setting every morning at 8am promptly. All are collected by 5pm. The children enjoy their time here and the girls' mother Donna ensures that they attend pony riding, swimming and ballet classes on alternate evenings when she collects them. Ranjit takes her baby to be cared for by her mother three times a week in the evenings, while she attends a gym class. Elaine, as a single mother, does not have any extended family, but she meets with her friends and their babies once a week in the evening at the local community centre crèche and attends the slimming club.

Reflective activity

It certainly seems like Jean and Joanne are investing well in their business.

»   *Think about the activities that Jean and Joanne have provided for the children. While they are investing in and changing the scope of their business, what else might they consider when supporting the co-construction of creativity and play?*

»   *Use your beautiful mind and list your creative ideas.*

Extended thinking

Donna seems to be lucky enough to be able to afford to take her children to activities outside of the setting. Ranjit and Elaine have their schedules too. Reflect on Gillis' (2008) point about islanding children.

»   *What are your views?*

»   *Are these mothers islanding their children?*

»   *Discuss how the childminders can creatively support these parents in varying the play experiences on a daily basis.*

Chapter reflections

This chapter has explored reflections upon the imagination, creativity and playfulness of young children. It challenged you to reflect upon how you use your imagination to nurture reflective thinking and your beautiful mind to make a difference to children and to you, to support children in developing their imagination and creativity beyond the norm and to imagine a more beautiful world than the one in which we live. Fisher's (2004) point that creativity underpins life progression demonstrates how powerful a theme this is, something which Malaguzzi recognised long ago. The connections that James and Brookfield (2014) skilfully make from creativity, to imagination, to play and reflection and demonstrates how closely these points are interlinked; it almost feels like without one you cannot have the other and that somehow they are combined as one. As an adult you can now reflect and ponder on whether we truly respect play as an all-encompassing genius. You can now consider your thoughts of one genius; the genius of play (Jenkinson, 2001); the genius of playfulness; creativity; imagination and reflection. You need to reflect upon your own practice and note if, when and why we suppress children in their pure play (Moyles, 2010), and to recognise that playful learning and teaching strategies must encompass the idea of pure play and playfulness. You need to reflect on the statement the children are just playing (Hallet, 2016) and show your knowledge of the learning context within the play. Most of all, you need to try to avoid being so fearful. You need to have confidence in your ability to recognise that there are times when children need to take risks in their play.

Extended reflections

As an adult you are challenged to recognise the diverse experiences and circumstances of children and the effects these may have on them, in terms of their ability and freedom to enjoy their play environments (Blundell, 2016). You are challenged to observe, keep children safe, but recognise and understand children's needs and support their resilience through times of hardship in their lives with play therapies. Above all, you are dared to reflect upon and recognise your ability and failings as adults in ensuring the co-construction of play. You have heard that children's creativity and play is essential to childhood and children's learning and development. You have also identified that play is not just a 'time filler' while you engage children in schedules or target setting. As adults you need to observe, co-construct and rejoice in the fact that you are supporting children in making a difference to their lives as well as their learning. This chapter should inspire you not to be dismissive of play, but to use our beautiful minds to make playfulness significant in a child's life. You will have noted that play can be used as a wonderful therapy for you as well but that play needs time (Thomson TV advertisement, 2014). Remember that children need time too, and that you need to change the adult-contrived trend of the islanding of childhood of which Gillis (2008, cited in Blundell, 2016) speaks.

Further reading

Blundell, D (2016) *Rethinking Children's Spaces and Places*. London: Bloomsbury Academy.

De Bono, E (2004) *How to Have a Beautiful Mind.* London: Random House.

Hallet, E (2016) *Early Years Practice for Educators and Teachers*. London: Sage.

Palmer, S (2015) *Toxic Childhood: How the Modern World is Damaging Our Children and What We Can Do About It* (Updated version). London: Orion.

Popper, S (2013) *Rethinking Superhero and Weapon Play*. Maidenhead, Berkshire: Open University Press.

References

Abbott, L and Nutbrown, C (eds) (2001) *Experiencing Reggio Emilia: Implications for Preschool Provision*. London: Oxford University Press.

Abbott, L (2001) Perceptions of Play – A Question of Priorities? in Abbott, L and Nutbrown, C (eds), *Experiencing Reggio Emilia: Implications for Preschool Provision*. Oxford: Oxford University Press, pp 8–20.

Barnardo's (2016) *Bringing Five to Thrive Alive*. [online] Available from: www.barnardos.org.uk/five-to-thrive-evaluation-report.pdf (accessed 20 November 2016).

Blundell, D (2016) *Rethinking Children's Spaces and Places*. London: Bloomsbury Academy.

De Bono, E (2004) *How to Have a Beautiful Mind.* London: Random House.

DfE (2014) *Statutory Framework for Early Years Foundation Stage*. [online] Available from: www.gov.uk/government/publications/early-years-foundation-stage-framework--2 (accessed 20 November 2016).

Edwards, C, Gandini, L and Forman, G (1998) *Hundred Languages of Children: Reggio Emila Approach: Advanced Reflections* (2nd edn). London: Ablex Publishing.

Fisher, R (2004) What is Creativity? in Fisher, R and Williams, M (eds), *Unlocking Creativity: A Teacher's Guide to Creativity Across the Curriculum*. London: David Fulton, pp 6–20.

Hallet, E (2016) *Early Years Practice for Educators and Teachers*. London: Sage.

Hawkes, H (1970) *Murder on the A34.* London: Random House.

HM Government (2015) *Channel Duty Guidance: Protecting Vulnerable People from being Drawn into Terrorism. Statutory Guidance*. London: Home Office. [online] Available from: www.gov.uk/government/uploads/system/uploads/attachment_data/file/425189/Channel_Duty_Guidance_April_2015.pdf (accessed 20 December 2016).

James, A and Brookfield, S D (2014) *Engaging Imagination: Helping Students to Become Creative and Reflective Thinkers*. New Jersey: Wiley and Sons.

Jenkinson, S (2001) *Genius of Play*: *Celebrating the Spirit of Childhood (Early Years)*. Gloucester: Hawthorn Press.

Lewis, C S (1950) *Chronicles of Narnia: The Lion, the Witch and the Wardrobe*. London: Harper Collins Ltd.

National Archives (2016) *Sexual Discrimination Act 1975.* [online] Available from: www.legislation.gov.uk/ukpga/1975/65 (accessed 20 June 2016).

Moyles, J (2010) Practitioner Reflection on Play and Playful Pedagogies, in Moyles, J (ed) *Thinking about Play: Developing a Reflective Approach.* London: Open University Press, pp 13–29.

Palmer, S (2006) *Toxic Childhood: How the Modern World is Damaging Our Children and What We Can Do About It.* London: Orion.

Palmer, S (2015) *Toxic Childhood: How the Modern World is Damaging Our Children and What We Can Do About It* (Updated version). London: Orion.

Popper, S (2013) *Rethinking Superhero and Weapon Play.* London: Open University Press.

Quinn, B (2016) Nursery 'raised fears of radicalisation over boy's cucumber drawing'. *The Guardian* (16 March 2016). [online] Available from: www.theguardian.com/uk-news/2016/mar/11/nursery-radicalisation-fears-boys-cucumber-drawing-cooker-bomb (accessed 20 December 2016).

Roberts, R (2006) *Self-Esteem and Early Learning: Key People from Birth to School.* London: PCP Sage.

Singer D G and Singer J K (1990) *The House of Make-Believe. Children's Play and the Developing Imagination.* London: Harvard University Press.

Tarrant, P and Holt, D (2016) *Metacognition in the Primary Classroom.* Oxford: Routledge.

Thomson TV Advertisement (2014) Thomson Holidays present Simon the Ogre. [online] Available from: www.youtu.be/JXNJA1yGn-8 (accessed 20 December 2016).

Thornton, L and Brunton, P (2014) Background to the Reggio Approach, in Green, S (series ed), *Bringing the Reggio Approach to Your Early Years Practice* (3rd ed). Routledge: London, pp 7–13.

Woods, A and Hall, V (2013) Exploring Outdoor Possibilities for All Children, in Woods, A (ed), *Child-Initiated Play and Learning: Planning for the Possibilities in the Early Years.* Oxford: Routledge, pp 50–67.

11 The reflective leader

JAYNE DALY

A beautiful body and a beautiful face age and grow old. A beautiful mind does not age and becomes ever more beautiful. A beautiful body and a beautiful face without a beautiful mind can be boring. A beautiful mind without a beautiful body or a beautiful face can still be attractive ... This means a mind that is attractive to others as well as yourself. It is not just a matter of sitting in a corner having beautiful thoughts. It is a beautiful mind in action. This action is not just that of solving complex problems, but the action of exploring a subject in discussion and conversation. It is in this context that others can see how beautiful your mind can be.

(De Bono, 2004, p 224)

Introduction

De Bono's view here can be used as a metaphor for the basis of a balanced approach as a reflective leader. Indeed, there are many times when, as early years leaders, we may need to stand back and re-evaluate how we approach early years care and education, and it is very easy to think we are alone in making key decisions. It is also easy for us to think that we have no leadership responsibilities, as we forget that as early years practitioners we lead and support the children in new discoveries and the next stage of their development. We may use that *beautiful mind* to develop children's curiosity, and to develop a rapport with our colleagues and external agencies in whatever situation because, as De Bono (2004) posits, only then do we understand the true views, capabilities, needs, values and feelings of others. But is this easy to do? What does leadership actually involve? Can everyone in early years be reflective in their leadership approach? Why is being a reflective leader in early years so important? These are questions that will be explored throughout the context of this chapter and we will revisit once more the ideologies that De Bono proposes.

Historical content

According to the Effective Provision of Pre-School Education Project (EPPE) carried out in 1997–2004 (Sylva et al, 2004), children in their earliest years' cognitive and social development were better supported by highly qualified practitioners and, furthermore, Siraj-Blatchford et al (2002), in the Researching Effective Pedagogy in the Early Years (REPEY) project, noted the differences in understanding of curriculum and effective pedagogy by those educators that were qualified to degree level status within the Private, Voluntary and Independent (PVI) sector. Following these reports in 2006, the then-Labour government introduced the graduate leadership status, providing capital for practitioners to gain their graduate status in the form of the Transformational Fund. Then, in 2007, the Graduate Leader Fund (DfE, 2013a) was introduced, in order for practitioners to gain Early Years Practitioner Status (EYPS) (DfE, 2013b). Managers of PVI settings were thrown into uncertainty about their roles and the significance of this change, as the shift moved from lead figures in early years settings being managers and deputy managers, to now being graduate leaders. Although managers would retain their positions in terms of their day-to-day responsibilities the main significant change would be that the graduate leader would be responsible for the planning and delivery of the curriculum for our children in their pre-school years (Ofsted, 2013). This uncertainty found many managers concerned about their status within the early years workforce, and some sought an opportunity to upgrade current qualifications (usually at level 3, but sometimes at level 2) to foundation degrees and full honours degrees to allow them to be able to go on to gain EYPS. Apart from issues of leadership, this also had its own personal implications which have been highlighted in Chapter 5 of this book.

Defining leadership and management

What does leadership mean to you? Is there a difference between the role of a manager and that of a leader? Think about leaders you have known; those that you aspire to and those that, for whatever reason, you do not. How do we define the difference between the reflective leader and the resourceful manager in early years? Is there a difference in particular leadership morals and values within early years environments because of the very nature of the role?

Kydd et al (2002, p 1) considers that:

> leading is about vision and strategy and providing inspiration to the people working in the organisation so that the aims of the organisation can be achieved. Managing is about putting the vision into practice and enabling the organisation to function.

Whalley (2012) deliberates the difficulties in setting apart the role of a leader from that of a manager within early years PVI sectors but hastily identifies that this may not be true of head teachers within a school setting. Whalley (2012) further determines the work of Law and Glover (2000) who are quick to define leadership, suggesting a more genial and inspiring approach than that of a manager, whom, they suggest, has a more instructive approach to meet the needs of the organisation and policy. Solly (2003, cited in Rodd 2006) concurs with this and advances this suggestion by highlighting the leader's role as all-encompassing, suggesting the importance of values and vision for the future that must include a commitment to continuous reflection and reflective practice. This, Solly (2003, cited in Rodd 2006) determines, is different from that of the role of a manager, who has high expectations of professionalism and clear communication channels. Northouse (2007) is able to take a step further, recognising the similarities of the leader and manager terminology. After all, he suggests, both work with people and both are concerned with positive outcomes and achievements. He does, however, concur with the notion that, some of these things apart, there is a need for specific roles.

Aubrey (2011) promotes the idea that the roles of management and leadership are separate. She tells us that where management is concerned, within an early years context, there is an emphasis on maintenance and upkeep rather than progression, whereas the contexts with a leadership focus are more concerned with a new vision that can be developed and nurtured for change. O'Sullivan (2009) identifies leadership as being mysterious, something which has yet to be defined, and reviews the work of Bennett et al (2003) who suggest that leadership is *a contested concept* (p 3). Currently, Murray and McDowall Clark (2013) argue that Nutbrown (2012), in her recent recommendations for improvement in quality, has not been specific in the leadership model she alludes to. What is clear, however, is that she does not promote a single leadership model for the future of early years.

Most would argue, therefore, that there is a need for administrative classification of the role of a leader as compared to that of a manager. Research appears to posit a defining shift in roles and responsibilities.

Goleman's (2002) work identifies the responsibilities of a good leader. He discusses the leadership qualities that are different to those of a manager, suggesting leaders *prime good feeling in those they lead* (p ix). This in turn, Goleman (2002) suggests, helps leaders to gain the best performance from their followers. This is something that we are constantly concerned about as leaders. Have we made the right impact on children and families through our leadership traits or skills and are these *good enough to make a difference*? (O'Sullivan, 2009, p 3). O'Sullivan continues by contemplating her own leadership experiences and notes the complexities of the role of a leader in early years today. She aspires to Goleman's (2002) point by highlighting that an effective leader cannot lead alone and must inspire their team to become reflective in their personal leadership practice.

CASE STUDY

Scenario 1: Asha

Asha is a nursery manager in a PVI setting. She has 12 years' experience at this setting leading and managing a team often at various levels in their career and training. Asha is under continuous pressure from the owners to effectively manage budgets, compile marketing strategies, set staff targets for improvement in quality, meet all legislative and policy requirements and hold together a very close team. Asha knows her team very well, after all many of them were working at the setting when she was a practising nursery nurse in the pre-school room. The team had actively encouraged Asha to take up this position and has supported her ever since. Asha is therefore able to effectively use the skills and knowledge of individuals well in order to enhance positive outcomes for the children and the business. This is because Asha is able to recognise not only the strengths and weaknesses of individuals but also when individuals are experiencing difficulties and is able to tap into their emotional state in order to support them when needed. This is what Goleman refers to as emotional intelligence.

Goleman (2002, p xii) posits:

> *For too long, managers have seen emotions at work as noise cluttering the rational operation of organisations. But the time for ignoring emotions, as irrelevant to the business, has passed.*

Asha has found that by supporting her team in this way she is able to adjust her style to promote personal mastery as noted by Senge (2006) but, more importantly, Asha is able to use her emotional intelligence to increase awareness of herself in terms of her compassionate and thoughtful approach to leadership and management which allows her reflective practice to build her own self-mastery, as Goleman (2002) suggests.

Reflective activity

Asha seems a perfect leader, doesn't she? Let's think about Goleman's theory. Go back to thinking about managers and leaders that you have had or, of course, your own management/leadership experiences. Ask yourself the following questions.

» *Is emotional intelligence something that we all possess? Or does Asha have a special ability/characteristic or leadership trait?*

» *Do you think it is possible for leaders such as Asha to continually reflect upon their behaviours and the behaviours of their teams in order to be open to using their emotional intelligence to its best in terms of getting the best out of others? Is this practical?*

» *Is Asha a reflective leader or is she a resourceful manager, getting the best results from the team because of her past experiences and knowledge of them?*

Extended thinking

Consider this chapter so far.

» *Do you think you possess a special ability to lead others including the children?*

» *What makes you think this? List examples.*

» *Or, do you think that leadership is not for you?*

» *Why do you suppose this is?*

» *What does your ideal leader look like?*

Theories of leadership: trait versus skill

Aubrey (2011) speculates that the traditional organisational/characteristic/style theories are largely becoming a thing of the past. It has been, as Aubrey suggests, debated by many whether leadership qualities are innate traits or nurtured by organisational training. Northouse (2007) also discusses the trait approach to leadership and notes the work of Stogdill (1948) who contemplated that, although a leader may appear to have a specific innate trait in one leadership situation, this may not be true in another. Northouse (2007, p 16) further argues that the trait leadership theory *is alive and well* in the twenty-first century. Kirkpatrick and Locke (1991) within their research developed Stogdill's theory of 1948 and 1974 and posited that leaders can either be born with or learn leadership traits. Table 11.1 shows the innate traits and characteristics from three studies undertaken by these researchers.

Table 11.1 Leadership traits

Stogdill (1948)	Stogdill (1974)	Kirkpatrick and Locke (1991)
Sociability	Sociability	Drive
Self-confidence	Influence	Motivation
Persistence	Tolerance	Confidence
Initiative	Co-operativeness	Cognitive ability
Responsibility	Responsibility	Task knowledge
Insight	Self-confidence	Integrity
Alertness	Initiative	
Intelligence	Insight	
	Achievement	
	Persistence	

Source: Adapted from Northouse (2007)

It is important to consider here that the trait leadership theory focuses on the leader rather than the followers. This theory recognises that the leader needs to have particular personal qualities in order for the organisation to be successful. It does not, however, focus on the impact that the trait leadership ideologies have upon the team members themselves. It is therefore worth remembering, as O'Sullivan (2009) reminds us, that not all leaders that society has aspired to were good people, although they were perceived as being *great leaders* (p 5).

Like the trait theory, the skills theory is also leader-centred in its approach. However, it differs from the trait theory because, rather than the idea that the leader possesses personality traits, the skills approach is based upon a nurtured approach to leadership. The idea here is that skills can be learned and developed by the leader. According to Katz's (1955) theory, the skills a person needs are based on a three-point system: technical skills (being able to apply themselves to a specific area of work); human or people skills; and conceptual skills which, as its name implies, is being able to deal with particular theoretical knowledge and ideas. The skills model has been developed more recently by the suggestion that person-ality and motivational traits do have a bearing on effective leadership. Northouse (2007) refers to Mumpford et al's (2000) theory which noted that particular personal attributes and competencies were needed in order for a leader to be successful. Figure 11.1 shows a brief model of the skills approach to effective leadership.

Personal attributes + Competencies = Good leadership outcomes

Figure 11.1 *Components skills model*
Source: Adapted from Northouse (2007)

It would be easy to assume that Asha has many of the traits/skills shown in Table 11.1, eg *sociability, persistence, personality, motivation, self-confidence, knowledge* and definitely *responsibility.* But surely, for Asha to possess traits such as *tolerance, influence* and *integrity,* there has to be an element of reflection and reflective practice to allow her to influ-ence others within her team to do the same? Reflecting back upon the metaphor from De Bono (2004, p 224), in response to O'Sullivan's (2009) point regarding the great leaders not always being good people, think about those people who may have been classed as 'great leaders'. Did they have the *beautiful mind in action*? Does Asha have a *beautiful mind in action* in terms of her leadership traits or characteristics? We must continue to reflect upon this point as we go through this chapter.

CASE STUDY

Scenario 2: Asha's project

One of the projects Asha has been assigned to by the setting owners recently is the introduc-tion of an extension for a new baby unit to be opened in three months' time. This will mean that there will be three new job roles created, but this will also mean that there will have to be some internal re-shuffling of the team in terms of their current roles. Asha knows that parents of the babies will want the close individual attention that they deserve. She knows that whoever she puts in charge of the baby unit needs to be highly approachable, reliable and friendly. Amna is an experienced room leader. She has worked for Asha for seven years, supervising the toddler room. Asha feels Amna is just the person for the role of baby room leader, given comments from parents during a recent Ofsted inspection. Asha approaches Amna with regard to this, hoping that Amna will agree, and knowing that she is also under pressure from the owners to get the right person for this role. Asha does not feel that she can open this role out to whoever gains the additional positions in the setting. She has considered this but feels that, in view of the current pressure she is under to make this new unit a success, she does not want to leave anything to chance. Amna's qualities can only mean one thing for Asha; she is the right person for this job and therefore she asks to see Amna to discuss this.

As Asha had predicted Amna is not happy about the change. She explains to Asha that she does not want to leave the toddler room. She has children and parents there that she has very good bonds with. Asha is able to show empathy for Amna's situation, and listens carefully to her opinion. She is then also able to persuade Amna that she should trust her and give her examples of the excellent practice Amna has shown, that makes her Asha's first choice, as well as giving clear reasons as to why she did not want to open this out to one of the new positions. Amna has great respect for Asha and she trusts her implicitly, but she still has many concerns about how this may work out if she were to accept and who would take over from her in the toddler room. Asha knows that Amna has a great talent for building relationships, she is welcoming and warm, and she knows Amna aspires to become a leader herself within a setting one day. She has recently completed her foundation degree in early childhood studies and will go on next year to top up to her full BA (Hons) degree. Asha obviously has a vision for the future of the setting and wants, of course, to support Amna in her future aspirations. It is down to her to persuade Amna that she is part of that vision, and that this is how she will fit into it, with support through the transition and change process. Asha realises that Amna needs some time to think about this situation and perhaps discuss it with her family and colleagues before she reaches a final decision.

This is obviously a difficult situation for both Amna and Asha. Think about some of the traits and/or skills that Asha has used in this scenario. She has shown good *social judgement*. She has most definitely tried to *influence* and *motivate*, she also seems to be *persistent* in her approach and has shown great *integrity* in her honesty towards Amna. Amna obviously appreciates that honesty.

Reflective activity

»   *How is Asha going to use her traits or skills to continue to support Amna into realising that she is part of the change process and can become part of the new vision within the setting?*

»   *If you were Amna would you be persuaded? What may or may not influence your decision?*

»   *Can all early years visions be effectively shared? Is this possible?*

Extended thinking

Think about where you work or your placement.

»   *Consider whether there is a shared vision. Yes or no?*

»   *What determines this?*

Theories of leadership: transformational versus transactional

Rodd (2006) considers that within the early years environment there is a clear need cultur-ally for the early years leader to be caring, compassionate, empathic, welcoming and courte-ous. She further alludes to the transformational style of leadership which Goleman (2002) advances, highlighting that in his opinion there are clear associations between the concept of emotional intelligence and the transformational style of leadership in its motivational, trustworthy and visionary stance. So what is transformational leadership? And how does this relate to an effective early years leader?

Burns (1978) was the first to note how effective leaders were able to relate to the motiva-tions of others and was able to clarify differences between two main types of leadership, these being *Transformational* and *Transactional.* He had developed his theory on the work of House (1976) who attributed to the charismatic leadership theory, suggesting that such leaders have charismatic characteristics, which have specific effects on their followers, but also have a self-awareness of their own moral codes and values. Bass (1985) based his work on transformational theory on the work of Burns (1978) and House (1976). He argues the transformational leadership model supports and motivates followers into realising potential goals for their future and also how this can impact upon the good of the team and the organi-sation. According to Kuhnert (1994), transformational leaders try to develop their followers to their individual and fullest potential and are key to motivating their followers into recognis-ing that their aspirations can be used for the greater good rather than for their own self-gain. From a much more up-to-date stance, Northouse (2007) recognises an *idealized influence* model in which he posits that followers trust in this leader's moral and ethical deportment so much they become influenced to follow the leader's vision and emulate him or her because they see this as how they wish to be.

The transactional leadership model (often associated with management models), on the other hand, concerns itself with giving reward or punishment to the followers in order to change organisational outcomes to benefit themselves. The contingent reward is given to the followers by the leader in order to benefit the leader and the organisation. On the flip side of this, within the transactional model, the leader may use negative reinforcement known as management-by-exception, whereby a leader may use active or passive management strate-gies to take remedial action in order to benefit themselves and the organisation. Table 11.2 shows the differences in leadership model styles.

Table 11.2 *Transactional/transformational leadership*

Transactional leadership model	Transformational leadership model
Followers perform better when chain of command is clear and certain	Inspires motivation
Rewards and punishment can motivate	Promotes intellectual stimulation
Followers need to obey instruction	Has consideration for individuals
Followers need careful monitoring	Can be an idealised influence

Source: Based on the work of Northouse (2007) and Bass and Avolio (2004)

Reflective activity

» Which model's characteristics are recognisable to you? Transactional? Transformational?

» Or have you experienced both?

» Which model would you prefer to be led by?

» Or would you say there needs to be a balance of both?

Extended thinking

Think about that ideal leader again that you thought about at the beginning of this chapter.

» What model characteristics best describe him/her and why? List your reasons.

Situational leadership model

Hersey and Blanchard (1969) developed a popular model of leadership known as the situational model. This model has since been developed and refined by many others, but overall the same principles apply, whereby the leader considers their style against the developmental level of their followers in order to adjust their leadership style (of which there are four: supporting; coaching; delegating; and directing) in order to meet their followers' requirements. It is possible to see in Figure 11.2 how the leader may adapt their style to offer the correct level of support as and when needed by adjusting their supportive behaviour against their directive behaviour. The lower the level of support needed, the more the leader can direct or delegate their followers to achieve required outcomes. The higher the level of support needed, the lower the level of direction required. In the latter situation, therefore, the leader can use their leadership skills to praise, listen and guide, until such a time as the followers are ready to move forward, break away from the close leadership contact and deal with a less supportive stance from the leader.

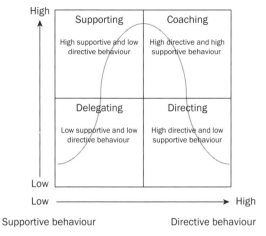

Figure 11.2 *Situational leadership model*
Source: Adapted from Northouse (2007)

Reflective activity

» *Will there be times during the new visionary changes of the setting when Asha may find it useful to adapt her leadership style to support/direct individuals?*

» *How will she ensure she continues to develop the* beautiful mind *that De Bono (2004) refers to within this process, ensuring that she shows herself as a* great leader *and also a* good person?

» *Can Asha support other aspiring leaders within the setting to develop a* beautiful mind in action *to ensure effective outcomes for the children?*

Extended thinking

» *Is the beautiful mind in action that De Bono promotes easy to achieve or is this ideological? Think about your reasons for your answer.*

CASE STUDY

Scenario 3: Amna

Amna has now had time to reflect upon the move to being leader of the baby unit. She has openly discussed this with her family and colleagues. It is apparent that her colleague in the toddler unit, Joe, is also aspiring to gain more experience in the leadership field, as he has persuaded Amna to take the position, and he will discuss with Asha the prospect of becoming the new toddler room leader. After all, he knows the children and parents well and has 'covered' for Amna in her absence. Both Joe and Amna go to Asha to discuss this. Asha is relieved and happy, not only about Amna but also that Joe seems to have read her mind! Asha knows that, with only two years' experience in the early years field, Joe will need lots of support, mentoring and coaching, but he is quick to learn and has recently completed his first year of foundation degree in early childhood studies. Asha also anticipates that there will be lots of change within the setting with the new plans and new staff. She also knows that she will need to be effective and reflective when using her mentoring and coaching skills in order to ensure that a passionate community-based model is strived for. Of course, to begin with, the shared vision (refer to Scenario 2) that she dreams of will not be easy to accomplish. Jones and Pound (2008) identify that there will be differences in accountability within the leadership roles within an early years setting, therefore it will be down to team leaders, like Asha, to have a firm main obligation to create a 'team spirit' (p 27) to ensure a coming together of common goals.

It is clear here that Asha is going to have lots to do. She is going to have three new staff that will need support and coaching to identify with the settings vision for the future. Of course this cannot be a shared vision until all of Asha's staff are comfortable and able to play their individual part. Amna is quite a way there; despite the fact that she is moving rooms her supportive need is quite low in comparison to that of Joe and the new staff members. Creating a new team for Asha as a leader is a challenge, and means that as O'Sullivan (2009) suggests a good leader *shows staff where they fit in so that everyone has a sense of purpose and worth and can find their place in the organisation* (p 7).

What does an early years leadership framework look like?

Murray and McDowall Clark (2013) note the complexities of identifying an early years leadership framework which would model itself on the *passionate care, to improve the education and well-being of young children* (p 289) as they allude to the work of Nutbrown (2012). This is not a new concept according to O'Sullivan (2009), who reminds us of the struggle of Maria Montessori when she set about finding a safe and warm place for the children of Naples with food, before she could even think of pedagogical practices.

Nutbrown (2012) suggests that as early years practitioners we should aspire to be leaders but, as Murray and McDowall Clark (2013) remind us, Nutbrown does not identify clearly what type of leadership model we should aspire to within early years care and education. Early Years Teachers (EYT) replaced the EYPS from September 2013. According to Murray and McDowall (2013) this change may be more concerned with the pedagogical framework rather than the professional stance of leadership care, as this may be lost in the transition. They go on to promote the involvement of all practitioners and staff in the leadership community as they noted from their study that, without exception, their participants spoke of being passionate about wanting the best for our children by effective mentoring and coaching of all staff regardless of their qualification, in order to connect to a shared vision.

Handy (1994) makes the poignant point that managers or leaders are not always open to *the world outside* (p 106) and that, although they may be central to what is going on in the organisation, they must not stay stagnant there in the centre. They must come out of their central location to be among their people in order to motivate them into understanding and sharing the idealistic vision that they dream of. Marshall et al (2003), however, posit that the vision of an organisation needs to be more than that of a group of lead figures deciding on what the vision or values will be, and that leaders need to be motivating others to agree or share this vision. The vision should involve a coming together of all parties, from the top down through the 'hierarchy' of the setting, to determine what is actually valued by all staff. Determining a vision statement is not the role of the manager or leader alone, but the role of everyone in order to build this *shared vision* that Senge (2006) considers.

By modelling her passionate leadership behaviour and giving Amna and Joe the opportunity to step out of their comfort zone, Asha hopes to inspire them to be part of the setting's leadership vision model. Asha will then be able to open her *beautiful mind* to other areas where her skills may be useful and make a difference. Reflecting back to the beginning of this chapter, De Bono (2004) asks us to involve others in our actions through our discussions and conversations. It is about spreading the good work within early childhood care and education and about mentoring others to aspire to do the same within a community-based reflective model.

Aubrey (2011) explores the notion of reflective practice through action research which she accredits to the work of Lewin (1946), Kolb's (1984) learning cycle and Schön's (1983) theory of *reflection on action*, discussed in Chapter 1 of this book. Aubrey (2011) suggests we are now moving away from the historical notion that theoretical knowledge was all that you needed to succeed in leadership and *reflecting in action* (Schön 1987, p 44) can be one way forward. We are, as early years leaders, persistently held answerable by current government legislation for the future life chances of our youngest children. This, according to O'Sullivan (2009) is a *heavy weight to bear* (p 5). Aubrey (2011) continues that we must be reflective leaders in action in order to try out new ways of working to identify successes and failures.

Aubrey (2011) notes the commitment of leaders and their teams to lifelong learning and an ability to be self-aware and self-reflect by learning from the 'real-life' experiences of others in a mentoring capacity. It is, of course, essential that an early years leadership mentor establishes not only a rapport with their following mentee but also the clear ground rules and boundaries that their relationship will need in order for success. Rogers (2008) highlights the importance of creating mutual trust on both the sides of the mentor and the mentee relationship in order for it to develop. Confidential issues may be discussed or personal cultural values may be explored as part of the 'getting to know each other' process, but the mutual respect you have for each other should be evident. As Rogers further identifies it is not up to individuals to judge or question each other as this is not the purpose of the mentor/mentee relationship.

Wallace and Gravells (2005, p 21) discuss the work of Carl Rogers (1983) as he highlights the *unconditional positive regard* the mentor may need to have for all mentees. Megginson and Clutterbuck (2005) concur and consider that the mentor should recognise that mentees will have behaviours that are different to their own, in many cases, and the mentor should be receptive to these, creating a non-judgemental atmosphere. Moon (2004) investigates the ideas of Goleman (1996) regarding emotional intelligence as they explore a clear emphasis on the concept that the management of emotions and feelings is vital before effective learning can take place.

It is important that Asha brings motivational and aspirational attention to her role as a mentor. It is possible to identify particular theoretical models to which Asha may refer. One which may suit her leadership style is the CARE (Comfort, Awareness, Reawakening, Empowerment) model described by Turnbull (2009) (and discussed in Chapter 5 of this book) which particularly highlights the social and emotional needs of the mentee. Turnbull's (2009) viewpoint is supported by Moon (2004) and Whitmore (2002) in their citations of the research done by Goleman (1996) in stressing the importance of understanding that the mentee may not be able to move forward in meeting their goals until their emotional needs are met. The CARE model, Turnbull (2009) observes, gives the mentor the flexibility to be able to use their skills to move backwards and forwards between the stages of the model to ensure the mentee has effective support. This model is relevant to Asha as a mentor because of her close bond and connections with her team and, of course, the leadership morals she imposes.

CASE STUDY

Scenario 4: New staff

The baby unit is now open following successful Ofsted approval. Asha has recruited three new staff to her team, Ellen, Maria and Raheela. Two of these new staff are newly qualified to level 3. Asha knows, within the current climate, that she and the rest of her experienced team must continue to support and develop their skills within a vocational stance. She also encourages them to go on to develop their theoretical knowledge to support their practice in a lifelong learning capacity, so that they may connect to the leadership vision of the whole team. One new member of the team, Raheela, is a qualified Forest Schools leader (yet another leader with individual skills) and there is now the exciting prospect of developing the curriculum to incorporate Forest Schools sessions and develop the setting curriculum. Amna and Joe are settling into their new leadership roles. It is interesting here how, although I mention these members of staff as being leaders in their own right, within the team there are many staff members who would not want that 'title' for fear of it taking them away from the children. O'Sullivan (2009) alludes to this, as do I at the beginning of this chapter. As practitioners within early years we do not see ourselves as leaders in many respects even though we lead children every day in a pedagogical sense. These are exciting times and Asha is full of enthusiasm and hope that she will be able to support and develop and direct this team in order to ensure effective outcomes for the children. Asha knows she has to develop a team that will create an environment that needs to be safe, calm, inviting, happy, stimulating, exciting and fun. She must continue to be passionate, be motivational and inspiring as well as developing her integrity as a leader.

Reflective activity

»   *Is developing this team easy to do? Will Asha need a transformative or transactional approach to leadership or both?*

»   *Does she need to be a resourceful manager or a reflective leader?*

Extended thinking

» *Give reasons for your answers to these reflective activity questions.*

Leadership and team development

Muir (1984) defines teamwork as:

> *the continuous interaction between a small group of clearly bonded people who share a common task, similar values and who hold distinctive knowledge and skills.*
>
> (p 170)

O'Neil (2003) argues, however, that this kind of interaction is not easy to accomplish and takes great time, effort and dedication in order to avoid problematic issues for leaders or managers. Developing and motivating staff to have a common and shared vision is not easy. Once again Goleman (2002) recognises this and identifies the role of the manager or leader in being aware of their own emotional intelligence and allowing this concept to be transferred to the team as a whole. Goleman (2002) suggests that, by the leader being aware of the *moods and needs* (p 229) of the team, s/he is able to divert conflict by pointing out to individuals when their fellow team members may be feeling emotionally unstable, thus diverting conflict as the team learns to support one another through use of their emotional intelligence. Rodd (2006) concurs with this theory somewhat, and suggests that this is the key to the leader motivating their teams in supporting them to look beyond egotistical thoughts.

O'Neill (2003) contemplates models of teamwork and identifies the views of Tuckman (1965), Adair (1988) and Belbin (1981) in terms of addressing the need for developing teams with team spirit. O'Neill goes on to identify through his research that some of the concepts underpinned by such theories are now open to much scrutiny within the educational context in terms of the leadership role in handling pressures and conflict in teams, or the impact change may have on already established teams. He further identifies that models very often have not taken into account the individual and cultural norms of the organisation in which the team is working.

Rodd (2006) considers the cultural norms and characteristics of the early years setting and suggests the transformational leadership style is very much based on the stereotypical attitudes of characters of the female nurturing instincts. As she suggests, it is well known that most early years practitioners are women. Mandell and Pherwani (2003) also reviewed the links between the transformational style of leadership and gender and argue that, although both display transformational traits and characteristics, the female often has higher levels of emotional intelligence. This is something that is disputed by Goleman (2002). Furthermore, Mandell and Pherwani (2003) consider the views of Bass (1990) who believes the transformational leader has motivational qualities that can be used to support their staff in achieving high expectations. Bottery (2004) disputes this, and argues that both transformational and transactional leaders are essential for effective leadership.

Motivation of teams, Bottery (2004) implies, is a function that continually grows with maturity. He reflects upon Maslow's (1954) hierarchy of needs and suggests that, as living standards have now changed, individuals within teams can now reach for the much higher levels of self-actualisation within this model. Anderson (2003) reviews the motivational theories of McClelland (1961), Herzberg (1966) and McGregor (1970), among others and argues that the theoretical theme of motivation seems to be linked to the idea that the individual needs reward. Extrinsic rewards, however (eg pay and benefits), within the education sector (particularly in early years) are mostly stagnant.

Therefore, this would suggest that what is needed to motivate us as early years practitioners comes from within; an intrinsic motivational experience. Asha's passion comes from within. She knows what her aspirations are for the children and needs to motivate and inspire her staff to reflect and to change with the times, something which O'Sullivan (2009) tells us we are becoming very good at within early years, as we constantly change to the meet the demands of current government policy within our practice, although, as her previous comments (in this chapter) suggest, this is not an easy task.

Leadership and professionalism

As a team leader Asha needs to aspire to ensuring the best outcomes for children and their families. She must listen to the families and the staff but, most of all, listen to the children themselves, as, she must not forget, they too are part of her team. Paige-Smith et al (2012) identify with family-centred practice, which includes how we must listen to children and model inclusive practices. Effective communication and professional integrity are part of that challenge when it comes to ensuring we are working together as reflective team leaders, which includes being part of a reflective and proactive team, within the child's community. Paige-Smith et al (2012) allude to the reflective practices of the professionals involved within a child's community and the collaboration of all involved to ensure positive outcomes for the child. O'Sullivan (2009) reminds us that it is easy in hindsight for us to reflect upon issues of poor leadership, communication or professionalism and look back with regret on how we handled a particular situation. Some of my own early leadership experiences emulate that feeling, but it is about being brave enough to step forward and say *I am prepared to change and develop my mind so that it becomes reflective and beautiful and to inspire and motivate you to do the same.*

Chapter reflections

It is easy to assume that leading others within early years is straightforward and that De Bono's (2004) idealistic viewpoint of having a beautiful mind in action is an all-encompassing strategy to successful leadership. The idea is idealistic, but I urge you to use this metaphor as a reflective tool while on your leadership journey, alongside reflective models that I mention in this chapter. Whilst we can refer to many theoretical ideals of traits, skills, models and styles of leadership (Burns 1978; Bass 1985; Kuhnert 1994; Northouse 2007) discussed throughout this chapter, it is clear that the mystery of early years leadership that O'Sullivan (2009) posits is a valid one. Whilst being a resourceful manager is important, in terms of responding to the ever-changing demands of government policy, we must open our minds to the reflective stance of the leadership role. We must explore our morals, values and, of course, our visions for the future within early years leadership practice. We must show the passion that Murray and McDowell (2013) allude to in order to ensure that we share our leadership vision with others, and include them in that journey. We must try to remove egotistical thoughts (Rodd, 2006) from our minds and the minds of those we lead and ensure they are aware of their own emotional intelligence (Goleman, 2002), which in turn will help to promote the transformational vision for the future. We must become great leaders of early years in supporting the individual care and pedagogical needs of children and their families, but, equally importantly, we must be approachable to them as good people. Being professional and having clear communication channels is not just the role of a manager (Solly 2003, cited in Rodd, 2006), the early years leader needs to be all-encompassing but must not shy away from the fact that s/he cannot do this alone. Coaching and mentoring others is important, the team you work with could be the leaders of the future, and we know too that their passion to succeed must come from within, so as coaches we must motivate and CARE (Turnbull, 2009). Look to others in your team on your leadership journey and use your beautiful mind in action within early years to inspire others to use theirs!

Extended reflections

» *Now you have read this chapter consider your beautiful mind in action at work or in placement. Is a beautiful mind in action easy to maintain? Did you achieve this or is this still work in progress? Do you now think differently because of your beautiful mind? What impact does this have on colleagues and the children?*

Further Reading

Rodd, J (2013) *Leadership in Early Childhood: The Pathway to Professionalism.* 4th edn. Maidenhead: Open University Press.

This is a fully revised and updated edition of a most scholarly text relating to leadership in the early years sector. Rodd recognises the need for visionary and ethical leadership, and she reflects upon the importance of political and cultural changes affecting early childhood services. In this book you will find useful cases studies which will enable you to engage with the text and relate theory to your practice.

References

Anderson, L (2003) A Leadership Approach to Managing People and Teams in Education, in Kydd, L, Anderson, L and Newton, W (eds) *Leading People and Teams in Education.* London: Paul Chapman Sage.

Aubrey, C (2011) *Leading and Managing in the Early Years.* London: Sage.

Bass, B M (1985) *Leadership and Performance beyond Expectations.* New York: Free Press.

Bass B M and Avolio B J (2004) *The Multifactor Leadership Questionnaire.* Sampler set and manual, 3rd edn. Redwood City, CA: Mind Garden.

Bennett, N, Wise, C, Woods, P and Harvey, J (2003) *Distributed Leadership: A Review of Literature.* Nottingham: College for School Leadership.

Bottery, M (2004) *The Challenges of Educational Leadership.* London: Paul Chapman.

Burns, J A (1978) *Leadership.* New York: Harper and Row.

De Bono, E (2004) *How to Have a Beautiful Mind.* London: McQuaig Group.

DfE (2013a) *Evaluation of the Graduate Leader Fund – Final Report.* Available from: www.education.gov.uk/publications/standard/publicationDetail/Page1/DFE-RR144 (accessed 23 April 2013).

DfE (2013b) *Graduate Leaders in Early Years: Early Years Professional status.* Available from: www.education.gov.uk/childrenandyoungpeople/earlylearningandchildcare/h00201345/graduate-leaders/eyps (accessed 23 April 2013).

Goleman, D (1996) *Emotional Intelligence.* London: Bloomsbury.

Goleman, D (2002) *The New Leaders Transforming the Art of Leadership into the Science of Results.* London: Time Warner.

Handy, C (1994) *The Empty Raincoat, Making Sense of the Future.* London: Random House.

Hersey, P and Blanchard, K (1969) *Management of Organisational Behaviour.* Englewood Cliffs, NJ: Prentice Hall.

House, R J (1976) A 1976 Theory of Charismatic Leadership, in Hunt, J and Larson, L L (eds), *Leadership: The Cutting Edge.* Carbondale, IL: South Illinois University Press.

Jones, C and Pound, L (2008) *Leadership and Management in the Early Years from Principles to Practice.* Maidenhead: Open University Press.

Katz, R (1955) Skills of an Effective Administrator. *Harvard Business Review,* 33(1): 33–42.

Kirkpatrick, S A and Locke, E A (1991) Leadership: Do Traits Matter? *The Executive* 5: 48–60.

Kuhnert, K W (1994) Transforming Leadership: Developing People through Delegation, in Bass, B M and Avolio, B J (eds), *Improving Organisational Effectiveness through Transformational Leadership.* Thousand Oaks, CA: Sage.

Kydd, L, Anderson, L and Newton, W (2002) *Leading People and Teams in Education.* London: Paul Chapman Sage.

Law, S and Glover, D (2000) *Educational Leadership and Learning.* Buckingham: Open University Press.

Mandell, B and Pherwani, S (2003) The Relationship Between Emotional Intelligence and Transformational Leadership Style: A Gender Comparison. *Journal of Business and Psychology,* 17(3): 387–404.

Marshall, S J, Adams, M J, Cameron, A and Sullivan, G (2003) Leading Academics Learning about their Professional Needs, in Kydd, L, Anderson, L and Newton, W (eds), *Leading People and Teams in Education.* London: Paul Chapman Sage.

Megginson, D and Clutterbuck, D (2005) *Techniques for Coaching and Mentoring.* Abingdon: Routledge.

Moon, J (2004) *A Handbook of Reflective and Experiential Learning, Theory and Practice.* Oxon: Paul Chapman Sage.

Muir, L (1984) *'Teamwork'* in Olsen, M R (ed), *Social Work and Mental Health*. London: Tavistock, 68–176.

Murray, J and McDowall Clark, R (2013) Reframing Leadership as a Participative Pedagogy: The Working Theories of Early Years Professionals: Early Years. *An International Research Journal*, 33(3): 289–301.

Northouse, P G (2007) *Leadership: Theory and Practice*, 4th edn. London: Sage.

Nutbrown, C (2012) Foundations for Quality: *The Independent Review of Early Education and Childcare Qualifications. Final Report.* Available from: www.education.gov.uk/ (accessed 28 July 2012).

Ofsted (2013) *Guide to Registration on the Childcare Register*. Manchester: Crown. Available from: www.ofsted.gov.uk/resources/guide-registration-childcare-register (accessed 23 April 2013).

O'Neill, J (2003) Managing through Teams, in Kydd, L, Anderson, L and Newton, W (eds), *Leading People and Teams in Education*. London: Paul Chapman Sage.

O'Sullivan, J (2009) *Leadership Skills in the Early Years: Making a Difference*. London: Continuum.

Paige-Smith, A, Rix, J and Craft, A (2012) Reflective Family-Centred Practices: Parents, Perspectives and Early Intervention, in Millar, L, Drury, R and Cable, C (eds), *Extending Professional Practice in the Early Years*. Milton Keynes: Open University Press.

Rodd, J (2006) *Leadership in Early Childhood*, 3rd edn. Maidenhead: Open University Press.

Rodd, J (2013) *Leadership in Early Childhood: The Pathway to Professionalism*. 4th edn. Maidenhead: Open University Press.

Rogers, J (2008) *Coaching Skills*. Maidenhead: Open University Press.

Schön, D A (1987) *Educating the Reflective Practitioner*. San Francisco, CA: Jossey-Bass.

Senge, P M (2006) *The Fifth Discipline. The Art and Practice of the Learning Organisation*. London: Random House.

Siraj-Blatchford, I, Sylva, K, Muttock, S, Gilden, R and Bell, D (2002) *Researching Effective Pedagogy in the Early Years* (REPEY). DfES Research Report 356. London: DfES, HMSO.

Sylva, K, Melhuish, E, Sammons, P, Siraj-Blatchford, I and Taggart, B (2004) *Effective Provision of Pre-School Education Project, Final Report: A Longitudal Study Funded by the DfES 1997–2004.* Nottingham: DFES Publications.

Turnbull, J (2009) *Coaching for Learning*. London: Continuum.

Wallace, S and Gravells, J (2005) *Mentoring in Further Education*. Exeter: Learning Matters.

Whalley, M E (2012) Leading and Managing in Early Years, in Millar, L, Drury, R, and Cable, C (eds) *Extending Professional Practice in the Early Years*. Milton Keynes: Open University Press.

Whitmore, J (2002) *Coaching for Performance*. 3rd edn. London: Nicolas Brealey.

12 Reflecting on the multi-professional team

CAROL HAYES, MANDY DUNCAN AND ANN WHITEHOUSE

'Well you know what grown-ups are,' said Dinah. 'They don't think the same way as we do. I expect when we grow up, we shall think like them, but let's hope we remember what it was like to think in the way that children do, and understand the boys and the girls that are growing up when we are men and women.'

(Enid Blyton, 1944, *The Island of Adventure*)

Introduction

What is a multi-professional team?

The tragic and unnecessary death of a child is always likely to provoke a response in us and, in February 2000, the death of Victoria Climbié so disgusted civilised society that the Green Paper, *Every Child Matters* (DfES, 2003) was produced following the Victoria Climbié Inquiry (Laming, 2003). The Laming report made 108 recommendations to strengthen the preventative services with the intention of preventing a repeat of the circumstances leading to the death of Victoria Climbié. The legislation that followed these documents was founded on the idea that the only way to do this was to have more effective co-operation between the agencies involved with vulnerable children, and the crucial phrase 'joined-up working', although around before this time, really came to the fore. The concept of multi-agency working can be traced back as far as the Children Act 1989 (Department of Health, 1989) and probably before, when it was seen as being good practice and placed at the centre of planning for local services, but it was revitalised in the Children Act 2004 (DfES), with Figure 12.1 showing how the government of the day believed that inter-agency working could be achieved by being located in children's centres and extended school settings.

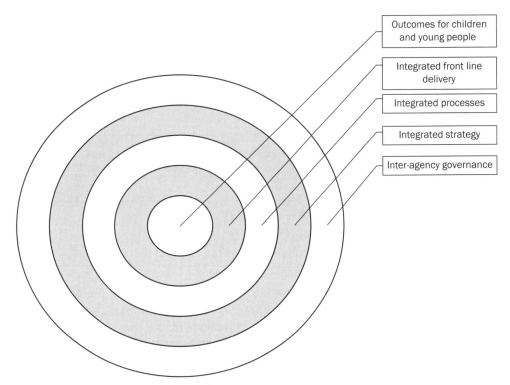

Outcomes for children and young people

Integrated front line delivery

Integrated processes

Integrated strategy

Inter-agency governance

Figure 12.1 *A model of whole system change*
Source: Adapted from DfES (2004)

Since 1989 we appear to have had a plethora of phrases appearing in the literature to describe the process of working together in partnership, for example:

- multi-agency working;

- inter-agency working;

- inter-professional working;

- multi-disciplinary working;

- inter-disciplinary working;

- partnership working;

- trans-disciplinary working;

- joined-up practice.

The list appears endless and there are probably many more terms that you have come across. A phrase used by Lloyd et al is that this is a *terminology quagmire* (2001, p 3). Whilst I am sure that the founders of these terms would all claim that they had a nuance of difference, to fit a particular circumstance and model of working, it seems that what is important, which-ever phrase we use, is that different professionals centred around the child are regularly and routinely talking and sharing vital and in-depth information, that they are working towards common goals and have a clear understanding of each other's roles, responsibilities and boundaries. This can be at either strategic or operational level. Kay and Fitzgerald (2016) suggest that the range of terminology is in fact only a way to indicate the level of integration and working together (see Figure 12.2).

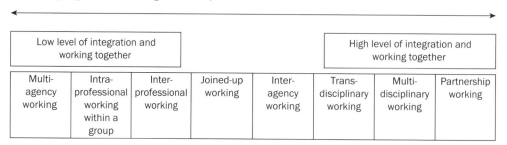

Figure 12.2 *Continuum of levels of service integration*
Source: Adapted from Fitzgerald and Kay (2008, p 7)

Working together across professional disciplines is always going to be complex but perhaps we are making it too complex with this variation in models and losing the essence of the need to work as a team around the child. As Fitzgerald and Kay (2008) suggest, it is probably not possible or even desirable to make these distinctions at the risk to the child and their families. Better to be able to retain the flexibility and fluidity of the range of models, including a multiple-service approach, but also acknowledge a single-service approach may be appropriate, depending upon the unique needs of the child and their family.

> This perpetuates the notion of interagency working as a virtuous solution to 'joined up' social problems and to under-acknowledge inter-agency working as a site of tensions and contradictions.
>
> (Warmington et al, 2004, p 48)

As well as differing terminology there are clearly differing models of team working. Atkinson et al (2002) suggest that there are five different models:

1.   decision-making groups;

2.   consultation and training groups to shape training and good practice;

3.   centre-based delivery, bringing different professionals together under one roof;

4.   a co-ordinated delivery team where one takes the lead role to co-ordinate the other professionals in the team;

5.   operational team delivery with professionals working together directly with the service user.

Atkinson et al (2002) suggest that these models are not exclusive and a team could flow into and out of them as required by their agreed common objectives. Although different agencies come together for different reasons and teams work together in different ways, essentially this is a process of different services with very different backgrounds coming together to pool their expertise and differing perspectives of the child and family. By doing so, they produce a shared level of responsibility for the management of the case in view. The study by Atkinson et al (2002) notes:

An overlap or a merging of roles indicated that boundaries between agencies had become blurred, and in the main this was felt to have been beneficial. However, others felt that maintaining distinct roles was crucial in allowing individual agencies to make a valuable and unique contribution to multi-agency working.

(p 11)

Reflective activity

Each one of you has contact with a range of healthcare and education professionals.

» *Consider your own family and list the services that you or your family have had contact with during the last year.*

» *What information did you need to share with each of them?*

» *How would you feel if the professionals talked together about the information that they now hold on you and your family?*

» *Would this information sharing have been beneficial to you or your family in any way?*

Challenges of working together

Trust

Kay and Fitzgerald (2016) identify trust as one of the most important elements for working with other people. If you are to work closely with a range of different professionals, roles that traditionally you took on may now be more appropriately assigned to others. You must be able to trust each other to provide the integrity, confidentiality and commitment that you would have yourself. You may need to trust others to take the lead role in a number of areas and trust their vision, skill and ability. If you are going to truly trust the partners in your working relationship you need to understand their professional roles, training and experience and they in turn need to understand yours. Each member of the team needs to understand all the other services and to create a shared vision to enable continuity and progression. This can only occur if each member of the team has a clear sense of who they are, a belief in their personal identity and a knowledge of how those they are in contact with perceive them. Anning et al (2006) suggest that, on another level, each team member brings a sense of professional identity and, at a third level, they bring a cultural and historical identity. These can be fluid and flexible as we change roles and responsibilities within the team. Thus, while trust can be a huge strength of multi-agency working it can also be an enormous barrier. Hudson (2005) suggests that the biggest conflicts and tensions within multi-agency teams occur due to the following issues.

• Professional identity – Who am I and do I fit the profile of my profession?

• Professional status – Do I fit the culturally perceived hierarchy? Do I put certain professions on a pedestal and thereby feel unable to communicate with them on an equal footing?

• Professional discretion and accountability – Can I meet the demands of confidentiality, trustworthiness and respect?

Overcoming these barriers demands a degree of professional transformation which requires each professional to feel safe and secure in their own self-awareness. Only then can there be a blurring of the edges of the knowledge base, and a shifting of the labels assumed or imposed upon them by other members of the team.

Relationships

The ability to communicate together is at the heart of that trust and the focus of working together. There are, as we have seen, enormous advantages to working together and sharing information, but it can be such a complex human process, with so many challenges to overcome, it is questionable whether it is possible in *all* cases. The main challenge is that each agency or professional within the team tends to see only one slice of the pie.

If we think of a pie, sliced into sections with each professional/agency taking one slice, it is then very hard to put the slices back into place to make the whole pie again. When you look at one slice it is hard to imagine what the whole pie looks like or to merge the pieces back together again. This is the same for a multi-agency team who, without strong channels of communication, can see only bits of a child from their professional perspective and find it hard to see him/her holistically and contextually.

> As simple as it sounds, cutting through interpersonal, social and cultural barriers to create a climate where people feel able to talk openly removes one of the biggest challenges to multi-agency working.
>
> (Siraj-Blatchford et al, 2007, p 129)

This suggests that relationships between the professionals in the team and their ability to communicate together will determine the success of the team objectives.

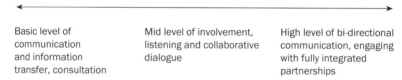

Figure 12.3 *Continuum of communication*

This continuum of communication shows how the strength of your interactions between team members can increase from a basic level to a high level as the relationships and trust develop. However, as with any continuum, you can move up and down this line as the context dictates, developing differing levels of communication with differing professions at different times, as those professionals start to assume their allocated team roles and responsibilities.

From 1999 onwards a new form of institution began springing up across England that was designed to improve outcomes for children. Funded by the government to the tune of £3 billion, Sure Start children's centres, which were initially rolled out in the most disadvantaged communities, were closely linked to the Labour government's aim to reduce child poverty and to the conviction that children's lives would be saved if the key agencies involved in children's welfare were enabled to share information and work in a more collaborative fashion under one roof (Jack, 2005). It is true that teams working in the same location will have opportunities for informal exchanges on the corridor or in the staff room, but the depth and validity of such exchanges needs to be considered. However, more than location, collaborative and communicative working structures need to be in place for this to work effectively. It is probably true that even with these structures in place, without the cultural shift of sharing and collaboration, this policy of integration will not work.

We have not so far considered the importance of relationships between families/parents and the professionals in the team. In a report by the DCSF (2008a, 2008b) it was clear that 92 per cent of parents do want to be involved with their children's services and over half wanted to be *very involved*. The only way that we can pull that 'pie' together is to include parents in the multi-agency team. Without the involvement of the child's 'prime educator' few initiatives or interventions will prove to be effective. Greco et al (2005) suggested that having parents involved with the multi-agency team keeps the group 'grounded' and focused upon the child and their family. Interestingly, in this study parents who had been involved with multi-agency teams felt they had been listened to and respected, yet still felt powerless to influence the direction of the findings, and most importantly the allocation of funding.

Working in trusting and meaningful partnership with parents is the most effective way to support children and families and has become one of the most important aspects of your role as an early childhood professional. As you are the members of the multi-agency team most likely to have regular contact with parents through informal interactions on a daily basis, the responsibility for building and maintaining relationships with them may predominantly fall upon you and your colleagues in the setting.

Reflective activity

To work effectively in partnership with parents, the early childhood professional will usually adopt a supportive and non-judgemental approach to gain their confidence, trust and respect.

» *Consider how your role as part of a multi agency team supporting a child may, in some circumstances, impact on the relationship you have built with their parents.*

Confidence

A recent study by Payler and Georgeson (2013), showed that while multi-agency working was effective in some settings in others it was non-existent, reflecting similar findings by Greco et al (2005). Both studies demonstrated that there was 'patchy' coverage and this was particularly so at practitioner level. This appears to defeat the whole concept of multi-agency working and of crossing professional boundaries and brings in issues of inequality of services for children and families which needs to be addressed. Payler and Georgeson (2013), suggested that one of the major inhibitors to multi-agency working was a lack of confidence in early years professionals, but if you are working in a setting which does not already engage with a range of other agencies and is isolationist, it is hard to see how you can develop that confidence to work with other professionals or that the setting could mentor their practitioners to offer training and self-belief.

CASE STUDY

Alice

Alice started attending The Elms pre-school nursery part time in September, soon after her third birthday when she became entitled to early education. The pre-school nursery is a non-maintained setting with charitable status. Alice lives on the local estate in a semi-rural town with her mother (Magda) and father (Daniel) who moved to England from their home country of Poland as a family when Alice was a baby. She has a baby brother (Jakub) who is six months old. Magda speaks and understands a little English, but relies on Daniel to read documents or fill in forms. Daniel works long hours to support the family and Magda relies on members of the local Polish community for support as she misses her parents and family.

After a few weeks in the nursery, her key worker (Kerri) has concerns that Alice may have some delay in several areas of her development. Kerri shares her concerns with the special educational needs co-ordinator (SENCO) on the team, who is also the deputy manager. After making an assessment based on observations of Alice, Kerri and the SENCO decide to contact the district SENCO for more expert advice – they have worked with her before when they needed to refer a child and know that she is experienced and approachable.

The district SENCO agrees to come and visit the nursery to see Alice and to support the team, but she is fully booked for the next six weeks. She recommends that in the meantime, the nursery team approach Alice's parents to explain their concerns to them and suggest that Alice might benefit from some extra support.

The key worker and SENCO invite Magda and Daniel to see them while Alice is playing in the pre-school. Magda comes alone as Daniel is at work. She appears to understand the team's concerns about Alice's development and admits she has noticed that she does not seem to be developing like other children. Magda tells Kerri afterwards that neither of the children sleep well and that she is exhausted. She intimates that she is having difficulty coping on her own for long periods. Kerri sympathises with Magda and suggests her health visitor could give some help and support.

The next day, however, Magda arrives to collect Alice with a Polish friend pushing the pram and tells Kerri that she is feeling much better today and her friend had reassured her that there is nothing wrong with Alice; she is just developing at her own pace.

Over the next few weeks, Kerri continues to communicate with Magda sharing Alice's successes as well as her developmental needs and sensitively asks Magda about Jakub and how everything is going at home. The SENCO arranges for the district SENCO to visit at a time when Daniel can take time off work and Kerri persuades them both to come and talk to the district SENCO after she has observed Alice.

Daniel and Magda talk to the district SENCO who shares the nursery team's concerns about Alice's development and suggests starting a Common Assessment Framework (CAF) process to access other professional support for Alice. Daniel thinks Alice has already started to make progress since starting at pre-school and is adamant that she will soon 'catch up' without additional support. Magda can now understand that Alice may benefit from support and would like some guidance on sleep patterns and toilet training but has to work hard to persuade her husband to consent to a CAF process.

The nursery SENCO starts the CAF process with the agreement and participation of both parents. Although she has been trained, this is the first time she has started the process and the district SENCO offers support. The following professionals are accessed to initially assess Alice's developmental needs and then provide relevant interventions to support her and the family where relevant:

- general practitioner (GP);
- health visitor;
- consultant paediatrician;
- clinical psychologist (child development centre);
- speech and language therapist;
- family support worker;
- key worker;
- nursery SENCO;
- district SENCO.

The nursery SENCO is selected as lead professional for the team at the first meeting.

Alice's speech and language delay is one of the areas of concern considered by the multi-professional team. The health visitor reports that some hearing loss in the left ear has been detected in a recent test. The GP has referred Alice to a consultant paediatrician who sent a report recommending a complex medical intervention. The speech and language therapist reports that an initial assessment performed at the child development centre shows that Alice's comprehension and receptive language was within normal limits but her expressive language is very much delayed. Alice will be offered a block of therapy sessions when a space becomes available. The key worker asks if they could have some guidance from the speech and language therapist on exercises they could do in the nursery while Alice is waiting for therapy. The district SENCO suggests Alice might benefit from Makaton and asks if the nursery staff are trained in signing. No one asks for the observations and assessments on Alice's language and communication development that Kerri has recently shared with the parents.

Reflective activity

Discuss aspects of the case study with colleagues.

»   *Consider the challenges Alice's parents are likely to face as the team around the child is established. How might they have felt upon being asked to come into the nursery?*

»   *Consider how Magda and Daniel's family heritage may influence their values and beliefs. How might their values and beliefs conflict with those of the professionals who are aiming to support them?*

»   *Consider how the key worker feels when the parent appears to have rejected the setting's assessment of Alice.*

»   *Reflect upon the levels of communication, trust and respect that this team appears to be exhibiting.*

»   *Have any professional boundaries been crossed in supporting Alice? Consider the effects this may have on individual professionals or their professions in general.*

Extended thinking

Use your own experiences of working within teams to reflect upon differences in professional cultures and the influence this may have on professionals' values and beliefs in practice.

»   *In what ways do they differ?*

»   *Why have differences developed?*

Consider your own professional identity and your status within the perceived hierarchy of professionals working within multi-agency teams.

»   *How may these views affect your participation in a team?*

»   *What actions could you take to improve your identity and status as a professional?*

The ethics of information sharing

'Information sharing', as you have seen above, is a concept that has become a key part of the political strategic response to the succession of high-profile child death inquiries which have highlighted the devastating consequences of failing to share information between agencies (DCFS, 2008a, 2008b). Police, health, social care and education services are now urged to work together to gather and share information about vulnerable children. In 2009 ContactPoint, a national online database of basic information on all children living in England, was launched by the Labour government. Only a year later it was decommissioned amid concerns that the level of scrutiny and surveillance inherent in the system was an infringement of the privacy and rights of children, young people and their families. Extensive use of electronic data collection and sharing of information in all walks of life has resulted in considerable debate in recent years. The Department for Constitutional Affairs (2006) Information Sharing Vision Statement, declared that:

information will be shared to expand opportunities for the most disadvantaged, fight crime and provide better public services for citizens and business, and in other instances where it is in the public interest.

(p 5)

Critics of information sharing, however, argue that it is dehumanising, invades privacy, increases stress and is open to abuse, particularly in the case of electronic databases which can be accessed by large numbers of people. This tension between personal privacy and public accountability produces one of the major ethical dilemmas facing modern society and is often felt acutely by those of us working with children and families in a multi-agency context (Ball and Webster, 2003). We are all now used to instant information, electronic banking, internet shopping and may feel safe and protected by CCTV (closed-circuit television) and other forms of surveillance. On the other hand, we may object to confidential information which is consensually shared with one party being passed onto others without consent. This however, is an everyday reality in the commercial world and it happens all the time, but how does it affect your right to privacy? The notion of rights is problematic in itself (Bannister, 2000). Possession of rights implies a duty on someone else to uphold these rights. The Universal Declaration of Human Rights (1948) states that all human beings are born free and equal in rights, but this is more of an ideal than a reality. People are not free but live within the rules and constraints of the societies and circumstances within which they find themselves and they are certainly not born equal as any examination of world poverty will reveal (LaFollette, 2003). The question then is whether the right to privacy is a moral imperative or rule that we should uphold in all circumstances regardless of the consequences.

Moral dilemma: is it ethical to share information about children and their families?

The deontological perspective

Immanuel Kant (1724–1804) was a German philosopher who argued from a deontological viewpoint that some acts are inherently right or wrong and people should act accordingly regardless of any good or bad consequences that might result. Kant said the main thing is not the level of good produced by an action but the nature of the action itself that is most important (MacIntyre, 1967). Central to his theory is the concept of 'goodwill' which is the will to do something morally worthy and involves doing one's duty simply because it is one's duty, out of respect for moral law. Kant argues for what he calls the 'categorical imperative'. This is a moral action that commands us unconditionally. To use information sharing as an example, you might believe that life would be better if certain information about you was not known to others. To take the right to privacy as a moral rule, however, would mean in deontological terms that you would have to believe that the sharing of information was not right in any circumstances at all, ever. If you believe that sharing information about other people is always wrong, this becomes your moral imperative or rule and your motive for obeying this rule comes from respect for the rule itself not for the consequences of it. If following the rule is motivated by self-interest or by a desire for the result, this has no inner worth. Deontologists, therefore, might argue that a person who has information that if shared with the police might foil a major terrorist plot, should not share it, even if hundreds of lives might be saved because to do so would mean that the moral rule had been broken which can never be good or lead to happiness (MacIntyre, 1967). In other words the preservation of our own virtue, through upholding the rule, outweighs even the preservation of other people's lives.

The utilitarian perspective

The utilitarian position holds that actions can never have intrinsic worth and the moral worth of any act can only be determined by its consequences. Jeremy Bentham (1748–1832) was an English philosopher who believed that the morality of an act should be judged in terms of the good that comes from it and that the correct course of action is the one that results in the greatest amount of good for the greatest number of people. Acts that produce pleasure and happiness for people are ones that are good and acts that diminish pleasure or promote pain are bad. Bentham criticised the concept of inalienable rights claiming that rights arise from tradition or government and that neither of these provide anything inalienable (Lyons, 1994). Indeed, utilitarians might argue about whether the rights of the individual should be a consideration at all as it is the good of society that should be the main consideration. The utilitarian perspective might hold that if you have information that might expose a terrorist plot, the correct course of action to take is to share that information with the police and in so doing save hundreds of lives. This will obviously have bad consequences for the terrorist who might go to jail but this course of action has clear benefits to society that will lead to more happiness for more people than if you keep the information to yourself.

CASE STUDY

Information sharing

You are the nominated child protection officer in a private day nursery. An early years practitioner has raised concerns about a four-year-old in the pre-school room. The girl often wears clothes, including shoes, that are too small for her and often arrives without a coat when the weather is cold. The child is very quiet, speaks very little to adults and has not really made any friends, preferring to watch the other children play. She has developmental delay in most areas and finds it difficult to concentrate. The child's father has parental responsibility and is the main carer. The early years practitioner is concerned that father and daughter do not seem to communicate much when he drops her off and picks her up from school. The family has no extended family support.

Reflective activity

» Relate each of the philosophical positions previously discussed to information sharing in the context of this case study.

» Would you share information about this child and her father? Why?

» If you choose to share information, what information would you share and who would you share it with?

Extended thinking

Reflect upon these two philosophical positions.

»   *What do you see as the main qualities and pitfalls of each position?*

Discussion

One of the most commonly cited advantages of sharing information about children and families is that it allows for early intervention which can prevent the escalation of problems and improve outcomes for children. Appropriate information sharing, therefore, could be seen to be a moral course of action from a utilitarian perspective as it leads to increased good in the form of better outcomes for the child and by extension her father. The official guidance does not take a deontological position that it is the duty of professionals to share information in all cases; instead it states that practitioners must use their professional judgement to decide whether to share information and what information to share (DCSF, 2008a, 2008b). However, for staff working with children and families, particularly in a safeguarding context, this can create a dilemma in itself, so when making decisions about whether to share information it is important to first establish a legal basis for this with regard to data protection, confidentiality and human rights. Any information relating to a living person who can be identified is protected by the Data Protection Act 1998 and should only be shared with that person's consent. Confidential information (any information that is of a private or sensitive nature and was given in the expectation that it would not be shared with others) is also protected in law and should not be shared unless there is informed consent from the person to do so. Consent should be given freely and should not be coerced by practitioners. It should never be assumed that consent is given in a situation where no response to the request to share information is forthcoming. Coercion reduces an individual's freedom and can thus be seen as an infringement of human rights under the Human Rights Act 1998. In the case of children, any child whom you assess to be able to fully understand the situation should be asked for consent to share information (generally over 12 years of age). This is not usually appropriate for younger children and whoever has parental responsibility for the child should therefore be asked to consent on their behalf. The only exception to this is if it is deemed to be in the public interest to breach confidentiality such as when sharing the information would protect a child or adult from risk of significant harm or where withholding information might interfere with the investigation of a serious crime. In situations where you make the decision to share information, only the necessary information should be shared and you should only share with the people or agencies that need to know (DCSF, 2008a, 2008b). Keeping all of this in mind, the decision to share information in relation to the case study above rests on one of two things: gaining consent from the child's father or sharing the information without consent in the belief that it is in the public interest to so in order to protect the child from significant harm. Therefore, according to the official guidance on information sharing, you should employ the utilitarian approach, as ultimately it is the consequence to the child and family that determines whether the act of sharing is good or bad.

Surveillance and control

Surveillance involves paying careful and close attention to a person or group of people for a particular reason and has become an accepted part of contemporary social life. The internet has created opportunities for individuals, private and public bodies to collect, organise and share information. It is questionable whether organisations can always be trusted to protect individual rights to privacy, however, and many of us no longer even know who holds information about us. Many organisations and institutions have become reliant on information technology but along with this comes a declining ability to protect that information (Davies, 1996). Issues such as identity theft, personal safety risks to young people who post personal information on social media sites, secondary use of information and incorrect information being stored against people's names are real problems in contemporary society.

In 2006 *A Report on the Surveillance Society* (Murakami Wood, 2006) described our society as one which routinely tracks and records our use of travel and public services, makes automated use of CCTV, analyses our shopping habits, monitors telephone calls, email and internet use and records financial transactions and personal information which is held by government and other agencies. You are often not aware you are being monitored and the report states that around 2,700 people have been wrongly identified as having criminal convictions. Pervasive surveillance, it seems, is likely to continue to accelerate in years to come although the report points out that even though the Home Office spent 78 per cent of its crime prevention budget on installing CCTV during the 1990s, CCTV schemes have apparently had a very limited effect on levels of violent crime and has simply displaced it (Waples and Gill, 2009).

In addition to offering co-location to key service providers, the aim of the original children's centres set up in each local community by the Labour government early in the 21st century, was to offer additional services such as debt and addiction counselling, adult education, birth control, breastfeeding advice and support for teenage mothers. They also provided universal child surveillance programmes to ensure that children and families were routinely assessed by staff for health and development needs, attachment and emotional disorders, social problems and parenting capacity. The drive to 'normalise' troubled families is cost-driven with a recent report by the Department for Communities and Local Government (2013) estimating that spending by local governments on troubled families is significantly more than that spent on average families. In West Cheshire, for example, a 'troubled' family costs the local authority £76,190 compared to just £7,795 for an average family. Families who cause and/or experience a complex mix of problems put a strain on the public purse and making sure children are in school, adults are in work, parenting is adequate and that crime and anti-social behaviour are reduced are therefore government priorities.

The Panopticon

In the late eighteenth century, through a series of letters to his father, Jeremy Bentham, a utilitarian philosopher, gave birth to the idea of the 'Panopticon' which he originally conceived as an architectural design for a prison (Bentham, [1791] 1995). The design was circular in structure containing a central control tower enabling a single inspector to see into all the cells which would be situated around the perimeter (see Figure 12.4). It was designed so that the prisoners inside would feel they were under constant surveillance even when they were not. Bentham believed it was not necessary for surveillance to actually be continuous, as long as the subjects being observed could not tell whether or not they were being watched at any given time. The mere fact of knowing they might be watched, he argued, would be sufficient to alter their behaviour. He believed he could transfer the same architectural design to gain power and control over a range of institutions and went on to say that the Panopticon was a suitable model:

> *Whether it be [for] that of punishing the incorrigible, guarding the insane, reforming the vicious, confining the suspected, employing the idle, maintaining the helpless, curing the sick, instructing the willing or training the rising race in the path of education.*
> (Bentham, [1791] 1995, p 2)

Bentham believed the Panopticon was the perfect architectural expression of the utilitarian goal of harmonising the desires of the self with the desires of society or the conscience. To be constantly under the eyes of the inspector would result in losing the power to do evil and consequently almost the thought of doing wrong. Bentham believed that people under an uncertain but invisible panoptic gaze exhibit a kind of anticipatory conformity with the rules, which eventually becomes internalised.

Figure 12.4 *The Panopticon design*

Reflective activity

»   *How could Bentham's ideas about the Panopticon be applied to multi-professional work with children?*

Discussion

Families are important to governments because they form the context within which most people have their material and emotional needs met and are enabled to work, be educated and make a contribution to society.

> *Strong families give children love, identity, a personal history and a secure base from which to explore and enjoy life as they grow up. Strong families also help build strong communities, so they are crucial for a successful society.*
>
> (DCSF, 2010, p 4)

Governments work on the principle that society is largely held together by families and changes in family processes and structure as well as increasing family instability presents challenges to governments, for example, in the form of the changing roles and contributions of men and women to the home and workplace, parental separation and divorce and the ability of families to care for their old and young members. The role the state should play in shaping family structure and behaviour through its economic and social policies is to a large extent dependent on the political ideology of the party in power. Left-wing policies advocate high levels of intervention in family life, often leading to the accusation of a 'nanny state' if governments are thought to interfere too extensively with personal and family life. The Conservative ideology, on the other hand, regards families as private institutions which should take responsibility for themselves to a greater degree. Previous Prime Minister David Cameron famously claimed in his 'Broken Society' speech, following the 2011 UK riots, that the *slow-motion moral collapse* that had taken place over the past few generations was largely due to families; parents who are not at home, those that don't care, those that have lost control and absent fathers. Whatever you think about Cameron's comments, it is clear to see that controlling and 'normalising' families is very important to governments in order to promote social cohesion; the ability of people in communities and the country as a whole, to collaborate in order to make progress towards common goals for the good of society. The children's centre model could be viewed as one way that this aim could be achieved and it incorporates a two-pronged strategy. Firstly, it targets the development and education of young children, increasing the chance that they will grow up into responsible and useful members of society and, secondly, it targets their parents by, for example, providing parenting classes and support to get back into the labour market which might result in less idleness and crime and the building of a more civil society. In this way children's centres could be seen to exemplify Bentham's idea of the inspection principle whereby parents are either referred to children's centre services by local authorities, as part of child protection plans to change their behaviour, or they may be subject to a more covert form of surveillance which takes place through attendance at universal services such as health visitor appointments or stay-and-play sessions. In either case families may feel as if they are being watched and judged and that the ultimate penalty for not conforming is the removal of their children into the care system. As we have seen, Bentham believed that if people felt they were under surveillance, they would alter their behaviour accordingly and would lose the will to commit an act of wrongdoing at all. Of course the extent to which covert surveillance takes place in children's centres is debateable but, if it takes place at all, the question of whether rights to privacy are being invaded becomes prominent as do issues of consent, autonomy and trust. You might see the children's centre approach simply as a sound means of monitoring parents, closely observing their children and sharing the information gained with those in authority or, on the other hand, you might view the children's centre as a more sinister and potent symbol of the kind of 'big brother' society we should strive to avoid. Munro (2005) argued that the multi-agency system has created an *alarming potential for panopticism* suggesting that it has provided governments with a powerful instrument for exercising discipline and power, and the various professionals that work with children and families take the role of 'inspectors' recording information about children and their families in order to share it with others in authority.

Foucault's (1980) reading and analysis of Bentham's Panopticon focused on the voluntary submission aspect of the design (Ward, 2005). His observations are in line with a contemporary society overrun with panoptical mechanisms in both physical and cyber space. Foucault believed that the idea behind the Panopticon represented an accurate model for modern forms of surveillance and control stating that:

> *There is no need for arms, physical violence, material constraints, just a gaze. An inspecting gaze, where each individual under its weight will end by internalising to the point that he is his own overseer.*
>
> (Foucault, 1980, p 155)

Foucault examined the relationship between discourse, knowledge and power. He believed that certain versions of events are given the rubber stamp of 'truth' in our society and have the effect of creating power by marginalising other ways of acting. The opportunity to succeed, therefore, depends upon acting in ways cognisant with currently accepted versions of knowledge, for example, parenting according to the professional 'prescription'. Furthermore, he believed that contemporary Western individuals have been created by modern institutional, social and cultural practices that allow particular discourses of 'the person' to become prominent. This results in people feeling that they possess or should possess certain traits and characteristics and therefore choosing socially favoured ways of acting that are ultimately governed, without force, by their own individual consciences. According to Furedi (2001) this has manifested itself today into a generation of paranoid parents who are so overwhelmed by the pressures of modern parenting that they cannot make even basic decisions such as when to toilet train their children without consulting the official orthodoxy which is transmitted via parenting magazines and manuals written by the 'experts'. Marx, before Foucault, explained this as the institutionalised beliefs and actions of groups of people which are sometimes inexplicable and incoherent and trap people within inadequate schemes of meaning, leaving them unable to imagine things any other way (Spivak, 1988). By the same token that certain types of knowledge are favoured, certain types are considered illegitimate or even disqualified, for example, cultural variations in parenting styles. The latter types of knowledge may still retain some popularity but are confined to the margins, opposing the accepted discourses that surround them which may be embedded within political systems, educational institutions and social organisations. To this end, Foucault (1980) advocated that practitioners be highly reflective and ask themselves certain questions such as what types of knowledge they seek to disqualify, what types they want to diminish and what theories or political stance they wish to advance through their work with children and families.

Presumably Bentham would have approved of children's centres and the growing list of other means of monitoring society. Although there was obviously little technology back in the 1700s, Bentham had already conceived of the idea of an identity tattoo, so it seems likely that he would be in favour of increased surveillance in the belief that people would act in a more socially responsible manner (Bentham, 1995). Perhaps the biggest problem we have living in an information society, is that we may feel we lack control over our personal information and therefore the very essence of ourselves. If the right to privacy is not taken to be a categorical imperative and enforced across multiple domains, everything is a matter of trust. But it is difficult to trust when computers can be hacked and those in authority can use information corruptly or pass it on to others without our consent or knowledge. How can families attending children's centres be sure the information they have shared will be used to their benefit and not as a means to their disempowerment, of relinquishing control to the 'professionals' who know best? Utilitarianism argues that it is the balance of good over bad that determines the desirability of the alternatives to this. Not only is a course of action that is expected to produce the greatest balance of good over bad desirable, but such actions are obligatory and even the most desirable course of action may have a negative impact on some parties. Therefore, certain organisational practices which adversely impact some service users can be justified as long as they produce the greatest balance of good over bad for society as a whole (Singer, 1991).

Information sharing and monitoring are now facts of life and arguments perhaps should now focus on the use or misuse of information-sharing techniques rather than the issue of information sharing itself. Monitoring, surveillance and information sharing might be considered inherently neutral tools for practitioners that may or may not be used unethically within the multi-professional system. Perhaps it could be argued that as long as the multi-professional approach emphasises communication in the design and implementation of monitoring systems, upholds strong laws to protect the individual and accepts accountability, it could offer a solution which proves satisfactory in both deontological and utilitarian terms. Utilitarianism, with its emphasis on consequences, does not adequately take into account individual rights and dignity. On the other hand deontology, with its focus on absolute obedience to moral duty, does not consider consequences and this belief makes the principle of universality invalid. People and circumstances will always be different. Discussion would therefore, perhaps, be better focused not on whether information sharing is ethical or unethical but rather on how information-sharing mechanisms might be administered more ethically in the future.

Chapter reflections

This chapter has attempted to examine some of the very real issues which surround the whole topic of multi-agency working, starting with the confusion of terminology and the ensuing difficulties of ensuring that all those involved with any team around the child really understand the premise of the process. Clearly the importance of this level of communication to the health and welfare of our children is paramount, but unless we really reflect upon the ethical, moral and practical problems that this process hinges upon, we could be sleepwalking into a situation which is so ineffective that it becomes literally a matter of life and death for the young children of our society.

Changes are needed to raise the skill level and awareness of the whole childcare, education and health-based workforce, if we are to create a seamless and integrated approach to working with children and families. This will require commitment and investment from governments and local authorities, as well as a commitment to eradicate poverty, ensure that education is available to all and ensure all children, globally, have access to health and social services. The only way that this is likely to happen, as we have discussed in this chapter, is to bring about a climate of trust and communicative relationships. This is going to demand that professionals working in the field go through not just a change of process and procedure, but a change in attitude to each other and to the child. At the heart of all that we do as professionals must be the child, their welfare, needs and aspirations; nothing must inhibit our belief in this. We can do this, but it requires that we step back and reflect upon our policies, procedures, hierarchies and possessiveness to develop trustful relationships and respectful interactions.

Extended reflections

» *After reading the discussion at the end of the chapter, extend your reflective account applying Bentham's concept of the Panopticon to multi-professional work with children by considering the extent to which you agree with the view that the multi-professional approach is fulfilling a government agenda to promote social cohesion through 'normalising' families.*

» *Does contributing to a multi-agency team compromise our professional values and beliefs regarding the importance of working in respectful and trusting partnerships with parents?*

» *Can the voice of the child be adequately heard within a complex multi-professional team and how can the early childhood professional become more effective as an advocate for young children and their families?*

» *Should we persevere in implementing the considerable changes required for multi-professional teams to work successfully or should our focus return to improving systems within individual services to make them more effective in responding to children's needs?*

Further reading

Fitzgerald, D and Kay, J (2016) *Working Together in Children's Services*, 2nd edition. Oxon: Routledge.

Whilst a very readable and practitioner-based text, this book addresses a range of theoretical perspectives and contexts which will introduce you to the key issues and essential skills for multi-agency working, and allow you to reflect upon and critically explore the benefits and barriers that arise when crossing professional boundaries.

References

Anning, A, Cottrell, D, Frost, N, Green, J and Robertson, M (2006) *Developing Multi-professional Teamwork for Integrated Children's Services*. Maidenhead: Open University Press.

Atkinson, M, Wilkin, A, Stott, A, Doherty, P and Kinder, K (2002) *Multi-agency Working: A Detailed Study*. Slough: NFER.

Ball, K and Webster, F (2003) *The Intensification of Surveillance, Crime, Terrorism and Warfare in the Information Age*. London: Pluto Press.

Bannister, D (2000) *Privacy and Human Rights. An International Survey of Privacy Laws and Developments*. Washington, DC: Epic.

Bentham, J ([1791] 1995) *The Panopticon Writings*. London: Verso.

Blyton, E (1944) *The Island of Adventure*. London: McMillian Children's Books.

Davies, S (1996) *Big Brother: Britain's Web of Surveillance and the New Technological Order*. London: Pan.

Department for Children, Schools and Families (DCSF) (2008a) *Information Sharing: Guidance for Practitioners and Managers*. Nottingham: DCSF.

DCSF (2008b) *The Impact of Parental Involvement of Children's Education*. Nottingham: Crown.

DCSF (2010) *Support for All: The Families and Relationships Green Paper*. London: HMSO.

Department for Communities and Local Government (2013) *The Cost of Troubled Families*. London: DCLG.

Department for Constitutional Affairs (2006) *Information Sharing Vision Statement*. London: Crown.

DfES (2003) *Every Child Matters – The Green Paper*. London: DfES.

DfES (2004) *The Children Act 2004*. London: HMSO.

Department of Health (1989) *The Children Act 1989*. London: HMSO.

Fitzgerald, D and Kay, J (2016) *Working Together in Children's Services*, 2nd edition. Oxon: Routledge.

Foucault, M (1980) *Power/Knowledge: Selected Interviews and Other Writings, 1972–1977*. London: Harvester Press.

Furedi, F (2001) *Paranoid Parenting*. London: Allen Lane.

Greco, V, Sloper, P, Webb, R and Beecham, J (2005) *An Exploration of Different Models of Multi-agency Partnerships in Key Worker Services for Disabled Children: Effectiveness and Costs*. York: DfES Publications.

Hudson, B (2005) Partnership Working and the Children's Services Agenda: Is It Feasible? *Journal of Integrated Care*, 13(2): 7–12.

Jack, G (2005) Assessing the Impact of Community Programmes Working with Children and Families in Disadvantaged Areas. *Child and Family Social Work*, 10: 293–304.

LaFollette, H (ed) (2003) *The Oxford Handbook of Practical Ethics*. Oxford: Oxford University Press.

Laming H (2003) *The Victoria Climbié Inquiry*. London: HMSO.

Lloyd, G, Stead, J and Kendrick, A (2001) *Hang on in There: A Study of Interagency Work to Prevent School Exclusion in Three Local Authorities*. London: NCB.

Lyons, D (1994) *Rights, Welfare and Mills Moral Theory*. Oxford: Oxford University Press.

MacIntyre, A (1967) *A Short History of Ethics*. London: Routledge.

Munro, E (2005) What Tools Do We Need to Improve Identification of Child Abuse? *Child Abuse Review*, 14(6): 374–88.

Murakami Wood, D (ed) (2006) A Report on the Surveillance Society for the Information Minister. Surveillance Studies Network. Available from: https://ico.org.uk/media/about-the-ico/documents/1042390/surveillance-society-full-report-2006.pdf (accessed 9 January 2017).

Payler, J and Georgeson, J (2013) Multiagency Working in the Early Years: Confidence, Competence and Context. *Early Years*, 33(4), 380–97.

Singer, P (ed) (1991) *A Companion to Ethics*. Oxford: Blackwell.

Siraj-Blatchford, I, Clarke, K and Needham, M (2007) *The Team around the Child: Multi-Agency Working in the Early Years*. Stoke-on-Trent: Trentham Books.

Spivak, G (1988) Can the Subaltern Speak? In Nelson, C and Grossberg, L (1988), *Marxism and the Interpretation of Culture*. London: Macmillan.

Universal Declaration of Human Rights (1948). Available from: www.un.org/en/universal-declaration-human-rights/index.html (accessed 9 January 2017).

Waples, S and Gill, M (2009) Does CCTV Displace Crime? *Criminology and Criminal Justice*, 9(2): 207–24.

Ward, L. (2005) *'Flags of Concern' on Child Database*. Guardian Unlimited, 28 October.

Warmington, P, Daniels, H, Edwards, A, Brown, S, Leadbetter, J, Martin, D and Middleton, D (2004) *TLRP111 Learning in and for Inter-agency Working, Inter-agency Collaboration: A Review of the Literature*. Bath: University of Bath, Learning in and for Interagency, working project.

13 Reflection and change

CAROL HAYES

There is nothing like looking, if you want to find something … You certainly usually find something, if you look, but it is not always quite the something you were after.

(J R R Tolkien, 1991, p 65)

Introduction

Do you remember the traditional nursery song about going on a bear hunt?

We're going on a bear hunt!
We're going to catch a big one!
I'm not afraid!
Are you?
Not me.

If you remember, the child goes on a scary journey to encounter a range of new and potentially dangerous situations, a tall mountain to climb, a jungle to push through, a wide river to swim across and a dark cave to explore. No doubt the thought of this journey conjured up images of werewolves, vampires and ghouls, causing goose pimples to rise on the back of the child's neck as s/he has to consider the new skills and knowledge that are needed to successfully achieve the journey. This is very like the scary journey that you might take when you embark on action research for the first time. You are entering the unknown, you are not even sure whether you have the knowledge and skills to complete the journey, and you are not sure quite what you will find. The Good, The Bad and The Ugly springs to mind because, when you reflect upon your practice and that of your setting, you see the things that are good, that you need to build upon and broadcast, but you also see the bad things that you need to improve, and the things that in one light are acceptable but, if viewed from other perspectives, can be ugly, and need careful rethinking and re-examination.

This chapter examines the whole concept of instigating change in the setting and, through a range of case studies, will examine the difficulties that you might encounter as a practitioner/ researcher.

Action research

The term 'action research' was first coined by Kurt Lewin in 1946 when he described it as:

comparative research on the conditions and effects of various forms of social action, using a spiral of steps, each of which is composed of a circle of planning, action and fact finding about the result of the action.

(Lewin, 1946, p 35)

Lewin believed in the empowerment of people, and felt that if they were involved in their own research and analysis process, and could see how the actions could directly affect themselves, they would be more likely to adopt the new ways of thinking in a form of self-reflective enquiry. This would then become a liberating process enabling all practitioners to see themselves as researchers, in control of their situations and environments. This he felt would in turn help to raise self-esteem and confidence. In 1988 Kemmis and McTaggart offered a different, but very comprehensive definition of action research:

Action Research is a form of collective self-reflective enquiry undertaken by participants in social and educational practices as well as their understanding of these practices and the situation in which these practices are carried out ... the approach is only Action Research when it is collective though it is important to realize that the Action Research of the group is achieved through critically examined action of individual group members.

(Kemmis and McTaggart, 1988, p 5)

In 1996 McTaggart suggested that action research was not a method of research or even a procedure for research but a:

series of commitments to observe and problematize through practice, a series of principles for conducting social enquiry.

(McTaggart, 1996, p 248)

Johnston and Nahmed-Williams talk about action research in the context of what they call the 'thinking professional' and see the whole process as one of a cyclical nature with no distinctive beginning and probably no end as the practice is constantly under review and the analysis to improve and develop it is open-ended.

In which the professional attempts to improve or develop practice in a cyclical way, by planning the next step of action or development as a result of analysis of the previous action or development.

(Johnston and Nahmad-Williams, 2009, p 9)

You can see that although this is an aid to reflection advocated by professions there is by no means a clearly agreed definition of its roots. I tend to favour the more simplistic definition by Cohen, Manion and Morrison (2011) who talk of it as a small scale intervention conducted in the 'real world' which entails a close examination of that intervention and its effects.

Figure 13.1 *The cyclical nature of action research*

However, although usually represented as a circle such as the one in Figure 13.1, it is probably more accurate to describe it as a spiral, as reflection on action, as your findings should lead to further questions and further actions in a continuing progression.

This concept of a spiral of action was further developed by McNiff (2002) who suggests that it offers the ability to deal with a number of problems at the same time by allowing the spirals to develop spin-off spirals and uses Figure 13.2 to illustrate her meaning.

Figure 13.2 *Spin-off spirals*
Source: McNiff (2002)

Rodd (2012) refers to action research as:

> *The tool for narrowing the gap between research and professional learning and fosters reflective practice.*

(Rodd, 2012, p 213)

She also suggests that strong links have been drawn between action research and quality improvement within settings. However, if action research is to develop flexible, quality settings the process needs the ability to be able to respond to the environment and allow practitioners to make sound professional judgements. Such judgements need to be based upon the practitioner's ability to analyse and use data systematically collated from the setting, and set this within their own knowledge gained from their wider reading and evaluation. In this way action research can be seen as part of the general idea of professionalism, an extension to professional work requiring an involved practitioner rather than a passive receiver of others' ideology.

There is general consensus that action research starts with the identification of an immediate problem or series of problems within a setting. This then becomes a practical problem-solving approach, and a research question or hypothesis arises from the analysis of this problem, thus allowing an action to be carried out. Action research can then be seen as self-reflective research with practitioners doing the research on themselves, enquiring into their own lives and examining their own practice within context (see Figure 13.3).

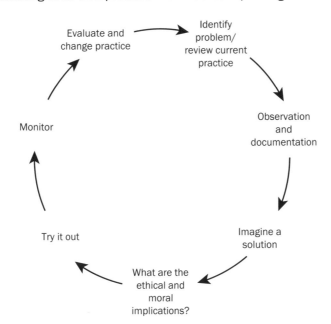

Figure 13.3 *Process of action research*

Set into this context you could, like Cohen, Manion and Morrison (2011), describe action research as a highly *political process* because it involves making changes that affect others. As a reflective practitioner with a political agenda, action research can result in a broader programme of changing practice and ultimately changing society. The researcher then becomes immersed in the whole social world in which they are studying. Kemmis, McTaggart and Nixon (2014) talk about shaping the social structures through the cultural/symbolic realm, the economic realm and the sociopolitical realm. The area selected for research will clearly be of interest to you, and this is likely to have been influenced by the reality that you inhabit, but this could affect the decisions you make about the research simply because of your involvement. In turn this could affect the way that you interpret and evaluate the data received. The implication of this is that you could unconsciously make the new understanding that you have of the issue fit into your current patterns of thinking and so, in the end, the process does not yield much substantial progress. If you are to embark on a piece of action research you will need to dig down and examine your own goals and the fundamentals of the interest that you initially bring to the project and then be brave enough to make changes, some of which may be substantial.

Participatory action research

Critical action research belongs to a family of different types of social research. Kemmis, McTaggart and Nixon (2014) talk about different generations of action research, progressively honing down their particular uses.

Participatory Action Research (PAR) is just one of these and is described by Kemmis et al (2014) as having three main features which distinguish it from other forms of action research.

* Shared ownership of the research.

* It demands a community based analysis to particular social problems.

* It is orientated to community action.

Kemmis et al talk of a *'spiral of self reflective cycles'* (p276) with overlapping stages involving:

1. Planning a change

2. Acting and observing the process and consequences of change.

3. Reflecting on these.

4. Re-planning.

5. Acting and observing again.

6. Reflecting again and so on.

What sets Participatory Action Research apart is the collaborative and social nature of the process, refuting those who say that action research is a solitary process.

> If practices are constituted in social interaction between people, changing practices is a social process. To be sure, one person may change so that others are obliged to react or respond differently to that individuals changed behavior, but the willing and committed involvement of those whose interactions constitute the practice is necessary in the end to secure and legitimate the change.
>
> (Kemmis, McTaggart and Nixon, 2014, p 277)

Reflective activity

» *Reflect on four characteristics of action research which make it distinct from other types of research.*

» *In what ways do these features appeal to you and why?*

Extended thinking

Compare and contrast the ideals of critical action research and Participatory Action Research.

» *What advantages or disadvantages can you see of PAR, as described by Kemmis, McTaggart and Nixon (2014)?*

» *Considering your own setting, how feasible would a collaborative approach be and how could you persuade colleagues of its value?*

Professional development

Professional development does not need to be just about courses led by others with more academic knowledge of the subject area. It can be more personal than that, and is arguably more useful if it relates directly to aspects of practice that you want to explore or improve. For some practitioners this re-evaluation can make the whole issue of professional development more approachable and accessible.

If you see action research as a regular part of your professional development, you can start with the question *How do I improve my practice?*, which is a very different approach to traditional training courses and education, where one 'expert' attempts to transmit his/her knowledge to the audience. Action research however, works on the basis of an acknowledgement of the value of the prior experience of you, the practitioner, and of your ability to participate in an active, flexible learning environment. To do this you need to take responsibility for your own learning through reflection. This in turn makes you accountable for your own practice, taking responsibility for your own planning, behaviour and thinking. Some practitioners may find this a scary prospect, especially if this is the first time that they have experienced that level of requirement to review and readjust their work practice.

Reflective activity

» *What do you see as the main advantages of action research? The first two have been done for you, can you think of two more?*

1 *Brings about changes in the practitioner's professional skills and abilities.*

2 *Increases levels of confidence, self-esteem and self-fulfillment.*

3

4

Extended thinking

» *If action research can bring about such changes to thinking and practice as is claimed, how objective do you think you can be if your findings prove to be critical of your own practice?*

» *If you are able to maintain that objectivity and bring about change, how realistic do you think it is to try to effect this on your own if colleagues are not able to take on board your findings?*

Challenges of action research

However important action research is to your reflective practice, as the practitioner/researcher you are likely to encounter some difficulties. The whole process of action research comes with its challenges, particularly for managers and room supervisors, unless they are prepared to learn with the people that they line manage. As already alluded to, some colleagues could see this as threatening and challenging to their personal authority, especially as it is likely to require a considerable amount of group consensus to implement. It is clear that any process involving change is likely to produce conflict from certain quarters if it challenges the status quo, and involves staff and the setting in upheaval and alteration. At some point it is inevitable that confrontation will occur and perhaps the hardest task is when the confrontation is with yourself as there must come a time when you confront your own prejudices, preconceptions and bias. This means being prepared to see your own shortcomings and not feeling affronted by a positive critique of your own long-standing beliefs and views.

It could be claimed that as a practitioner you are unlikely to be an experienced researcher and undertaking research is potentially a complex minefield, so to commence truly reliable and valid research you would need extensive training, and that without this the whole process could end up as nothing more than 'navel gazing' and idle self-contemplation. It is also true that there is that need for realism already discussed, and you will need to ask yourself whether the problem is capable of improvement or even whether it is within your remit to be able to achieve that. Alongside this it would be true to say that this type of research can be time consuming when you consider your normal workload, and you will have to reflect upon and weigh up the potential long-term benefits to your practice and to the children and families that you work with, before embarking upon the project. This will then require considerable preparatory planning to ensure that the time taken with the research is 'cost effective'.

Another potential difficulty is how to bring your colleagues on board, as a project that does not receive appropriate support from colleagues and management can be demoralising and counterproductive, so a well-planned and well-organised project will rely on your good interpersonal communication skills and relationships.

Reflective activity

» *Working with a trusted colleague, can you suggest ways to overcome the difficulties of action research as listed above?*

Extended thinking

While action research may well be a useful tool for practitioners to effect change in pedagogy, practice and understanding, it could be argued that it is only going to happen within the constraints of the national system and government guidelines.

Perhaps the focus should be upon the early years setting as an organisation with structures set within a social, economic and educational environment.

The responsibility for improvement needs to be understood within a wider context of 'the buck stops here'. An ideology of individualism regards the setting as only as good as the 'sum of its parts'. This implies that the practitioners within the system have responsibility and autonomy over their practice.

» *Do you think that this is really so?*

» *How engaged with the decision-making process do you feel, both at a local and at a national level?*

» *Should responsibility for quality improvement in a setting be placed not only on practitioners, but also on settings as a whole and upon the government ideology of the day?*

McNiff (2002) suggests that the whole premise of action research can be summed up in one phrase, *How can I improve my work?* This implies a very personal approach to the process and it is clearly a very self-critical and reflective approach because it starts with the idea that what you are doing as a practitioner is not perfect, it is not the best that it can be, but that you can strive to move forward, reviewing and changing all the time. McNiff (2002) does not propose this as a one-off piece of research which may or may not change practice, but as a continuous and evolving process. This is a very 'adult' and mature approach to practice. It differs from that of the young, newly qualified, level 3 practitioner who believes that, having done the course, they have 'arrived' and are the expert in the field with no further need for professional development. They may see their course as an end to their learning rather than the basis from which to start their education.

In these terms this can be a very personal journey which, by your personal action, you *can* influence others and thereby bring a change within the setting. However, Lowe (2007) sees this as very much a group process from the start. Lowe claims that the first step to action research is to get the research group together (similar to PAR as described above). In practice it is debatable whether this is necessary and whether, as McNiff (2002) believes, if you start from a personal perspective you encourage others to come on board as you develop the role as group leader/facilitator. It is important in those very early stages of the research planning to see the project as a whole and to reflect upon what obstacles you might meet along the way and what you will do at the culmination of the project. For example, who will need to know about the results of your research and how you will inform them and where this might ultimately lead further research.

This is the way that knowledge evolves, a process of learning from others and reworking existing knowledge in new ways.

(McNiff, 2002, p 2)

This evaluation of learning then develops from *How can I improve my work?* into *How can we improve our work?* Clearly this level of self-criticality demands that you are constantly reviewing your own drives, your own values and your own philosophy of early years practice upon which to base your proposition for change.

Griffiths and Kaday (2004) talk about a GROW model of reflection and change:

- **G**oal
- **R**eality
- **O**bstacles/options and
- **W**ay forward

The goal encourages you to consider where you want to be from where you are now. Reality encourages you to examine where you are currently, your current practice and how you feel about it. Obstacles and options make you consider what is preventing you from achieving that goal and what the options are to negotiate these obstacles. Finally, the way forward is exactly that, setting targets to help you to take steps towards these goals. This clearly demonstrates a well-planned, well-considered and well-constructed approach to action research.

CASE STUDY

Jennifer

Jennifer is a manager of a small, inner-city, private day nursery. She is aware that in the last few months there has been deterioration in the children's behaviour at meal times, at times it is difficult to get the children to sit at the tables and they seem to take no notice of the staff telling them not to eat with their fingers but to use the spoons. Staff try to get the meal time over in as short a time as possible so that they can also go for breaks and have their meals. At their last Ofsted inspection the report suggested that the support for these children was limited and this was a possible *area for improvement*.

Reflective activity

Consider how you can use the GROW model to reflect on this case study.

» *What goals do you think that Jennifer should have?*

Goals	1.
	2.
	3.

»   *What issues in her current practice could she focus upon?*

Reality	1.
	2.
	3.

»   *What possible obstacles do you think she might encounter and how could these be overcome?*

Obstacles	1.	Options	1.
	2.		2.
	3.		3.

»   *Offer three steps that you think will be the way forward for Jennifer and her staff and place these in order of priority.*

Way forward	1.
	2.
	3.

Extended thinking

Consider the following questions.

»   *How will you know when a goal that you have identified has been achieved?*

»   *What if this goal conflicts with other objectives of the setting?*

»   *If there is more than one goal how will you prioritise them for attention?*

A reflective research buddy

The practitioner/researcher is a relatively new phenomena for early years and can potentially be a lonely journey in the initial stages. However, using another knowledgeable person to work with, that you can call your 'research buddy', is helpful and can expand the remit of the journey to include areas not otherwise considered. Your reflective research buddy needs to be someone you trust whom you can invite to look at your research and offer constructive feedback. This helps to ensure that your changes to practice are more objective, less opinion based and more evidence based. Your reflective research buddy can be there to help you to ground your research. So this needs to be someone whose opinions you value, but not necessarily someone with the same ideas or ethos. It may be that you will need more than one reflective research buddy or that they can be assigned to particular projects for which they have some expertise. This does need to be someone who has the time and willingness to meet with you regularly to discuss your research data and to offer alternative views of the results of the research. Your reflective research buddy will need to listen to your ideas, challenge them and help you to find solutions. McNiff (2002) calls this sort of relationship a 'dialogue of equals' where you are both learning together. You can also become a reflective research buddy for other colleagues, and this will contribute to your own personal learning journey and help to create a community of lifelong learners, developing and enhancing knowledge, and producing a collective research community. This enables the learning to be grounded in practice but allows you to develop your own theories to underpin your entire ethos and philosophy of practice. This is a genuine partnership of colleagues and cannot work on the deferential model where the researcher uses the reflective research buddy as an advisor or sees them as a more powerful body with 'all the answers'. Rodd (2012) describes this as part of the process of establishing a 'research culture' within the setting:

> An environment in which intellectual interest and scientific curiosity exist and are evident ... values theoretical and research based knowledge which relates to child development and learning processes, intellectual and instructional methods and human resource management.
>
> (Rodd, 2012, p 211)

If settings are going to be responsive to the needs of their children and families they should be nurturing a research culture as Rodd suggests, one that values theory and research-based knowledge. This may be a new ideal to early years settings in this country and will take a considerable shift of emphasis from one of deference to the so-called 'experts' in the field, and in related fields such as psychology, sociology and education, to one of a questioning and sceptical nature where there is increasing respect for those in the specialist early years arena. One which, furthermore, draws upon a greater diversity of subject specialists such as economics, politics, law, anthropology, etc.

It is possible that as individuals we have preferred reflective styles. For example, some would rather write down their thoughts in diaries and journals, while others prefer to talk and engage in verbal discourse but, however we prefer to communicate, the reflective research buddy needs to be someone who will pose challenging questions and strive to understand the articulation of your thoughts. This is no 'cosy chat' but someone who will probe and help you to consider alternative ways to change things, allowing you to find your own solutions to problems, confronting negative intentions or behaviour and helping you to clarify your thoughts and organise your feelings.

CASE STUDY

Melanie

Melanie is the manager of the Tiny Tots children's centre. Almost half of the children who attend do not have English as their first language, and most have a very limited grasp of the English language. This has started to worry Michelle and her staff as it is making communication between the children in the setting more and more difficult and this is in turn affecting their behaviour. This is a 120-place nursery and in the 2–3 year-old age group there are two parallel groups of children with 20 children in the Orange group and 18 in the Yellow group. Melanie calls a meeting of all the staff to discuss some of the difficulties that they have encountered and the problems that they feel they are presented with on a day-to-day basis. She asks them to reflect upon their present practice and the processes so far in place.

Reflective activity

»   *Can you suggest any way that Melanie and her staff can undertake an action research project to enable them to have a better understanding of how children in the group are dealing with the communication and behavioural difficulties?*

Extended thinking

»   *How can Melanie maintain the focus of the research throughout her staff?*

»   *How can she manage the time constraints?*

»   *How can she deal with any preconceived ideas and presumed foreknowledge of the solutions?*

Validity and trustworthiness

It is always difficult to ascertain the validity of research, but this is particularly so for the sort of small-scale project in action research. Action research is often depicted as falling within an interpretivist paradigm and being qualitative in character, that is an attempt to understand the meaning or significance of an issue to a person or small group of people, rather than a numerical interpretation of the world. It is important to note that this is not always the case and quantitative data can prove very useful wherever it is appropriate and available.

However, it is true to say that in reality most action research does fall into an interpretivist paradigm of research, with the researcher starting from a very open-ended perspective looking for a depth of data rather than quantity, and attempting to understand phenomena in context-specific settings.

There are certainly some researchers, such as Punch and Oancea (2014), who would question whether validity is possible in action research but others, such as Lincoln and Guba (1986), have recognised the need for some form of quality check or measure to this type of research, and have adopted terms such as 'rigour' and 'trustworthiness' to establish some confidence in the findings of research that is essentially subjective in nature. Lincoln and Guba (1986) claim that to establish trustworthiness involves an examination of four areas.

1   **Credibility** – The integrity and truthfulness of the research.

2   **Transferability** – Whether the results can be generalised to other settings.

3   **Dependability** – Whether the processes are open to scrutiny with a detailed description of the research process.

4   **Confirmability** – All outcomes are evidence based.

Elliott (1991) suggests that the validity of action research is unlikely to be generated by scientific tests of truth, but rather on how it helps you to act with greater skill and intellectual independence.

> *In Action Research 'theories' are not validated independently and then applied to practice. They are validated through practice.*
>
> (Elliott, 1991, p 69)

However, Punch and Oancea (2014) identify a further aspect to the difficulties encountered with the validity of action research and proposes separating the action from the research. They suggest that if the researcher is frequently also the researched, this can bring with it difficulties of validity and credibility and they believe that most practitioners do not have the research skills necessary for such a task. To overcome this they recommend separating the practitioner from the action research and suggest that although there must be close collaboration between the researcher and the practitioner they should not be one and the same person. Punch and Oancea call this 'collaborative participation'. Through the collaboration and participation of the research and the researched, Punch and Oancea (2014) believe that a community of learners can be developed to enhance the trustworthiness of the research and allow more sceptical professional researchers to see this approach as valid and reliable material.

CASE STUDY

Melanie and story-telling

Melanie from the Tiny Tots children's centre is sure that story-telling could be used to improve all of the children's vocabulary, in particular their use of descriptive adjectives, and bring together the English and non-English speaking children in the groups. She persuaded the staff of the need to test out her hypothesis that story-telling can improve children's descriptive contextual vocabulary.

Reflective activity

» *Suggest a research methodology which could be employed by Melanie and the staff to test out the hypothesis.*

» *How can they ensure the validity of the proposed research?*

» *What ethical considerations would need to be implemented to ensure that this research is ethical and fair?*

Extended thinking

Validity is an important element of any research. Does the research do 'what it says on the tin'? Does it measure what it purports to measure? Rather than considering validity as a single concept more modern research has shown that it can come in many differing forms. Cohen, Manion and Morrison (2011) give twenty different forms of validity from concurrent validity, through cultural validity to theoretical validity. Of course not all these apply to all research projects.

Cohen, Manion and Morrison (2011) talk about the 'Hawthorne effect' on validity. They query whether there are times when the research itself causes a difference or change in behaviour.

» *In what way do you think that the 'Hawthorne effect' could influence the research methods employed by Melanie and her staff?*

Spreading the news

For action research to be successful it is clear that interpersonal communication skills need to be of the highest importance. This is a method of research which can be empowering to the practitioners who engage with it and the research data has the potential to bring about change, but this cannot be realised without that dialogue and community of practice. The only way to bring about meaningful change is to share the data and findings with colleagues and to discuss prospectively and retrospectively the issues that emerge. Action research is not done *to* you but requires active involvement and discourse with the whole process. This manner of communication may not only be with the other staff directly involved with the research process, but may be appropriate to a wider audience as dissemination of your findings may be appropriate and of interest to other practitioners. If you look back to the various manifestations of the reflective cycle you will see that an important part is the dissemination of the findings, sharing the new information and new insights to the original problem. Initially this is likely to be discussion at staff meetings or more formal continuing professional development sessions but, to improve the accessibility of the research, could also include websites, blogs and other social media. Kellett reminds us that:

> *Children have a fundamental human right to quality research about their childhood and their lives. Therefore they have a fundamental right to appropriate dissemination of that research.*
>
> (Kellett, 2010, p 77)

Kellett also suggests that we have an ethical duty to provide feedback, at an accessible level and findings to children and adults who have participated in the research. However, this is to assume that dissemination is a one-way, top-down flow of information from the researcher or the expert to the listeners or passive receivers. There is, however, a more interactive approach to dissemination, which appears to fit well with the action research process, that is a two-way flow of information inviting the audience to be involved with interpreting the data and providing options for solutions. This is likely to be a more productive approach and could potentially lead to further research and investigation with a co-construction of understanding and ideas. This also has the advantage of gaining others' perspectives and support, but also providing feedback in a less threatening situation. Rodd (2012) reminds us that practitioners are human beings that have a psychological need to 'belong', to find a place within a group, and to feel significant within that group. Only when all that is in place will they feel connected and able to contribute to the needs of the group. This can only be achieved through clear interaction and communication between the members of the team. Developing communicative relationships within the team will create a harmonious and mutually supportive group that fosters that sense of belonging and that feeling of significance within the setting. This, in turn, enables the criticality of reflection and trust that binds teams together rather than forces them apart.

One possible barrier to dissemination is the concern of the practitioner/researcher about exposing themselves to critical peer review and whether their peers will see the research as competent and trustworthy. So a key component of the planning for any piece of action research needs to be an indication of how the results will be transmitted within the team once the research starts to achieve results, and at what point this will be appropriate. So the most important part of dissemination is honesty, integrity, respect and trust, with an absolute belief that you have something of value to contribute.

Undoubtedly the main benefit of action research will be to the participants in the research. However, writing a report or an article for a practitioner magazine also offers a free flow of information and provides you with evidence of what was completed. It could potentially be compiled into a portfolio for possible certification at a later date. It is important to remember that any conclusions reached within your practice and the action research conducted are probably exclusive to your setting and unlikely to equate directly to other settings, although there may be indicators for further, wider-scale research. It is likely that you will be left asking more questions than you answered and this is undoubtedly a 'healthy' approach, making you realise that the more you know the more you understand that you do not know. This is the first step to true professionalism of your practice.

Knowledge is power

This view of reflective practice moves us towards a concept of a 'research community' or, as Hallet describes it, *a community of learners*, where staff develop their practice by sharing their experiences, understanding and interests through discussion. In this way Hallet says:

> Reflection has the capacity for transformation … Reflective practice loosens predictable outcomes, exposes the practitioner to new perspectives, possibilities and understanding.
>
> (Hallet, 2013, p 94)

This moves us to a reflective approach which does not simply ask *what is right or good practice?* but a more inquisitorial *in what way can we create effective learning environments?*

It is about finding ways to articulate change in a format that allows positive changes to be made however unpredictable that change may be.

Knowledge and understanding gained from action research enables you to develop the intellectual and emotional power within yourself to instigate change. This empowerment enables you to be more effective both personally and professionally as you begin to comprehend what underpins your practice and gives you a forum to communicate that understanding. action research encourages a participatory form of research with those being researched also taking an active role in the process and gaining a wider understanding of the underlying philosophy of the practice. This produces a shift in the power process within the research, gives the participants an important 'voice' within the research, and has the potential to 'democratise' the whole research process.

CASE STUDY

Melanie's action research

Melanie and her team from the Tiny Tots children's centre met after nursery one day and discussed 50 common words which they felt were important to all the children in the nursery, and would be useful for them to be able to use confidently. They then reviewed the story books in the two nursery rooms. They selected ten books that contained a selection of the 50 words that were repeated in context throughout the texts. All books had accompanying illustrations to reinforce the meaning of the words chosen. They labelled two parallel groups A and B. Group B was to be used as a control group and would not be introduced to the ten selected texts until after the research period was completed. Both groups were read stories each day in the way that they always had in the past. Group A was the experimental group and the three staff in the room agreed to read the ten stories throughout the three-week experimental period using repetition and emphasis to highlight the selected 50 words, when they appeared in the books. Group A would have two story sessions in a three-hour period, one where all the children came together at circle time and one where only interested children would attend on the mat with a member of staff. All ten books were out in the Group A reading area for children to handle at their will.

All the staff at the Tiny Tots children's centre agreed to undertake a series of observations of the children. It was decided by the team that these should be both formal narrative observations and incidental records when children were heard to use any of the 50 words in their everyday play. This was noted on a tally chart on the wall of the nursery. The formal and informal observations were conducted with both Group A and Group B (the control group). When all the observations were completed the staff in the two rooms came together to discuss their results and assess whether the selected 50 words were more commonly heard from the children in the research group (Group A) or the control group (Group B).

Reflective activity

Working with a colleague consider this case study.

» *Can you suggest any inherent difficulties with the research design?*

» *Can you devise another research strategy and test Melanie's hypothesis?*

» *Do you think that the observers should have had some training in how to observe, or at least some discussion prior to the commitment about what to observe? Explain your answer.*

» *How else could the team have recorded the results of their observations?*

» *How many observations do you think they will need?*

The results of this research could be of interest to the other rooms within the children's centre.

» *How do you suggest that Melanie disseminate the results to all the other staff?*

» *Could these results also be applicable to other nurseries within the area even though they are not in the same mixed cultural area of Tiny Tots?*

» *How applicable would the results be to other nursery settings outside of the area? If you think that they might be useful, how could Melanie disseminate the information to other nurseries?*

» *What recommendations do you think that Melanie could make to the team regarding the teaching and learning within the children's centre on the strength of the results?*

» *If changes are to be made, how could Melanie persuade her staff to change their ways of working to improve the way that the centre deals with such large numbers of non-English speaking children and families?*

» *If action research is really a cyclical process with no end, what do you think is the next step for Melanie and her staff?*

» *What continuing professional development would you recommend for the staff in this children's centre?*

Extended thinking

Participant observation is a useful tool for small scale action research, however Cohen, Manion and Morrison (2011) suggest that it is also 'subtly intrusive' as it requires the detached researcher to also be an empathetic and sympathetic participant.

» *How can Melanie and her staff ensure the reliability of the qualitative research?*

» *Why is this necessary?*

Change management

The first step to changing the practice in a setting is to understand how to manage the change with each individual within the site. To make this change successfully each practitioner needs to be convinced of the need for change and have a willingness to participate to support that change. Clearly the practitioners need to know *how* to change, and understand that they have the ability to implement that change. It is also important to consider from the start of the research process what will be needed to sustain and maintain that change. When you are considering change within a setting you need to understand that the change takes place at two levels, firstly the individual and then the setting. Settings do not change but practitioners do. No matter what action research is undertaken, the change resulting from it can only be successfully completed if the individuals within the setting work towards it. Change happens one person at a time, so tools such as communication, planning and professional development all form a vital part of the reflective and progressive cycle.

Before any change can occur the fear of change must be overcome. For most people any change in their usual routine and way of tackling things can be frightening. It is the issue of moving into the unknown which brings with it fear of a loss of control, a realisation that an activity that they have been doing in a certain way or at a certain time in the past, may not have been the best way and it requires a challenge to their thoughts and theories. This can also bring with it a level of guilt and a challenge to their professionalism, as they start to understand that reflecting and changing their practices is their own professional responsibility which they may have neglected for some time.

One of the most written-about models for managing change is that of John Kotter (1996). Originally designed for business organisations, this model can now be applied to most early years settings. Kotter proposed the following eight-stage process for managing change.

1   Establish a sense of urgency: demonstrate to the team that change needs to happen.

2   Create the guiding group: identify a number of colleagues with the right mix of skills to work together to help to implement the change.

3   Develop the vision or strategy.

4   Communicate a vision for change.

5   Empower broad-based action: consider the current practice that may be impeding change and encourage staff to come up with original solutions.

6   Generate short-term aims: create some achievable goals that enable colleagues to celebrate their work and the individuals who made it possible.

7   Consolidate gains and generate more change: use these short-term gains to generate long-term success and adopt a reflective attitude.

8   Anchor new approaches in the culture of the setting: consider how to embed the new ways of working into the ethos, culture and philosophy of the setting.

Kotter (1996) suggested that if you try to force change upon colleagues they are likely to push against it and rebel as they feel manipulated, thereby causing conflict and resistance. It is possible that different people will react differently to change depending upon their personality type and personal circumstances. The early years 'industry' is possibly unusual in that it tends to have many staff with a strong moral philosophy for their work, unlike those working in offices and factories. Those working with children and families have a strong philosophical rationale to their practice which has been built up over time and probably originates from their own upbringing, culture and training. This will be hard to change and it may be hard to persuade them to rethink their individual attitudes and skills and what underpins their whole practice.

Another issue to consider before successfully implementing change is the age of the participants. Eric Erikson's psycho-social theory originally postulated in the 1950s (Erikson, 1993) suggests that people's priorities and motivations are different depending on their stage in life, their personal circumstances and their qualifications. This will require confident and sensitive management of the people involved with or affected by the change.

Change is a necessary part of action research and it is important that the setting and the individuals within it are responsive to that change, with the capacity to be adaptable and flexible. Change is vital to the success of the setting and the stress and challenge created by that change can motivate teams and build self-esteem and optimal performance. However, too much stress and challenge can lower performance, decrease motivation and deplete energy levels. Once again, open and honest communication is the key to allowing colleagues to express their concerns and anxieties about the potential changes. Engaging the staff with the action research will give those participating a level of empowerment which can alleviate the potential for fear and stress caused by the change and will harness a trusting relationship within the team, thereby building confidence in their own ability to manage the change.

Chapter reflections

It can be seen in this chapter that useful, valid research does not need to be global, national or government-sponsored but that small-scale research within a setting can be just as influential to the practitioners and children within that setting. National policy development is invariably top-down, with dictates coming from senior positions in the government, for example the Early Years Foundation Stage (DfE, 2014) where decisions are taken by party political politicians and laid down in legislation requiring all early years settings to comply. However, we have seen that policy can also be developed from the bottom up. Research influencing policy in a setting which is shown to work is often the context for policy development at local and eventually national levels. An example of this may be the debate concerning parent partnership programmes. So action research can influence not only practice but also the theory underpinning early years care and education, enabling other practitioners to readily access the ideas and make practice more reflective. This in turn enables you to justify your practice to others in a reasoned manner because you can show the data and evidence collected in a critically reflective fashion.

Action research, as the name suggests, is about action and research. It is possible to have research without action and action without research but action research is about the links and integration that exist between the two, the 'doing' with the enquiry. This is not a process that seeks to discover new theoretical knowledge for its own sake, but it does search for practical, applicable solutions to very specific problems. If early years practitioners refuse to grasp the nettle of action research they will potentially inhibit their capacity for evidence-based change and will miss the opportunity to influence early years theoretical underpinning, thereby undermining their own role and status. This will surely damage the credibility of early years practitioners to be seen as professionals with a distinctive, specialist knowledge base. This leaves practitioners vulnerable to having their whole philosophy and ethos controlled by researchers and academics from outside practice or by those who have lost contact with practice. This creates the potential for a gap to open up and become increasingly wide between those involved in research in the early years field and those in practice. The challenge for practitioners is to narrow that gap by context-driven research, enabling innovative and flexible practice to improve the enabling environments for young children and their families. Only then can practitioners in early years begin to command sufficient respect from other professionals to truly take a step towards recognition of the professionalisation of those working with the very youngest and most important children.

Extended reflections

» *This chapter refers to a potential gap between theory and practice, between the theorist and the practitioners. How do you think that you can bridge that gap, and how helpful can a reciprocation between theory and practice be?*

Guidelines for good practice in action research

- Consider what evidence there is for a particular difficulty, problem or desirable improvement.

- Decide upon the question you want to explore and if possible consult with colleagues and fellow researchers.

- Decide upon the details of the methods to be used and the overall methodology.

- Make sure that your enquiry methods do not disrupt the lives of children and their families.

- Make sure that your enquiry methods preserve the anonymity and/or confidentiality of those involved with the research, and that your research is ethically sound.

- Make it clear that involvement with the research is voluntary and anyone who wishes to opt out of it is at liberty to do so.

- Make an evaluative and analytical study of the previous literature relating to the subject area. This may inform the design of your research and allow you to relate your findings to some of the theories that inform the topic.

• Explore your existing knowledge and your current rationale for the practice and examine whether this is compatible with what you and the staff are actually doing in the setting.

Reflective activity

» *Work again with a colleague from your venue that you trust and feel comfortable with, to come up with a reflective question that would be suitable for an action research project in your early years setting.*

» *Suggest an appropriate methodology for such a project.*

» *Who will be involved and why?*

» *How will the research findings, whatever they are, affect future practice?*

» *How will you disseminate your findings?*

Extended thinking

Martin (2011) reminds you that reflective practice is about watching yourself at work and without this it is hard to establish positive professional development. The basis of this she claims is developing a culture of 'curiosity'. This means engaging regularly with a range of generic questions, which she grades from less powerful questions to more powerful questions.

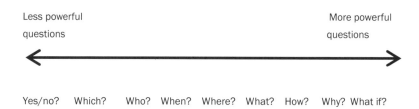

Figure 13.4 *Power of questions. Adapted from Martin (2011).*

» *Why do you think that Martin (2011) graded the questions in this manner?*

Further reading

Brock, A, (ed) (2015) *The Early Years Reflective Practice Handbook*. Oxon: Routledge.

This is a well edited book, using experts from across the field of early years. The book really does examine the professional role of the early years practitioner and sets this within a wider political sphere. There is a wealth of practice guidance as well as a sound theoretical underpinning which seeks to explain practice in the 'real world'.

This is an excellent handbook for any early years practitioner looking to understand how reflective practice can be part of their every day experiences with children, promoting quality and self-motivated learning.

References

Brock, A (2015) *The Early Years Reflective Practice Handbook*. Oxon: Routledge.

Cohen, L, Manion, L and Morrison, K (2011) *Research Methods in Education*. 7th edn. Oxon: Routledge.

DfE (2014) *Statutory Framework for the Early Years Foundation Stage*: Setting the standards for learning, development and care for children from birth to five. London: Crown.

Elliott, J (1991) *Action Research for Educational Change*. Buckingham: Open University Press.

Erikson, E (1993) *Childhood and Society*. New York: WW Norton and Company.

Griffiths, B and Kaday, C (2004) *Grow Your Own Carrot*. London: Hodder Headline.

Hallet, E (2013) *The Reflective Early Years Practitioner*. London: Sage.

Johnston, J and Nahmad-Williams (2009) *Early Childhood Studies*. Harlow: Pearson Educational.

Kellett, M (2010) *Rethinking Children and Research: Attitudes in Contemporary Society*. London: Continuum.

Kemmis, S, McTaggart, R and Nixon, R (2014) *The Action Research Planner. Doing Critical Participatory Action Research*. Queensland: Springer.

Kotter, J (1996) *Leading Change*. Boston, MA: Harvard Business School.

Lewin, K (1946) Action Research and Minority Problems. *Journal of Social Issues*, 2: 34–46.

Lincoln, Y and Guba, E (1986) But Is It Rigorous? Trustworthiness and Authenticity in Naturalistic Evaluation. *New Directions for Program Evaluation*, 73–84.

Lowe, M (2007) *Beginning Research*. Oxon: Routledge.

Martin, M (2011) *The Bamboo Project*. Available from: www.michelemmartin.com/thebamboo projectblog/reflec.html (accessed 16 June 2016).

McNiff, J (2002) Action Research for Professional Development: Concise Advice for New Action Researchers, in www.jeanmcniff.com/ar-booklet-asp (accessed 13 November 2011).

McTaggart, R (1996) Issues for Participatory Action Research, in Zuber-Skerritt, O (ed), *New Direction in Action Research*. London: Falmer Press.

Punch, K F and Oancea, A E (2014) *Introduction to Research Methods in Education*. London: Sage.

Rodd, J (2012) *Leadership in Early Childhood* (4th edn). Maidenhead: Open University Press.

Tolkien, J R R (1991) *The Hobbit* (4th edn). London: Unwin Paperbacks.

Index

Page numbers in italics are figures; with 't' are tables.